★ THE ★
HARD
WAY

★ THE ★
HARD
WAY

The Odyssey of a Weekly Newspaper Editor

Alexander B. Brook

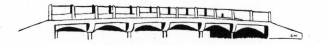

Bridge Works Publishing Co.
Bridgehampton, New York

Printed in the United States of America
1   2   3   4   5   6   7   8   9
First Edition

Library of Congress Cataloging-in-Publication Data

Brook, Alexander B. (Alexander Bacon),
The hard way : the odyssey of a weekly newspaper editor / by
Alexander B. Brook.
p.   cm.
ISBN 1-882593-00-6 (alk. paper) :
1. Brook, Alexander B. (Alexander Bacon), 1922-   .   2. Editors-
United States—20th century—Biography.
I. Title
PN4874.B72A3   1993
070.4′1′092—dc20
[B]   AC   92-39425
CIP

To the memory of my mother,
Peggy Bacon Brook,
an inspiration, example and supporter for 66 years

———————————

CONTENTS

Foreword

Alexander ("Sandy") Brook left the life of a New York City business executive to pursue a dream—owning and editing a weekly newspaper in Kennebunk, Maine. He found confrontation and conflict, struggle and sacrifice. He encountered awesome political and commercial pressures that threatened his newspaper's very existence. But he prevailed. He built a newspaper that brought him pride, and that brought him prizes, and that eventually brought him profits, too.

The press is widely criticized today for sins, real or imagined, ranging from bias and inaccuracy to arrogance and insensitivity. *The Hard Way* is the story of how one editor and publisher made integrity and truthfulness his passport to success.

Sandy Brook bought the *Kennebunk Star*, a shoddy, money-losing, 1,254-circulation weekly, for $30,000, all of it borrowed. This is the story of how, over 20 years, driven by love for his community, a crusading ardor and an enduring entrepreneurial spirit, Brook multiplied the *Star*'s circulation more than tenfold, won an array of regional and national awards for journalistic excellence and public service, expanded the paper's geographic reach and rechristened it the *York County Coast Star*, and increased its value to $1.6 million at the time it was sold in 1977. Today the *Star* is owned by *The New York Times*.

The Hard Way is more than a story of the intimate inner workings of a weekly newspaper and the people who report its news, sell its advertising and circulation, and keep its presses running. It is a story of the sociology and politics of an American small town and its citizens.

Sandy Brook and his newspaper encounter, in the pages of *The Hard Way*, arrogant and corrupt politicians, and businessmen abusers of the environment. They encounter the ugly forces of prejudice. Brook takes us with him as he goes to war to save the salt marshes, the beaches and the fragile and scenic river fronts from uncontrolled development. He takes us with him as he challenges the vindictive misuse of political power. In other chapters, he takes us with him as he tries to deal delicately with a school principal, a churchman and a Rotarian friend who, each in a different way, has been offended by the *Star*'s approach to journalism.

There are scoundrels in this tale, as there would be in a story about what goes on beneath the surface of any American town, small or large. Some are inclined to swindling, some to lawsuits, some to boycotts—directed at the *Star*. But there are heroes as well—such as Herman Cohen, whose noisy one-man revolution toppled a town government and provided a stirring lesson in democracy at work.

The Hard Way examines the role of a small newspaper in our democracy as few, if any, books about the press have done. It does this with warmth and poignancy, for the civics lesson is essentially a study of human nature. Most of all, though, *The Hard Way* is the story of one newspaperman's courage and sacrifice in his search for self-discovery and fulfillment.

Warren H. Phillips
Chairman 1978–91, Dow Jones & Co.,
Publisher of *The Wall Street Journal*.

QUEBEC

MAINE

VERMONT

Augusta

NEW
HAMPSHIRE

Portland

NEW
YORK

Kennebunk
YORK COUNTY

ATLANTIC

OCEAN

Portsmouth

Boston

MASSACHUSETTS

CONNECTICUT

R.I.

N.Y.C.

Long Island

100 Miles

★ I ★

★ 1 ★

Heading North

I grew up scorning suit-and-tie commuters, particularly Wall Street Man. But there I was, in 1957, dressed like all the rest of them, commuting 90 minutes each way from Basking Ridge, New Jersey, a state low on my preference list, to Manhattan, where I worked for Francisco Sugar, whose stock was traded on the New York Stock Exchange, a few blocks from my office. I had never wanted to be a businessman, or even to get rich, but here I was, Assistant to the President, in it for the money. I had wanted to be a writer, but hadn't written for seven years.

I was hating life at Francisco. A doctor told me the burning in my gut was an ulcer. On weekends Anneke and I drove as far from home as time permitted, with Megan, 5, Lisbet, 3, and Eben, 1, in tow. We spent all I earned and had nothing but a mortgaged house and car, a household of effects, and a modest checkbook balance to show for our unappealing life. At work the office politics, in the guise of an aging workaholic vice president I had been hired to understudy, were not good.

One morning in mid-December I read the paper as usual on the crowded Lackawanna commuter train, crushed my way into a Hudson Tube car, and walked across lower Manhattan with the flood of the morning crowd. On my desk I found a letter I was expecting from John Cole. He'd be flying east from Ohio for Christmas and would drop in then to discuss what I had in mind. My letter, he wrote, had caught him with his morale down.

John was my age, 35, and had been a year behind me at Yale. Like me, he was a would-be writer working at a corporate job to sustain his family: a wife, Cynthia in his case, and two young children. Also like me, he had done some commercial fishing and some part-time weekly newspaper reporting. My letter spoke of a potential shrimp-fishing business in Cuba, an auxiliary use for Francisco's new Camagüey port facilities. I thought John might research the shrimp fleet idea and then, if it looked promising, manage the operation for us. In his letter he was agreeing to meet with some other company officers about it.

After those meetings, John and I went out for an after-work drink. From what he'd heard, John said, yes, he might be interested. He'd do just about anything for a change. How were things with me?

So far as they went, I said, OK. Then later on: maybe just fair. Then later still: actually, to get right into the bush, lousy. Maybe, I suggested tentatively, there was something we could do together. Where . . . ? How about Maine? God, John said, that would be salvation. But what could we do?

I didn't know — maybe something in the fishing line. Or — how about if I could find a weekly newspaper to buy? Would he come to Maine with me? You bet! Save my life, was John's reaction to that.

The Maine town I knew best from school and college summers was Ogunquit — not yet the tourist trap it was to become — on the coast of Maine's southernmost county, York. I thought I could get my Ogunquit artist friend, Dave von Schlegell, to look around York County for us. As we talked the future started glowing within, like liquor taking hold.

Two days after I called Dave he called back. The little York weekly newspaper wasn't for sale, but the *Kennebunk Star*, only ten miles north of Ogunquit, happened to be. The two elderly owners, sons of its long-deceased founder, Lester Watson, were ready to call it quits. They wanted too much for it, though, and Dave allowed as how he didn't think I'd want it at any price. But why didn't I come up and look around some more from Base Camp von Schlegell?

I called the Watson brothers and made the eight-hour New Jersey-to-Maine drive after work on Friday. Next morning I found Garden Street, shadowless under a grim overcast, angling off the section of Route 1 that doubled as Kennebunk's Main Street. From the shabby displays in those shop windows that weren't blank, it was clear that Kennebunk's forty-five hundred inhabitants didn't do much of their shopping in town.

Garden Street, about a block and a half long, dead-ended at the antique red-brick Kesslen Shoe factory, Kennebunk's major employer. Across the factory facade, overlooking Route 1 to the south, the Kennebunk-Kennebunkport Chamber of Commerce maintained a large sign that read: "Welcome to Kennebunk, Only Town in the World So Named."

The home of Star Print, Inc., an oblong, 30-by-60-foot, two-story frame structure with flat tarred roof, proclaimed itself too, but more modestly. Through rips in the pink-tan asphalt shingles yellow clapboards were visible. It stood alone between Greene's Garage and a small radio repair shop, facing the rear entrances to a small eatery and several struggling Main Street shops.

I climbed five weatherworn steps under the Star Print sign to a recessed landing and hesitated. Through a window in the door to my left I could see an idle black typesetting machine. The middle door led to four two-room rentals upstairs. Through the door to my right I could see two rolltop desks, three chairs, a table, and a chunky green object — perhaps a small bureau. Obviously the room was either some kind of office or the repair space for a used furniture outlet.

With a sense of destiny I turned the knob and stepped warily into a 12-foot-square room. A ceiling bulb competed wanly with the pale December light sifting through three grimy windows. Unpainted floorboards, dark with Garden Street grit, supported the old desks, apparently used only as filing cabinets and repositories for the same sorts of paper scraps that overflowed three grocery cartons. The chunky piece turned out to be a waist-high safe, whose back and top had once been painted the same acid green as the office trim. Scuffed patches in the wall paint revealed a flowered wallpaper beneath. Tattered, pull-less yellow window shades fluttered lightly at various levels and angles. Like the desks, two old wood-and-cane armchairs and one straight chair seemed to serve mostly as auxiliary filing cabinets. The room was innocent of all but lepidopteran and arthropodal life.

Through a door frame leading into the back shop one youngish and one elderly woman, both in aprons, chattered over some sort of piecework. The plump, younger one called out, "Perley — somebody in the office," and then two old men were ambling toward me.

I have in my memory an ineradicable image of Willis and Perley Watson staring at me, watery-eyed, over the surface of a homemade type cabinet. Neither smiled, ever, during our discussions. Willis, the elder brother, the publisher, slope-shouldered, heavier than Perley, white-haired, "kindly," spoke quickly with an unobtrusive Maine accent, vowels liquid and consonants mushy. He kept running off nervously to fuss around the tables where the women were working. Perley, gaunt, long-jawed, like Willis of medium height, high-shouldered and long-armed, stared coldly through rimless glasses. A cigarette burned perilously close to the dry skin of middle finger and permanently bent forefinger. I had never seen such dark nicotine stains. The big features that hung heavily on Perley's face bones and balding skull betrayed nothing. The voice was deep but flat, and Perley released it level and measured. His stare was impersonal, reptilian. He responded briefly to my unenlightened questions, volunteering nothing, betraying neither the least desire to sell nor the merest hint of warmth. He measured me as he measured his voice. I made the naive mistake of trying to soften our conversation with a smile, twice. Obviously I knew nothing about Kennebunk, or paper, or ink, or printing. Or advertising, or local affairs. Or bookkeeping, or where the money came from. I mentioned that I had once, nine years before, written a few stories for a small weekly newspaper, but this was of negative import — there was no reporting in the *Star*. Obviously I had no way of judging the merits of the business I had come to evaluate. Obviously, I was no trader. I had about as much maneuverability in that contest as a stilt-walker in a snowbank.

The brothers showed me the shop. There was the turn-of-the-century, two-page, sheet-fed Whitlock newspaper press, which could theoretically make 750 impressions an hour, and the flimsy Omaha folder. There was the operational 54-year-old Intertype hot-lead machine for linecasting body copy, and there was the Ludlow typecasting machine for ad and job work display lines, at 11 the newest and by far the most valuable piece of shop equipment. There were the three small hand-fed platen job presses for printing such things as billheads and leaflets, the true old-timers of the machinery family, and a Kluge automatic job press of undetermined vintage. There was an old drill press, used for routing ad-mat castings — or rather no longer used, I was to learn, because its motor was shot — and an antique Virkotype for raised lettering that the brothers claimed would run but that I never afterward had either the demand or the desire to test.

In cabinets around the walls were about three hundred drawers of beat-up foundry and wood type, most of it last used when the newspaper was set by hand. Several marble composing stones, black with eighty years of news ink, rested on crude cabinets with more type drawers and galley racks. Scattered about were the other equipment odds and ends, including a miter box, a backsaw, a bin of picture glass and cheap wood molding — the brothers were also in the picture-framing business. A few grime-ridden fluorescent fixtures dangled on chains, but most of the rays that shone on that incredible manufacturing jungle came from bare bulbs hanging on their wiring. The Celotex ceiling squares curled downward or were missing in large areas, exposing the pipes whose drippings had unstuck them.

We reached the cellar by a crooked set of stairs in a rear corner. Headroom was five feet under the beams. The only cobweb-free aisle was a well-worn path leading to a motor, which drove the newspaper press overhead by means of a long, flapping leather belt reaching up through a hole in the shop floor. I was to learn that the absence of cobwebs along its approach attested to the fact that the belt kept slipping off its drive-pulley during pressruns.

Willis was a collector of Collier Brothers caliber, only one remove from the legendary Kennebunk lady in whose attic was found a large carton labeled "Pieces of String Too Short to Use." The cellar was crammed with such potentially useful items as crippled lawn furniture, trunks full of old business correspondence, framed memento prints and family photographs, discarded toys and other memorabilia, pickling jars and empty cigar boxes by the hundreds, sash weights. It tempts me to say that the cellar contained as useful an assortment as the shop upstairs, an observation I defend by including among the upstairs paraphernalia the many petrified sandwiches, still in their waxed wrappers, abandoned behind reams of moldy bond, the tin boxes of bent type-spacers, the jumbled hellboxes, and the empty beer bottles and pint whiskey bottles, some not quite empty, left by Perley behind unused items and forgotten — 18 bushels of them when I got around to housecleaning — and the three 10-gallon potato-chip tins filled to within an inch of their brims with congealed masses of the uniformly one-inch-long chewed-up ends of Willis's cigars.

Willis, Perley, and I wandered into each corner. We admired each trusty piece of equipment in turn. Five minutes later our tour was complete; no further scrutiny seemed either kind or necessary. Why try to learn that the register of a press couldn't be adjusted, or that a motor was shot, or that the Kluge automatic job press hadn't worked in years?

We stood at a type cabinet while the women worked and chattered, the brothers on one side, I on the other. They just waited, Perley motionless, Willis distracted. In the embarrassing silence I began. Their price?

Thirty thousand dollars.

Pretty high — it was nice, but was it really worth that much?

Some people thought so.

Anyone else interested?

Oh, yes.

Well . . . could I see the books?

What did I have in mind?

Just year-end financial statements. Profit and loss. Balance sheet. Whatever they had.

Well, I could have a look at the subscription drawer, and count the cards. The bookkeeping was all journal entries. Perley kept the journals and made out the tax returns. I could see last year's income tax statement.

I'd like to see that, if they didn't mind. While Perley ambled to the office to consult the "files," Willis and I weighed the probabilities of snow. When Perley returned he handed me a document. It was sketchy.

The brothers declared net income of $2,600 on annual sales of $23,400. Did they pay themselves salaries, or was that it? I never asked, and I never learned.

What would a bad year be like?

Oh, it was a good, steady business.

What did I get for $30,000 — did the building go with it?

Not likely. The building was for sale for $30,000 all by itself, if I wanted it. If I didn't, they'd give me a five-year renewable lease on the downstairs for $75 a month.

I'd think it over, I told them, but I didn't have any money.

They'd take a $25,000 second mortgage at 4 percent, they said, for 25 years. All I had to do was raise $5,000.

I told them I had nothing till we sold our New Jersey house, and I'd need all that money for working capital.

The bank would go for a $5,000 first mortgage, they said.

I'd still have to think about it.

Don't take too much time, they said. They were going to sell it soon to one of the crowd that wanted it.

I might make them an offer. Would they consider something less? Nope.

I waited for a protest, at least, that the *Star* was worthy of its price tag. None came.

★ 2 ★

New Owners

Back in Basking Ridge I told Anneke how promising everything looked. I swore how straight our children would grow in Maine, how much the background of the sea would mean to them later, how our dull lives would be revived in self-respect and salt air. I waxed dithyrambic about Maine people, not yet spoiled by quick pace and fast buck.

I wrote to John, back in Ohio, and he wrote back something lyrical.

Just give him two weeks' notice — he'd be with me! The combination of our talents and desires would make things hum.

I called old friend and one-time part-time employer Doug Gardner. Doug, I said, do me a favor. Come up with me to Maine and have a look at Star Print, Inc. Use your 25 years of experience as a small-town job printer and weekly publisher to tell me what it's worth. You'll have all you can handle of the best scotch, thickest steaks, and fattest cigars, to go with a couple of days away from it all with an old friend and admirer. Sure, Doug said, lead on. But hold it for two weeks — things were busy.

Two weeks later, on a Thursday, I rose early and was in Sag Harbor, Long Island, by eight. Doug was in his *Express* office, ready to go, zipped into a leather jacket over plaid shirt held together at his 18-inch neck with a string tie and its martini-with-olive slide. He was about 55 then, six-feet-four, 240 pounds, dark straight hair, enormous head, one walleye, pocked skin, heavy features, voice like a diaphone. He had a big thermos of coffee, and I had a fifth of the cream he always laced it with. We stopped to get a dozen cigars and headed across the sound on the ferry to New London, and on up toward Providence.

I helped Doug kill about half the scotch before lunch, the rest of it before Boston. We had some more with our steak dinners and drove on to the von Schlegells. Dave and Mary thought Doug was great, and we all had quite an evening.

Next morning, after a few shots of cream in a few coffees, Doug rode up with me to Kennebunk. It was Town Report time, and Willis and Perley Watson were helping four women hand-fold and glue covers. Doug and I met the two regular employees, typesetter Paul Bannon and pressman-compositor Tom Dickson. Doug looked the shop over and talked briefly with the Watson brothers. Then we went out for coffee-and.

Well, Doug said, it wasn't much for equipment, he'd have to say that. And it was a hell of a price — the place had been used hard. If I was looking for value, forget it. But the area was bigger than the newspaper; it had potential, and with some sweat, it might work.

I made a 1:30 appointment with Robert Stinson, the youngish cashier at the locally owned commercial bank on Main Street, Ocean National. All I wanted, I told Stinson, was a $5,000 first-mortgage loan, secured by all the contents of Star Print. My working capital would consist of separation pay from Francisco and an undetermined amount from our house, when it sold. We discussed my lack of printing and newspapering experience, but I pleaded ancillary skills, good health, and determination. I was prepared for a struggle. If I failed, the material effects at Star Print should cover the loan. I wouldn't fail.

Stinson was skeptical. After listening patiently, at last he said he knew the Watsons' business and couldn't see the economics coming together, or even the $5,000 in collateral value. He was sympathetic, but he couldn't recommend the loan to his directors.

I found Doug and recited my sad narrative. We had a cup of coffee together, about half coffee. Would it do any good, Doug asked, if he offered to cosign?

Back we went to the bank. I was wishing that Doug hadn't worn his martini slide and hoping he'd stay a good ten feet from Stinson. I needn't have worried. Stinson saw a hard-working, hard-living man who knew what he was talking about. Doug told Stinson it was good enough for him to cosign for the $5,000, with his business behind it.

In that case, Stinson thought his directors might listen.

Doug and I had another coffee in the car, this time without the coffee. "Doug," I said . . .

"Drink up," he said, "you're three behind."

I returned to Garden Street and told the Watsons the deal was moving. The bankers would meet Monday, and when I got the answer I'd call them. If all went well, I'd be back next Saturday, and we could make final arrangements. They nodded. We went over the terms. They'd keep the receivables and payables. I was buying assets and good will. Closing would be two weeks from Monday, at the bank. Good.

I drove Doug home, then myself, and spent the weekend dreaming. Monday afternoon Stinson called to say the directors had approved the loan. I immediately gave Francisco my notice. Anneke would put the house on the market the next morning. I called John, who gave his own notice. We agreed to meet in Kennebunk Monday, March 17, closing day. I'd find us a place to stay for a couple of months before our families arrived.

Next weekend Anneke and I drove up together. The physical embodiment of my dream project startled her, she allowed later, but she was 29, and trusting. I formalized the bank loan, shook hands with the brothers, and found a rent. For $60 a month we'd have an unfurnished caretaker's cottage down a hill on the grounds of a Victorian mansion on elm-lined Summer Street.

At 10:30 the next morning, back in Basking Ridge, I was out saying my farewells to the gardens. I heard the telephone ring inside the house, then stop. The next moment Anneke was at the door, wild-eyed, motioning me in. It was Bob Stinson at Ocean National. Willis and Perley had offered my same terms to Perley's son, George, then working as a typesetter in Portland. They had told Stinson George had first refusal. George had applied to Stinson for a loan. WHAT!?

In 15 minutes I was back in the car in a change of clothes, with a toothbrush in my pocket. Six hours later, nonstop, I was at the von Schlegells' again, and next morning I was standing on the Star Print stoop when the Watsons arrived to open. They were surprised to see me back so soon. Yes, they had offered it to George, Perley said matter-of-factly, "but he couldn't swing it."

Were there other heirs presumptive in the woodwork? No, the *Star* was mine, the brothers said, but they had decided I'd have to reduce principal by two thousand dollars a year instead of one. The barrel I was over was slippery, and headed for the falls, and the brothers knew that was where they had me. I simply turned around and drove the normal eight hours back to Basking Ridge.

Saturday March 15, two days before Deal Day, I started up to Maine alone, pulling a U-Haul trailer stuffed with the densest of the Brook family's possessions, the first phase of our move. Because of my tow, I had to take the long route up the Jersey side of the Hudson to West Point, then across toward Boston. My 1954 Ford was in challenging harness. I was climbing an icy, two-mile, curvaceous hill on a divided parkway east of the Hudson — almost to its top in first gear — when the hill steepened for the crest, and the Ford simply stopped. On brakes and outrigger mirrors I was an hour and a half backing the trailer to the bottom, against traffic. Backtracking to a longer alternate route lost more time; when I reached Massachusetts, night had fallen, and it had started to snow. The snow and wind fell and rose, respectively, until the radio weatherman certified it as an Ides of March blizzard. Before I reached New Hampshire the U-Haul was whipping back and forth on what I could see of the road, swinging the Ford's rear end with it, tires skidding front and rear, and me compensating wildly at the wheel. Fortunately I was alone on the snow-blind highway, there being few people in New England that night as single-purposed as I.

It was nine when I reached Kennebunk and pulled into the un-plowed driveway to the cottage. It must have snowed all that day in Maine. I snatched the duffel I'd had the foresight to stuff with a flashlight and my old Navy-issue winter flight gear, pulled on hip boots, and started down to the house. In places the snow went to my waist; if I'd been trying for drifts I'd have gone over my head.

I let myself into an ice chest. Neither electricity, meaning the furnace, nor water had been turned on. The house was bare except for one wicker porch chair. I pulled on my sheepskin-lined pants, boots, helmet, and jacket, and propped myself in the chair by the window facing the driveway. John was due that night or the next morning. I kept a candle in the window, for heat as much as a beacon, and tried to sleep.

Next morning the sun shone. Late that afternoon John called. His worn-out car had broken down in Massachusetts, so he wouldn't make day one, signing day, the day for owner's inspection and talks with inherited employees. The first edition of the *Kennebunk Star* under new management was due out Thursday, first printing jobs next day. OK.

Paul Bannon, single, about 25, set the body copy for the newspaper and nondisplay copy for ads and job work with hairline matrices on the Intertype relic. He sat on a sawed-off kitchen chair in the corner behind his machine, where the floor was worn down half an inch, cursing and babying it good-humoredly, if you can baby something twice your age. Paul was quite tall, loose-limbed, with sleepy eyes and a rather puffy face. His manner was engagingly informal, and his outlook — carefree and uncritical — sustained a working-Irish wit and sense of the ridiculous.

Tom Dickson, the compositor and pressman, thirtyish, was somewhat shorter than Paul, more muscular but less athletic, a man of inner tensions who walked upright with small, quick steps. His hair was coarse, curly, and blond, his features small, his stare wary and myopic. Tom's wife, homebound with two young children in a rustic outback house, shared his passion for a small, fervid Christian sect, and Tom's recreation and enthusiasms were centered on the public's immorality and on the sect's little church, where he was a lay preacher.

I spent the first morning signing papers, talking with the Watsons and Stinson, and making the transfer. Making the transfer included learning which of the basement odds and ends did not belong to me and which Willis wanted to keep (all of them). The afternoon I spent mostly with Dickson and Bannon learning how to publish a newspaper and run a printing business. By that evening I knew how, and started to work at it. At five the other two left. I grabbed a hamburger at Congdon's across Garden Street and let myself back into the shop, the proprietor alone at last.

First I reinspected the office. Window sashes and sills had been painted once, long ago, but were now degenerate gray wood. One of the steam radiators worked noisily and one didn't, but there was a three-inch hot pipe up one wall that fed the radiators in the apartments upstairs, so the office was warm to stifling. I could hear two radios competing overhead. On the other side of a partition serving as the office's interior wall was a much smaller space, a walk-through to the shop with a window in it: the inner sanctum, where Publisher Willis had repaired to clip obituaries from other newspapers and cull the daily mail for releases from self-serving corporations and national ad agencies, and the publicity supplied by the secretaries of the local religious and social organizations.

I wandered into the shop and turned on the lights — one switch did it all. The nighttime shop, empty of activity and dark in the corners, exhaled a decay superimposed on its daytime cachexia. The machines that had been robustly clattering earlier were silent now, frail and exhausted in repose. The ceiling Celotex, curling grimily downward, cast horizontal shadows. Outside in the dark it had started to snow again, and flakes were ticking at the windows.

I picked my way around the clutter to the rear of the shop, where printing papers were stored. What hadn't been spoiled by leakage from the ceiling pipes was deep in printing dust, brittle and discolored. I switched on the cellar light and descended the swaying stairway, bending to clear the ceiling, and stepped into an inch of water at the bottom. The furnace, a lumpy Neanderthal monster, squatted ominously before me.

I worked my way upstairs again, picked my way around the machinery and back to the office. I sat down in one of the cane swivel chairs and leaned back too quickly — the spring was shot. If the wall hadn't been there, I'd have gone over backward. I tested the wall to see if it was safe to lean against, and let myself back again, tentatively. I gazed about me to the left. I gazed about me to the right. It was mine.

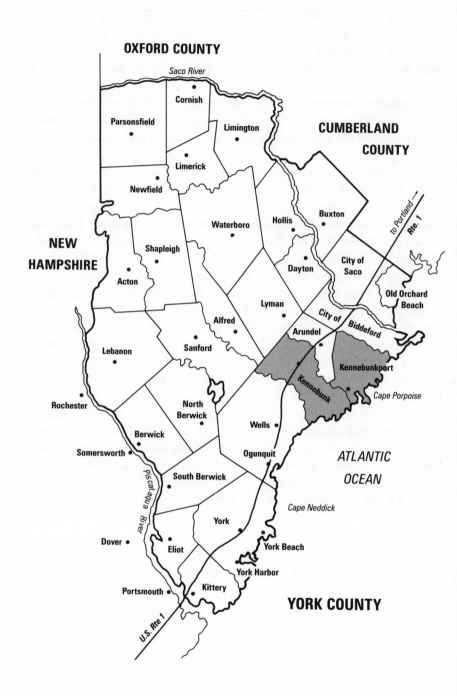

★ 3 ★

Maine

Maine is larger than the five other New England states combined. If you are driving from Philadelphia to Madawaska, Maine, when you get to Kennebunk you have gone only halfway. By virtue of its thousands of bays, creeks, islands, and peninsulas, Maine has so much coastline that if it were straightened out, it would reach from Kennebunk to San Francisco. Most of Maine, the inland bulge that juts up into Canada, is a wilderness of sixteen hundred substantial lakes and innumerable ponds — left when the glaciers of the last ice age receded — huge forests, wetlands, wild rivers, and mountains. To the north is French Canada; to the east and south is the ocean; beyond the wilderness to the west is sparsely populated rural New Hampshire.

Maine's earliest peoples were Amerinds of small tribes with names unfamiliar today beyond Maine's borders. Her first white infiltrators were explorers and itinerant trappers, but her first settlers were British fisherfolk, whose transitory island and shorefront communities were harassed by the Amerinds. The first permanent settlers were fugitives from Massachusetts Bay Colony "justice" seeking freedom from moral or religious strictures, men and women who crossed the Piscataqua River from what is now Portsmouth, New Hampshire, and called their settlements Kittery, Eliot, and York. The route they took became the King's Highway, never much more than a horse path.

These early settlers gradually yielded majority to timber-cutters and sawmill operators. Builders of boats and ships followed. Many privateers and cargo schooners took shape in the famous yards of the Kennebunks, vessels with oak ribs, fir planks, and pine spars felled as trees in local forests, lumbered in local sawmills, and fashioned by local shipwrights. Merchant maritime princes and sailing captains built grand wooden homes in the centers of the towns on both sides of the Kennebunk River.

Slowly, then rapidly, steam replaced wind as propulsion power on the ocean, and the proud local shipbuilding industry atrophied, then closed. The age of steam brought railroads and an exciting mobility.

The old King's Highway became the Boston Post Road, then U.S. Route 1, paved "down east" all the way to Eastport, first town in America to see the sun rise, and in the other, nameless, direction all the way to Key West. Newly accessible, the York County coast beckoned to barons of industry and finance, who built summer homes there and were able to join their families by rail in a single day from Boston, or overnight on a New York Pullman. Many summer hotels rose along the shore to house the genteel elderly, the trial-vacation families, and guests of the wealthy.

With their steamer trunks and pets in the baggage cars, the summer families arrived in late June on the Boston & Maine, whose picturesque station buildings along the line became the liveliest places in town. Passenger groups were met by cottage caretakers or hotel greeters in their jitneys and whisked grandly away. The Maine vacation industry was born.

The newcomers to Maine learned to love her. Their sons and daughters returned whenever they could, and the old folks prepared for retirement by winterizing their cottages and stretching their vacations from three months to five. These families became the more integrated and permanent summer residents who contributed to the culture of their second communities, amply supporting public buildings, museums, and theaters. Summer activity became the gaiety of parasols, tennis courts, canoeing on the rivers, and class-boat racing. The day after Labor Day the coastal towns emptied of revelers, and the natives turned again to their workaday pursuits and preparations for the long dark winters.

A whole new native industry of caretaking, landscaping, and estate and hotel maintenance flourished in this new culture, so the transition from a shipbuilding economy was made without prolonged privation. Kennebunk retained its population of about 4,000, and Kennebunkport its 1,500, into the early 1900s and the dawn of their industrial age.

With its two reliable rivers, the Kennebunk and the Mousam, the town that had supported sawmills was hospitable to the new world of the factory. Shoe factories — shops, they are still called — counter shops, twine and netting mills, a flour mill, a Leatheroid factory, and a maker of sliver cans for the textile mills, gave stability to the economy of the Kennebunks and sustained their people's work-inspired respectability. Separated by three miles of countryside from the beaches, with their summer glitter, the central village of Kennebunk led its own tree-shaded life. Its industrious people became uncommonly fond of their town, and several were inspired to write versions of its history.

Kennebunk settled around its highway and mills, Kennebunkport around its two harbors, one at the mouth of the Kennebunk River, the other at a broader body of water sheltered by islands at Cape Porpoise. After the turn of the century, when summer cottages became increasingly popular, colonies of summer homes sprouted. Writers, artists, and theater people settled into the community at the Port even more permanently than the wealthy captains of industry had done. No factories came to "The Port," ever. If Kennebunk had a modestly solid respectability, Kennebunkport may be said to have had a modestly racy gentility.

The centers of both communities were graced by tall churches and grand Revolutionary, Federal, and Georgian dwellings. Their main thoroughfares were lined with American elms, planted by far-sighted patriarchs. The elms grew huge and stately, their gothic branches arching to form shaded aisles for the traveler, their leaves sifting sunlight to dapple the lawns and clapboards of the mansions ranged behind them, and the shops downtown.

French Canadians looking for work inmigrated to Maine three generations and more ago, settling near the mills and factories — textile, shoe, and paper. Industrial Lewiston, Maine's third largest city, is mostly French Canadian in tone and character. Biddeford, largest of the two York County cities, is preponderantly bilingual Franco-American. A drab but proudly bustling community of 19,000, Biddeford is separated from York County's other, smaller city, Saco (pronounced Sah-co) only by the Saco River, which starts as a bubbling spring in New Hampshire's White Mountains and runs sweet and pure for most of its length until it accepts the factory waste in Biddeford and empties into the Atlantic.

When they came to Maine and were introduced to American politics, the Franco-Americans gravitated as one to the Democratic persuasion. To this day almost no Biddeford citizen would think of voting Republican for even the most trivial office-seeker, or admit it if the thought occurred. No Republicans bother to run for office in Biddeford, where 19 of 20 voters check only the straight Democratic box in all elections, local and otherwise. The rural Yankee folk in the other county towns have traditionally voted with equal fervor the straight Republican ticket.

In recent decades, however, the rural areas have been infiltrated by people from the predominantly Democratic centers to the south. The small-towner has learned to split his ticket and has become harder to classify. Meanwhile, the Biddeford Democrat has broadened his political stripe not so much as a hairline. The outsider, unfamiliar with local political realities, will hear the early rural returns and conclude that the county is landsliding for the Republicans. When the big, round Biddeford vote drops in late, he will be in for a shock.

Even today, fewer than a million people live in Maine, and three-fourths of them live in the lower third of the state, near the coast. Maine's great forests are owned by paper companies, but the men who cut the timber mostly work for and by themselves, selling what they cut to the pulp-users and sawmills, and most of the farmers are independent, small-acreage men. Potatoes are grown in the acid soil of the largest and northernmost county, Aroostook. Fishing, Maine's third major industry, is mostly done from one-man lobster boats or small draggers and gill-netters. The Maine character, neither belligerent nor yielding, has been further etched by the rigors of the five-month winters and the vigors of the other seasons. The insularity of Mainers, and their resulting poverty, have given them their own accent and vernacular, and kept alive social customs and traditional mannerisms that are quaintly funny to Metropolitan Man. "Does it matter which road I take to get to Millinocket?" asks the driver of the shiny car with New York plates stopped at the Maine crossroad, and the farmer standing there answers: "Not to me, it don't."

Gradually, most of the factories of Kennebunk died and came down, as their products obsolesced. Gradually, the highways that had strangled the railroads strangled the summer hotels too. The vacationer became tourist, more transient and less attractive, but, as the local manufacturing industry withered, more precious. Maine's greatest financial preoccupation became capturing this personage, who kept the euphemism "vacationer." The vacationers flocked to the watering places, and York County, which boasts many of Maine's finest beaches, with quartz pounded finer than the sand in an hourglass, bore the brunt of the new invasion.

The tastes of the tourists vulgarized the local offerings into fried clams, "giftes," and suntan lotions. Tourists came in greater numbers from farther afield, mobile working-class people who could now afford to spend their two-week holidays and blow their fifty-week savings in Maine. Route 1 became Maine's alimentary canal through which the tourists passed, and its borders bloomed with crass shops and competitive signs. The working communities were compromised by the new tourist-trappers, who hired local people and taught them to be nice to customers, change their sheets, stuff their mouths, and pump their gas.

The economy of the seaside towns developed an annual boom-and-bust cycle. Natives forfeited their short warm season to the tourists, working frantically to make enough money to last them through the winter. Promising native sons and daughters left home to seek their fortunes. The pleasant old-fashioned merchants in their downtown shops languished, or closed their doors. Empty storefront windows and reduced rents lured new merchant hopefuls to struggle and fail, to be replaced by urban fugitives or retired people looking for supplemental income from retailing, most of them doomed to dearth or failure.

In the mid-1950s textile manufacturer Goodall, the second-largest county employer, vacated its vast brick mills, and Sanford, the largest York County town, supported by Goodall, doggedly searching for replacement industry, became the "Town That Wouldn't Die". Within weeks of our arrival, textile-machinery maker Saco-Lowell, third-largest county employer, left too, and the largest of all, West Point Pepperell, was beginning the department-by-department move south to cheaper labor, tax exemptions, modern plants, and lower fuel bills that has left it a remnant industry in Biddeford today.

By 1958 the fortunes of the Kennebunks were at lowest ebb. It was to these communities that John and I had introduced ourselves with such enthusiasm during those blizzard-ridden Ides of March.

★ 4 ★

Partners at the Creation

John Cole arrived, haggard from his trip but brimming with optimism, during another snowstorm in the middle of the night. Sound asleep, I didn't hear his knocking above the storm and didn't know he'd arrived till morning. He was cautioned not to judge his future by what he was about to see, and entered the plant not visibly shaken.

The Watsons had refined the system they were prepared to teach us down to a few self-serving routines that ignored the imaginative and discriminatory sensibilities of our two principal sources of custom: the business people who had run out of billheads or business cards, and the advertisers who wanted to remind a limited audience of what they sold, where they did business, and what their names were. There was a third, suborder of customer, the readers, meaning the $2-a-year subscribers and people who bought the *Star* over the counter at any of half a dozen stores at 5 cents the copy. Of the three customer varieties these last were the least likely to give us trouble. They either subscribed through civic habit or paid their nickels to learn which townsfolk had died or to find their own names listed as club secretaries or recently installed Noble Grands. The newspaper didn't pretend to satisfy more complicated curiosities.

I have often returned to our first issue and the issue before it. Both were four-page broadsheet, meaning one folded sheet. In our first issue we had 51 inches of legal advertising, 17 classifieds, and about 190 column inches of display advertising at 40 cents per column inch, so total ad revenue in prospect amounted to $109. Circulation the week before had been 1,254, but about 350 of the mailed copies were sent free to Watson friends, advertisers, potential advertisers, or people whose expired Addressograph slugs had inadvertently been left in the slug file. Circulation revenue would be about $45, bringing total anticipated newspaper income to about $8,000 a year. Printing gross was less than that. What did Perley's $23,400 figure for 1957 gross income include? Upstairs rents? Willis's town clerk fees? The questions were academic; ignoring capital improvements, I'd need at least triple that to break even.

Except for some free illustrated ad mats and worn zinc logos in standing ads, the *Star* had been unillustrated all its long life. The nearest engravers were in Portland, and five-day service was the best that could be assured. Illustration was a luxury the brothers had never seriously considered.

The newspaper was universally gray. One or two headlines a week, headings, really, were set more than one column wide, their lengths dictated more by words like *Kennebunkport* than by the importance of the stories. The final Watson issue featured three brief obituaries at the top of Page One, a short Webhannet Club release entitled simply "Webhannet Club," and eight other miniscule releases from clubs and official groups. Boilerplate filler inside included two mats with tips to motorists from the Dodge Safety Consultant, three free "Did You Know?" mats, and several others inviting people to do such things as buy savings bonds, support the Heart Fund, and join the female branch of the Marine Corps. Sprinkled about as fillers were seven ads for Star printing and advertising.

Inside reading matter consisted mainly of three columns written by local housewives for 5 cents per column inch, one each for Kennebunk, Kennebunkport, and Wells, devoting a sentence or a paragraph each to the hospitalizations, parties, whist games, baby showers, and the comings and goings of local people visiting friends and relatives. John and I were ecstatic — if nine hundred people would actually buy the paper each week for these, watch our smoke!

At eight that evening of John's first day, we stopped work and drove five miles to the nearest restaurant still serving that late, the Cozy Corner, just across the Route 1 line in Wells, a rough truck stop with a counter, some booths, a pinball machine, and a jukebox. Like the Kennebunks, Wells and its village corporation of Ogunquit were dry, but at Cozy Corner the liveliness belied the law. In the steam and hubbub we ordered hamburg platters and raised water glasses. Now we knew enough about what we had gotten into to discuss our respective roles.

John was a synthesis of uncomplicated outdoor enthusiasms and liberal intellectualism, lean, long-armed and legged, dark hair, slow shuffle, rather gaunt face. His broad-ranged, expressive voice erupted in quick, spontaneous laughter, responding to ideas as well as to wit. His friendships were made easily among people drawn to him by his charm, who rewarded him with intellectual stimulation or mutual enthusiasms. He was in Maine to be a writer and editor — but then, so was I. I owned the business, so I had to be publisher, a title without appeal. I wanted to be editor, and after a tense silence, John agreed to be managing editor. We would take the same salary, $5,000 a year, and we'd get the same raises when they became practical. I'd manage business affairs, job printing, and circulation. John would sell advertising and oversee layout and newspaper preparation. We'd share the writing and whatever else came up, meaning editing correspondence, serving customers, answering calls, proofreading, housekeeping, maintenance, mailing, delivery, and other operational duties. Agreed.

Now, how would we make things work? What could we do, short of spending money we didn't have, to improve the newspaper and pay the bills? Obviously, we had to attract a larger audience and increase ad linage. We were neither salesmen nor promoters, so we ignored the usual solutions: subscription drives and advertising gimmicks. To gain readers — the key to gaining ad linage — we'd write our best and trust the readers to respond. We'd start an editorial column immediately. We'd use none of the stuff that had stuffed the *Star* of the past, devoting our news-hole exclusively to local events.

There must be illustration. We rented a Polaroid camera, and John took two snapshots next day, serving notice on our readers of more to come. John learned that a sister weekly newspaper 11 miles inland, the *Sanford Tribune,* had a Scan-a-Graver, a machine that engraved in dots on plastic. We arranged to deliver our photos and wait while the machine did its work. Leasing a Scan-a-Graver was out of the question.

Our first-issue lead story was our own, the buying of the *Star*. I kept it short. I wrote two editorials, one saluting the outgoing Watsons, the other introducing ourselves and our aims. Those editorials, our two illustrations, a few reported events, and some two-column headlines were enough change for the first week.

Friday night, after putting the newspaper to bed, John and I spent our first relaxed hour gloating over it, our very first publication, the start of an exciting new career for both of us. Next morning a Portland banker living in Kennebunk dropped in to become our first new subscriber. Following him, one by one, locals of all descriptions came by to look us over, wish us well, or warn us about what would, and what wouldn't, go down well in our pages with the unique set of individuals that made up the population thereabouts. The stands were sold out by Sunday, so we boldly raised next week's pressrun by 50 copies. Smoke!

John and I arrived at the shop at 6 each morning and worked till 11 at night, when we'd open a can of something, eat it, and fall into bed. Over the weekend we cleaned the plant as much as was practical, short of scraping off its walls and ceilings. We carted load after load of debris to the dump, cleaned up the toilet under the stairs, worked out a billing process, learned to set type on the Ludlow, cut paper, and hand-feed the small presses.

By dint of John's first sales efforts, by Tuesday we decided to make our second issue the first six-pager in *Star* history. We wrote a long illustrated story about a high school exchange concert and four or five short ones on other subjects. John and I drove down to the ocean at the height of yet another wild northeaster and got soaked taking a Polaroid snap of a big green one socking the crumbling sea wall. Damage to the wall precipitated a town financial crisis and our first reports of small-town government troubleshooting. That second issue we gleefully swept all advertising off Page One — forever. We used only one small house ad, and the last pieces of boilerplate in my time.

The extra two pages added a dozen overtime hours for Tom and Paul, and more than that for John and me. We had to learn how the old Whitlock press worked when half-size sheets were fed into it, and how the Omaha folder worked when the half-sheets were fed into the larger ones from the side delivery, never before used.

Tom Dickson stood on the pressman's platform, sullenly flipping the flimsy half-sheets apart and coaxing them one by one into the cylinder clamps from an improvised side-stop. We cut down a flat carton and taped it into the delivery well. The half-sheets spanned only one side of the long rake on the delivery fly and tended to shoot out free, and float. I caught each sheet as it floated down, urging it gently onto the deepening pile.

We had four pressruns instead of two that week, and hectic wasn't the half of it. The sheets would enter the clamps a hair imperfectly, tear, and jam up at the feed, or wrap around the cylinder. Tom's foot would hit the impression plunger, and his finger the switch. A grim glaze would cover his lensed eyes as he grabbed a rag and type-wash can, or I did, and we all cussed to make things easier while the cylinder was washed off and the mutilated sheet of paper and its scraps were picked from the bowels of the press.

Then hands were washed, and away we'd go again. Sometimes we managed 50 impressions without a jam-up. Between them the drive belt would slip off the motor pulley in the cellar, and John or I would run down, clamber over the dank earth bent like chimpanzees, get the belt back on, and climb back to daylight. Meanwhile the phone would ring in the office, or a voice from the office would shout "Anybody here?" or a fuse would blow, or the Intertype would squirt molten lead onto Paul's sleeve.

Never had I experienced such hullabaloo. From behind his machine Paul shouted derogatory suggestions — sometimes sustained humorous boos — to us and customers alike. Tom simply fumed. I'm sure he'd already made up his mind to quit. We told Tom and Paul we'd hold to six pages from then on, or bust. They agreed: bust.

★ 5 ★

The Bishop and World Politics

Our third issue almost busted us. Wednesday afternoon we had our first brush with the weekly typesetting phenomenon known as the day-before-publication breakdown. With little more warning than the tired sound of someone lying down on an old bedspring, our veteran hot-metal machine collapsed into near coma, victim of a sort of degenerative Intertype arteriosclerosis. After producing a record number of lines of body copy to fill six eight-column broadsheet pages, the old girl simply lost her sense of mechanical order and started swallowing matrices, spitting lead, and ignoring Paul's irreverent instructions.

Two hours of diagnostic probing proved futile. We called a friend of
Paul's, the mechanical foreman at the daily *Biddeford Journal,* who
brought his tool kit down after supper. He, Paul, John, and I spent the
next five hours working grimly over the Intertype like doctors around an
operating table. Several times we completed the cycle of taking her apart
and putting her together again, until finally the old girl revived and
remembered how she made lines of type from molten lead. Even extending our deadline as far as we could push the post office, by then there
weren't enough hours left to fill the pages. Our vow to use no more
boilerplate was so new it was breakproof. We found an antique advertising cut of a pretty boy in checked knicker suit and matching cap casting
for trout from a species of White Rock rock, planted it in the front-page
chase under the fold, set HAPPY EASTER in our largest wood type,
five inches deep across the bottom of the page, filled the ink fountains,
cranked up the old Whitlock, and let her thunder.

We ran a six-column headline, "Northeast Gale Bangs Coast,"
with two subheads, one of them, "Selectmen Meet to Map Sea-Wall
Repairs as Second Giant Tide Makes Toward Flood." Below those
purple headlines, on came our storm story sequels.

Our first critical editorial, one of four that week, will strike the
sophisticated reader unacquainted with rural audience reaction as neither startling nor heavy-handed, but it sent the Kennebunks into a sort of
Red Alert. The *Star* had appeared each week for 80 years innocent of all
moral exhortation or critical comment on local affairs. "Baccalaureate"
was mild as mother's milk compared to what would come. Although it
crossed my mind that it might irritate some readers, I don't remember
hesitating before hanging it on the copy hook by the Intertype. Good
Catholic Bannon set it in metal, shaking his head and whistling know-
ingly.

We read the text of Bishop Feeney's statement enjoining local
Catholic children to boycott Baccalaureate services in Kennebunk
High School. By holding the services in the auditorium this year
rather than in one of the local churches the school authorities were
trying to avoid offending the sensibilities of any religious group,
particularly that represented by Bishop Feeney. This, apparently,
was not enough, and Bishop Feeney is arguing on the astonishing
grounds of religious tolerance that no child of the Catholic faith
should attend non-secular services. The children who follow his
injunction will be denied this innocent pleasure and introduced to
the sensation of being different from their friends at an age when
such sensations are particularly painful.

But even this is not the main issue. More important is the fact that a wedge between faiths is hereby driven one stroke deeper, and that religious tolerance, which Bishop Feeney believes is best served by segregation of what is, in these communities, a minority group, is dealt a wound that may take years of patient understanding to heal. The same argument for segregation is advanced elsewhere by those who feel that by following a separate-but-equal course trouble may be avoided and tolerance flourish. Well, it just doesn't work that way.

In a single short editorial, a brash young newcomer was lecturing the head man of Maine's largest single religious denomination about tolerance, ethics, and wisdom, and urging the local education system to reject his thoughtless interference.

The local reaction taught me an early lesson, and, surprisingly, the lesson was not harsh but encouraging. First, the editorial got people discussing a local event; second, it got them talking about the *Star;* third, it got results that displeased no one — the bishop rescinded his instructions; fourth, it regained for the newspaper some of the respect it had lost long before, and set it at the center of community affairs, where it belonged. We sold out on the stands, and again raised the pressrun for the following week.

John's editorial that week was a well-done short piece of philosophical observation unrelated, except in a circumstantial way, to the local scene, and was the cause of short-lived tension between us. It was called "Trapped in Paradise," and it described John's thoughts on seeing two flies trapped with a chocolate cake under a plastic dome on the counter of Congdon's Restaurant. John was pleased with it, and when we got together for post-publication mortems he asked me how I'd liked it. Fine, I said, but I hoped there would be no more like it in our editorial columns, which should be reserved for comment on local affairs — they were not repositories for fragments of homespun philosophy. Until we began writing personal columns, no more like it appeared.

Most of my unwritten policy manual was developed that way — brickbat by brickbat. We wouldn't write essays except on the Maine scene, or comment on national or international affairs unless local people had a hand in shaping them. We would do only what we could do better than any other publication on earth, meaning telling our readers about their hometowns.

Neither John nor I was a trained journalist. We felt uncomfortable with who-what-when-where leads, pyramiding of information, one-thought sentencing, one-sentence paragraphing, formula words, and one-note tonality. I assumed that the style taught in journalism schools was designed to help mediocre writers write accurately, and mediocre readers to scan newspapers and stop reading when their level of interest had been reached. Journalese has the ancillary practical function of permitting the make-up man in the composing room to fill arbitrary sections of the news-hole by cutting reports from the bottom up without structural damage. I wanted our readers to have the full reports, regardless of composing-room difficulties.

Some weekly news stories are best told in the journalistic style, of course. I felt that others should be written casually, others in the short-story mode, others preceded by background information or episodic reminders. Unjournalistically, I wanted our scenes set in context, visually and chronologically. Weather, time of day, appearance or demeanor of the participants, the secondary scenario in the room or along the road, the attitudes of the role-players — all might be introduced in a weekly's pages to root the reader firmly at the center of the action. The reader could only care to read the results of the local budget board's deliberations if he could be part of the meeting audience, sense the currents and feel the waves. He would have to be collaborator before he found any pleasure in the contentious discussion over a $200 appropriation for Memorial Day festivities. Journalese would never do it. He would have to be given all the essential information, all the argument available to the school board before he could make up his mind about the need for new band uniforms, or what to do about smoking in the johns.

I divide weekly newspaper readers into four groups. In Group A are the intellectuals, the professionals, and the wealthy refined. They are hardest to interest partly because their critical judgment is most rarefied, partly because they tend to be independent of local opinion and less vulnerable to local decision making. Until the editor can persuade them otherwise, most of them look on the local weekly as a quaint joke. To interest them the editor must pay constant attention to his craft. They are his golden egg.

Group B contains the local activists, newsmakers, community leaders — the ones who react with greatest alacrity to editorials and "hard news" of the community. They are the publisher's chicken.

Groups C and D contain the lower three-fifths of the population, educationally and economically. The merest comparative bargain-basement marketplace, the free shopping guide, will interest Group D. Group C readers will buy the next step up from the shopper if they find some leavening tidbits of community information in it. They don't demand hard news. They want to know the new dump hours, where the next church supper will be held, who got married. For the most part they are elderly people on fixed or modest incomes who have already gathered around them most of what they need, or people with workaday interests, neither particularly ambitious, involved, intellectually curious, nor able to buy much more than staples and secondhand goods. Advertisers will pay only the lowest rates to reach them. For them the publisher needs no editorial staff. He can maintain a subsistence-level income, as the Watsons had, by providing nothing but releases and correspondence. But Groups C and D are his ordinary egg, ignored at his peril.

Someone sees an opportunity for a second hardware store in town because the competition is weak, or a doughnut shop where none has existed. If his offering is good and attractively marketed, the public will buy. But before the hardware or doughnut sellers will buy the publisher's wares, his advertising, the publisher must have an audience of his own that can afford to buy. To capture more than Groups C and D the weekly publisher must more than double his efforts by providing interesting stories about his community. To get his chicken, he must cultivate his egg.

The chicken-and-egg dichotomy makes progress painfully slow. Many publishers succumb to the severity of the business climate or take the easy way out. The easy way out involves some sort of free distribution to guarantee the circulation numbers that will interest advertisers, and it leads to a professional dead end. The best way, the hard way, is to hatch the egg into a chicken that will lay more eggs.

Over the years of my later experience I came slowly to a solid appreciation for the people of the lower groups. Without really knowing why, they responded to the best writing of the reporters I hired, those who paid careful attention to clarity, the first element of style; accuracy, the first element of journalism; completeness, the first element of trust; and imagination, the first element of excitement.

When the people of Groups C and D were given these things, they enjoyed their reading more. Quality, it seems, is not merely a frill demanded by the intellectuals in Group A. Like proper punctuation, the stringencies of style were developed to promote understanding, not to provide dull courses for undergraduates, or appeal for refined tastes. When they could follow the thread of the news easily the members of my basic audience enjoyed learning what went on in their communities, conversing authoritatively about it, and gaining local stature thereby. Many came to assume active community leadership roles, and their local savvy gave them leadership dimensions denied to more educated newcomers. And lo, they often turned out to be quicker of mind, more devoted to the finer points of ethic, more straightforward in their dealings, and more valuable as citizens than the highbrows and the rich.

It took me years to learn it, but when a newspaper strives to interest a sophisticated audience, its most satisfying response comes from others near the center of the readership spectrum. Those need only strong meat — they are their own condiment, the salt of the earth.

Business Burdens

Traffic in and out of a newspaper office by foot or telephone is heavy, constant, and oblivious to the usual office-traffic lulls, prandial, after-hour, and weekend. There was no avoiding it, we needed a receptionist-bookkeeper-secretary-buffer. Janice Reynolds became the first of these, unruffled by the inefficient turmoil. Now we were five.

Printing business was picking up as the tourist season approached, offering an illusion of future profitability. But our expenses were greater in every dimension than the Watsons' had been. I had soon learned that our printing competition up Main Street was not the run-down operation the Watsons had denigrated. The Arundel Print Shop owners were a Harvard man and his wife who employed three first-rate people. Their work commanded higher prices than ours, and with reason. It was plain that Star printing was no more profitable than the newspaper. The standard weekly newspaperman's dilemma of that day faced me: to print job work, or not to print?

If one bought a relatively old weekly, chances were, in 1958 and for a decade after, that a printing business would come with it. The newspaper was set in metal and printed on a letterpress, meaning weight and lugging things. Typesetting and composition were done where the press was, on the premises. The male employees needed full-time work. Because advertisers demand last-minute attention, most ads were sold within a day or two of publication, and for timeliness most copy was set the same way. So the publisher kept enough shop help to set and print the paper in two days. To take up the off-days' slack, he gave the trained men job printing to do. The smaller the weekly, the truer this was, in the old hot-metal days.

They are two quite different enthusiasms, printing and news-papering — making money by manufacturing and trying to lead a community with one's thoughts. Newspaper shops approach their job work with a no-frills sense of mass-production deadlines. Quality control in the combination shop becomes a ghastly, losing, long-distance sack race.

Today the answer to the question, To print, or not to print? should always be, Not to print. In 1958 conditions simply didn't permit me that option, nor would they for ten more years. And by that time the job-work volume and the capital investment it represented, made dropping it psychologically unthinkable.

The need to continue job printing, and the sight of the Arundel Print Shop half a lap ahead, made investment in some sort of automatic job press inescapable. I was advised that the smallest Heidelberg platen press was the right beginner's choice. I walked up to see Bob Stinson at the Ocean National Bank to borrow enough for the down payment.

There was an incidental part of the business to which I hadn't given much thought, and that was keeping track of the money. Before bankers will talk seriously they want to see some performance figures — fixed costs, variables, billing breakdowns, projections. Things like that. I had nothing but billing totals and payroll records, and this seemed to worry Stinson. How could I tell how I was doing? Didn't I care?

Well, sure, I cared. But the figures simply didn't matter. Obviously I'd lose money till volume doubled or tripled. Raising volume without increasing expenses took all my energy; I had no time for record keeping. Well, Stinson told me, his directors had to have more than this. Maybe I should wait before buying a press. Meanwhile, get the records in shape.

One of the tenants overhead was a grizzled old widower, crippled from eastern ranch chores. His son, Norris, worked in Kennebunk for a local insurance cooperative. After visiting his father one Sunday, Norris found me alone in the office. His friend, Bob Stinson, was worried about me. Accounting and bookkeeping were his line of work, and he'd like to get me started, no charge. I refused by reflex, but Norris insisted. He put together all the loose bills and billing slips from the desk drawer and tried to talk some sense into me. I could listen only with one ear, the other being cocked to catch the sound of the wheel rim coming off Time's winged chariot. There seemed no point in reconstructing the obvious. I was spending no more than I had to spend to expand a business that had to be expanded. I was working as long and hard as I could to keep from having to pay someone else. There were no possible economies, and there was no future in treading water. Why try to learn the break-even point? Would that make me do a single thing I wasn't already doing?

I followed some of Norris's advice, but I knew I wouldn't satisfy the bankers. I paid no bills I couldn't stall off, until I had enough for the down payment. In early June, there was the Heidelberg, electrified and operational.

Within days I had a visit from a man who taught printing at Saco's high school. He had a student about to graduate, the best he'd ever had, Robert Bissonnette, 17, known as Bezo. Bezo, an extraordinarily quick mechanical study, came on at $1.05 an hour, no fringes, no benefits. Eleven years later he was married, father of four, titular boss of the 40 production people, master of every machine, and the nicest guy around. Now we were six.

Bezo was taught to run the new Heidelberg and to help compositor Tom Dickson at the composing stones. When Tom left two months later, I had no idea where to find a replacement. The day after Tom left, a large man of about 50 with a lean gray face, long torso with pregnant paunch, long, dripping nose and close manner — a drifter, obviously — dropped in looking for work. Frank Adams was a printer, he said, and did seem to have some familiarity with it. I hired him on the spot, but none of us felt comfortable. He kept to himself in a rented room, stayed through the winter, pulled one dubious con act on me, and then, one early summer day, vanished. Soon after he left, an FBI man called. Did I know a man calling himself Frank Adams, latest alias for a check-forger who had learned his printing at a penitentiary?

At the work peak of the year, again we were shorthanded. Three days after Adams left, a young art student appeared at the office looking for work, a warm body. Jerry and his new wife had rented a summer house with another young artist couple, expecting to live pretty much on roots and berries. I told him to report for work after he'd had some lunch.

Bezo taught Jerry some of the rough jobs, including how to run the hand presses. Jerry managed to mash his thumb in one of them, but kept going till it healed. He failed to show up for work one Friday after Labor Day, but came in Saturday, distraught and empty-eyed. His wife and unemployed friend had run off together, and he, Jerry, was leaving that day. I offered some friendly counsel, and he left. I put my head in my hands, fighting despair. I was working around the clock, around the week, a nest of nerves.

Two hours later I was in the shop alone, frantically tackling Jerry's printing orders. As I worked, a broad-shouldered man of about 30 wandered in, introducing himself with a thick Scots burr as Bill Dawson. The day before, he'd had a disagreement with his employers at the *Sanford Tribune,* the large weekly newspaper and printing shop 11 miles inland. He had been assistant to the production manager, compositor for the newspaper and job work. Did we need anyone? Bill stayed on for about eight years before he opened his own shop in Kennebunk.

That same fall typesetter Paul Bannon told me his younger brother was getting himself in trouble back home in Boston and his parents were unwell. So Paul too had to go. Finding someone willing to hire into a ramshackle Maine shop to operate a dilapidated Intertype at what we could afford to pay was a desperate proposition. I advertised in a couple of Maine dailies and had just one reply. George Pulkkinen's father had seen the ad and called his son in Connecticut, where he was a Linotype operator.

George loved Maine and wanted to return with his wife, Fay. He was short, good-looking, ruggedly constructed, obviously bright, cordial, direct. He spent half an hour with Paul learning the kinks in our machine and doing some setting. "This guy is good," Paul told me privately.

George and I went out and sat on the front stoop in mild autumn sunshine. I had to sell him on us, not the other way around. In Connecticut he had been making half again as much as I could pay him, operating much newer machines in one of the classiest shops in New England. I told him things were as he saw them, for a start, but we were growing. I talked about Kennebunk like a Chamber of Commerce secretary. George asked some questions, then agreed without comment to wages and terms, and in two weeks we had a farewell party for Paul. In 1980, as associate publisher, George Pulkkinen celebrated his twentieth anniversary with the *Star*.

The Arundel Print Shop had a small offset duplicator called a Multilith, which gave them quality on most jobs we couldn't match. When I told the old Watson brothers I was thinking about offset they told me it had no future. Printing volume was on the rise; the newspaper had grown to 10 and 12 pages. We were straining, getting deeper in hock to finance companies and suppliers. Payables were three to six months in arrears, double receivables. I bought a Multilith, a small camera, and a platemaker, all used, all on time payments, and hired Fernand Loranger, who had run a Multilith at Saco-Lowell before the machinery-maker moved south. Like Bill Dawson, Fern stayed on for about eight years before starting a shop of his own. Now we were seven.

By the next spring we had grown enough to need another man.

Another star Saco High School pupil, Larry Hill, joined us and moved up the *Star* ladder during the rest of my 18 years with the paper, becoming foreman of our web-offset newspaper press department. Now we were eight.

On Thursday nights, while Bezo ran off the last pages on the Whitlock and Bill Dawson, Larry Hill, and Fern Loranger got a start on the week's job work, typesetter George Pulkkinen and I would man the folder, John Cole would collate, bundle for the stands, and bag for the post office, while part-timer Rita Welch, the plump younger woman who had been in the shop when I first came to dicker with the Watsons, ran the Addressograph and gathered sections. Rita was fast and tireless. She is the only woman I've ever known who was a grandmother at 32. She became the leader of the paper-day crew, a changing gaggle of girls and boys who came down after high school each Thursday. We'd chuck the mailbags out the loading platform's French doors into my Ford's trunk — in memory, it was always snowing. I'd drive them uptown and throw them on the post office's rear platform. Then John and I would head our separate ways to deliver to the newsstands, fielding the good-natured ribbing about the lateness of the hour from the folks hanging around the mom-and-pop stores waiting for us. We kept adding new drops.

The work was unrelenting. The first year we grossed $35,000, the next $52,000. Receivables went up to $15,000, payables to $35,000, and long-term debt to nearly $50,000, figures more than adequate to support a bankruptcy. Yet we were growing. If we could just grow enough to bring fixed costs per unit down to a profit point we might skim over the hump. I could see no end to capital spending.

Every slow-paying deadbeat in the area became a steady customer. We payed so little attention to the books that by the time we knew it, their bills had become hopelessly large. Those first two years, every machine in the place developed death rattle. There was always a supplier's rep hanging around asking me why I couldn't pay a little more a lot faster, nearly ensuring my crack-up, usurping time I needed to get enough done to be able to pay him at all.

I worked from 7 in the morning to between 11 P.M. and 3 A.M. every weekday, from 8 A.M. till 10 at night every Saturday, and 10-hour Sundays, every single one, with half a day off at Christmas, no others. I never stopped for lunch, taking a single sandwich to work and eating it standing up, when I remembered to eat it at all. For two years I was so wound up and worried that I couldn't sleep when I went to bed, and more often than not I was in bed no more than three hours anyway. I never stopped for coffee, never ate supper till I got home late at night, never stopped working to talk for pleasure; never, except for Saturday nights here or there, can I remember doing a single thing but work in total, blind frenzy. For 11 years I never took so much as a single two-day weekend off or a vacation of a single day.

It seems ridiculous as I look back, demented. Failure was a shattering, impossible prospect. But how could I not fail? If I got sick, I was lost. If I lost an employee and couldn't replace him immediately, I was lost. If the bank or a finance company or a supplier squeezed me and found me dry, I was lost. I was lost anyway, maybe. What would I do if the *Star* failed? I couldn't turn back this late in my game. I, who had begun life with so many advantages, would have failed at a dinky operation. I had to win, but at the end of those first two years, with all the effort I gave it, my back was to the wall.

★ **II** ★

★ 7 ★

Expansion

What kept me sane was hope, and what kept hope sane was the stirring of life in the roots of the newspaper, just showing its spikes above ground. The pages themselves were messy and unappetizing, but there was more than enough meat on them to justify the outlay of a nickel. We served surprises every week, and a sense of community oscillation.

Encouraged by the response to the newspaper in the Kennebunks, I was expanding coverage south into Wells and Ogunquit. Circulation had grown to 3,000 in the summer, and there were always countryfolk waiting at the newsstands Thursday nights, complaining if we were late, as we almost always were. We had taken such toddling first steps that the enthusiasm startled me. Everywhere John or I went people crowded around to argue or to learn why we felt as we did, or to tell us the news behind the news, which might have kept us from our misinterpretations.

Effervescent author Bill Clark, who wrote a column under his "Deacon Seat" logo, and lobsterman Alvin Fisher, who wrote his flavorful "Tide Lines," became frequent drop-in visitors at the old plant. They, George Stevens, and occasionally others, animatedly gathered around the grimy old composing stones after the paper went to bed Thursdays to play poker and drink beer with the shop crew.

I mentioned George Stevens. This extraordinary man was about 42, youngest of six siblings from a strapping family of rollicking eccentrics. Norman, George's oldest brother, a tall, gnarled countryman renowned for the intensity of his conversation, was a selectman. Norman's son, Frank, ham-handed, gentle, formidable, was now chief of police. George himself had a grown son by an early marriage, but was now single, supported mostly by a service disability pension. By trade he was a free-lance news cameraman of considerable skill but little application for the money-making game, and little feeling for it.

George was irrepressible, broad, big-boned, full of mirthful highs and great brooding lows. We published some of George's photos and asked for more. He was so set up by the local response that he recklessly up and quit free-lancing for all his former newspaper customers. George scorned the convenience and versatility of 35 millimeter, preferring his clumsy 2¼-by-2¼ Speed-Graphic, noble badge of the news cameraman's trade. The grain of his prints was very fine, his hand rock-steady, and his darkroom technique sure. George took over our expanding newsstand and post office delivery chores and continued without a break for many years. He also volunteered to sell merchant signature support on illustrated full-page ads for local high school teams. Little by little he would piece together as much of a living from the *Star* as he cared to put himself out for.

Each winter George's American Legion post staged a variety minstrel show to raise charity money. Seeing his drinking buddies cavorting on stage in sloppy costume sent George into a form of hilarity denied to most of us. One day he burst in with the cataclysmic intelligence that waning interest had made his fellow-legionnaires decide to cancel production plans; the minstrel show was on the rocks. John persuaded George to return to his legionnaires and offer to be the one-man show committee, with the promise of enough *Star* hoopla to put the 1959 show in the record books.

George became the irrepressible impressario, "Imp" for short. By show time Kennebunk was in great good humor, and in four towns "George the Imp" was on everyone's lips. Each week we ran front-page Barnum-esque progress reports. George was everywhere, the big butterer-up and egger-on man, and the comic relief. Town Hall was sold out a week early for its matinee and two evening performances, meaning that at least half the dead-of-winter population in town would see the show. The newspaper was making the news.

John and I attended meetings of budget boards, planning boards, school boards, selectmen, and whatever committees were newsworthy. Our reports were embellished with quotes of unintentional as well as intentional humor, inept as well as ept remarks, and intercommittee squabbling.

I was at first staggered by the local reaction to mild editorial criticism. But when public work, paid or unpaid, affected the quality of local life, I thought it should be judged by the highest standards. We had begun immediately to inspect the workings of local government and the quality of the schools. We interviewed candidates for municipal office, stating our preferences and elaborating. If the townspeople were shocked, the snubbed candidates and their families were outraged.

The towns were run by a few easily identified people, unofficial as well as official, who enjoyed their powers but obfuscated their public actions. No one outside Town Hall knew how responsibilities were handled, what options were available, what decisions were made, or even how things worked. Meetings were unagendaed, unattended, and informally scheduled. Most local elections were uncontested. Committee vacancies were filled with cronies.

What the public can't see can't interest it. Ignorant of the facts, unable to question or vote intelligently, the public interest dies and control of government coagulates. Town Hall fills up with bumblers and demagogues. John and I reported on the civic leaders, turning them into newsmakers in spite of themselves. Some enjoyed the attention, others didn't. When newspapers do their jobs, the elected bumblers and yes-men avoid the limelight, and suspicions form.

All this is, of course, generally understood. But small communities rarely apply such understanding to themselves. Most community newspaper publishers are local businessmen, like their fellow clubmen, and are guided by the same self-serving interests. All these people are made elaborately uncomfortable by printed criticism. To save himself unpleasantness, even ostracism, the weekly publisher usually avoids criticizing community leaders, confining his comment to boosterism. You can say anything you want to an acquaintance on a street corner — and deny it later. But in print . . . Lordy! In my first "Anniversary Thoughts" editorial I was moved to write defensively:

> Good people, if we have stepped on toes it is because we're not good dancers. But we didn't come to dance with you. We came to work with you, and on our first birthday we rededicate ourselves to the real interests of the towns and villages we serve.

Each week we gained supporters and detractors. The refrain of the detractors was: "You guys have your nerve coming in here and telling us how to run our towns!" We argued, and learned from our arguments. Sometimes our sights shifted, sometimes not. As outsiders, our views were, if not insightful, at least fresh. What the insiders saw was often clouded by preconception. When our critics accused us of unfair advantage with our newspaper megaphone, we'd point to the letters column and urge them to use it.

"Hello, is this the editor? I'm calling about your screwed-up story on the licensing hearing."

"Who is this, please?"

"Never mind who this is. I want a full retraction, and so does my lawyer."

"What part of the story was wrong?"

"All of it. It was all wrong."

"The part that said the meeting was held Thursday?"

"No, but just about everything else."

Gradually I learn that it is the fourth paragraph that has offended my caller, and then that it is the second sentence of it, in which the man who must be my caller has been quoted. Sometimes John or I had heard it wrong, but often the caller had misread the sentence, or had meant to say something he hadn't said, or had simply found out later that what he did say contained an error in judgment he wanted to purge from the record. Or else he had deliberately tried to mislead his audience but hadn't thought his words were being recorded. Over the phone I'd listen and agree to correct the mistake if I thought this were warranted. If not, I'd offer the letters column, or if things got mean, suggest a specific hack lawyer and hang up.

We learned that a story may be rendered worthless by a single unverifiable assertion, or an inaccurate quotation or one erroneously attributed. Even harmless, insignificant errors of interpretation arouse the reader's derision, and sometimes his abuse. Clarity and accuracy *must* be cardinal principles.

★ 8 ★

Bruised Rotarians

That second summer sales boomed, and the season was hectic. Circulation averaged 3,100, and the newspaper was 12 and 14 pages, meaning six or eight pressruns, 30 to 40 hours of rolling time for the screeching Whitlock. I was taking about every other run on the press platform, or catching the 2-page sections off the delivery fly, and then spending 4 hours on the folder.

Bill Bishop of the *Reading* (Mass.) *Chronicle* advertised a Premier press for sale, a somewhat faster version of the Whitlock that printed four pages at a pass rather than two, the potential effect being to cut our press time by two-thirds and folder time in half. Bill and I settled, no dickering, for $1,500.

Next Friday the Premier arrived on a flatbed. That sweltering July night, after the last sheet of our final run had flown off the fly of the Whitlock, two short, thick-armed men from the Saco Junkyard, who had been observing our pandemonium expressionlessly from the wings, approached the old girl with sledgehammers and two-foot wrenches, spat on their hands, and ripped her apart, root and branch, while the rest of us lugged the pieces out the French doors onto a brutally rusted six-wheeler George Stevens had borrowed for us. At 3 A.M., after our beery, sweating, hooting wrecking party, I drove the groaning truck to Saco and left it for morning.

Monday the Premier set-up man arrived, and the race against time began. By our first-run deadline on Wednesday, where the Whitlock had screeched its last, there stood the Premier, rolling with the *Star,* a thing of pride, if not exactly of beauty. Beauty was in the eye of the beholden.

The Premier permitted us to change to a Thursday dateline, as our advertisers had been pressing us to do. Halftone reproduction was superior too, in fact quite rich, and page makeup flexibility was improved. No longer was it necessary for us to sprint our cellar laps — the Premier's motor was attached to the press.

When that second summer ended, September came on like a cool drink. After Labor Day, Maine's playtime crowds melt away, and the locals pick up the skeins of their lives from the drawers they dropped them in three months before, busy themselves with back-to-school and battening down for the winter, take up the long needle of committee work, and get down to knitting. But before the local boards and committees shift into high gear, before budget work starts and the corn of November electioneering heats up and pops, there is a time of activity doldrums when the Maine weekly must stimulate its own news.

John began preparations for a *Star* meet-the-candidates night that would fill Town Hall. He became a Youth Center member, and in reporting its meetings got into a published squabble with his fellow members, the five most prominent local ministers, who nitpicked his reports of what they said in righteous letters to the editor. I began covering the activities of the Wells Harbor Committee, whose members were trying to get the Army Corps of Engineers to dredge the marshy mouth of the Webhannet River. John was promoting a similar dredging of the Kennebunk River harbor, organizing a group that met in the *Star* office with our district congressman.

1959 was the year of the first stirrings of environmental awareness in the Maine Legislature. The then newly formed Maine Water Improvement Commission began issuing ultimatums to southern Maine coastal communities to clean up their water. The *Star* was awarded partial credit for the affirmative Kennebunk vote to build a sewer, and total condemnation by the strident antisewer Taxpayers' Group. In Kennebunkport it was the officials and committee members, aghast at the cost of digging a sewer below the frost line in the ledgy riverfront village, who dragged their feet for years before our reporting and editorial campaign helped put them to rout, and the Port built its sewer. Our differences were the roots of bitterness between the newspaper and official Kennebunkport that lasted for more than a decade.

More money changed hands in Maine's coastal towns in 13 summer weeks than in all the other 39. Summer advertising flooded us into extra pages, and summer circulation lengthened our pressruns. Our regular printing customers, used to our cut-rate prices, doubled their orders, leaving no time for the summer traders accustomed to paying higher prices elsewhere and willing to pay even more for prompt service. The summer flood forced us to hire more help, but we couldn't afford trained people. Anticipating growth, we kept trainees on in relative idleness after summer was over.

We weren't alone. Shopkeepers and service people also kept larger staff and inventories than winter custom warranted. Their debtors couldn't afford to pay them in the lean season, so they couldn't afford to pay us. The tourist-trappers who skimmed the cream from our pitcher spent it where they did their winter trapping. The locals were annually doused with summer money and bled dry during the long off-season.

The little shops on Kennebunk's Main Street, miles from the summer action, clung precariously to life. Shop selections were skimpy and high-priced because trading was slow, driving custom out of town. Failures were frequent, and every bankrupt owed the rest of us near-bankrupts money. Empty Main Street storefronts encouraged a sort of commercial musical chairs game in which new players were lured by low rents to take the plunge into merchandising. Some managed a tuck somersault with half-gainer, but there were plenty of plain old belly flops.

The Chamber of Commerce was as dead as the winter economy. Almost all its puny budget was spent advertising for tourists and keeping them spending when they came. I argued for a subcommittee of industry, an argument ignored by my fellow directors, most of them tourist business operators, until a couple of respected Main Street merchants were persuaded, and an Industry Committee was formed. Our major accomplishment was a three-year, eventually successful effort to bring a plastics molding firm to Kennebunk — a company that is still the town's largest employer.

A year or so after we had arrived in Kennebunk, John and I were visited by a committee of two from the local Rotary Club. They already had the tentative approval of the sixty or so chapter members, we were told, so we were as good as in. The Rotarians were the big club in town — all the captains of business were Rotarians. They met for lunch Thursdays.

We feigned regret — Thursdays were tough for us. No problem, we were told, we could "make up" on Fridays or Mondays, in Biddeford or Sanford. Attendance was a big thing in Rotary.

We protested lamely: we ate while we worked. Lunch away from town was out of the question.

Oh, come on — everybody stopped for lunch! We couldn't snub our friends in the business community. That was true enough, financially speaking.

In due course we were indoctrinated, and each of us attended a few luncheons, singing the old songbook songs, paying our quarter fines for arriving late, listening to the guest speakers, and exchanging banter with our fellow clubmen. Even if we had passionately desired Rotary luncheons, we couldn't have been regular. Soon, giving up the charade, we stopped attending and waited for the inevitable boom to fall, our snobbery now a matter of record.

But before we were drummed out of membership, Rotary Club secretary and author of the chatty Rotary newsletter, George Whittier, who owned Whittier's Greenhouse, had contrived a friendly social initiative, an after-work drink. Whittier was a small, lively man in his late fifties, with a roan mustache, brisk wit, and pre-Kennebunk experience that passed locally for cosmopolitan. Our talk was enlivened by George's Big Apple reminiscences and the surprise of common acquaintanceships.

Conviviality, but not extended social contact, survived our removal from Rotary, whose membership was focal to Whittier's life. About a year after our visit, ill health forced George's resignation from the club. I recalled his early cordiality and was moved to write an interior-rhymed, humorous editorial tribute in prose form called "Idle Thoughts," taking the usual doggerel-writer's liberties with fact and construction. I half expected some forgiving Rotarian, maybe even George himself, to mention it, but none did.

Several months later, during a temporary remission in his illness, George casually offered another afternoon drink. I was happy to accept. We chatted for half an hour before he remarked off-handedly that I really shouldn't have insulted the Rotarians that way, for my own good if nothing else. The critical editorial, he reminded me — couldn't remember just how it went — the one that accused the Rotarians of sleeping after their Thursday luncheons. They all returned to work after Rotary, George said pointedly.

I was still puzzled. You mean the rhymed editorial, I asked, the one I wrote when you resigned? The humorous one?

No, George said, he must have missed that one. The one he meant wasn't rhymed, and the Rotarians certainly hadn't thought it was funny. He himself had been somewhat annoyed, he had to confess.

I wanted to make sure: he must mean the rhymed editorial?

No, the one about the Rotarians napping after lunch.

Finally, George got to his feet, saying he might be able to lay his hands on it. He was pretty sure he'd kept it — remembered coming across it recently. He walked to the telephone table, opened the drawer and, registering mild surprise, picked up the clipping on top. He handed it to me. "You can see for yourself that it isn't rhymed."

So I read some of it aloud to him, with the following pauses:

April has come again with its sote shoures, / and some shoures not so sote, / up from the deepest Missoures / and the northernmost Dakote, / and in the street outside the *Star* office there's a seven-foot pool, / hilarious trap for many an April fool. / Up the street they come, and the muddy water looks about two inches deep, / but it's really a foot, and the first car, some old heap, / hits bottom and nearly busts a spring. . . . /

And we sit here feeling lazy, thinking, that's it, Spring / busting out all over, even a bit (dare we say it?) early, / with the ice out of the rivers and the boys feeling boyish, and the girls girly. /

Up in the greenhouses, Brown Street and Whittier's, / the calla lilies are about yea high, and just between us, can you imagine anything prettier / than one in the teeth of George Whittier / doing an adagio among the boxes of seedlings? / While he's given us a lot of needlings, / we'd sooner get into a piano-playing contest with Victor Borge / than engage in a wit-slinging contest with George. / "He's witty, and you'll all agree, / he's rather Whittier than we." / Speaking of George, we've just learned that he's resigning / as Secretary of the dining / and after-luncheon-soporifically-reclining / Rotary Club whose wheels have spun, / with George lashed securely to the wheel, for one / . . . .

There was more of it, ending with a tribute to George, but the damage was in the above, and it was enduring. Levity can be dangerous.

That October Perley Watson died, painfully, of cirrhosis in his home behind the *Star,* a gray and gut-wracked figure, uncomplaining and uncompromising, an ornery old soldier.

And on January 10 my father phoned me from his home in Sag Harbor, the Long Island town where Doug Gardner published his weekly *Express*. Less than two years after he had cosigned my note at Ocean National, Doug had died of a heart attack. He had gone to a party with his wife, Vicky, eaten and drunk and boomed and laughed as usual, and had gone home complaining to Vicky of pain in his chest. She had wanted to call a doctor, but Doug said no, he'd just sleep it off. He slept, and died in his sleep.

I walked to the front room, sat down by the window of my first night's cold vigil in Kennebunk, stared up the snowy hill, and was overtaken by sobbing I couldn't control.

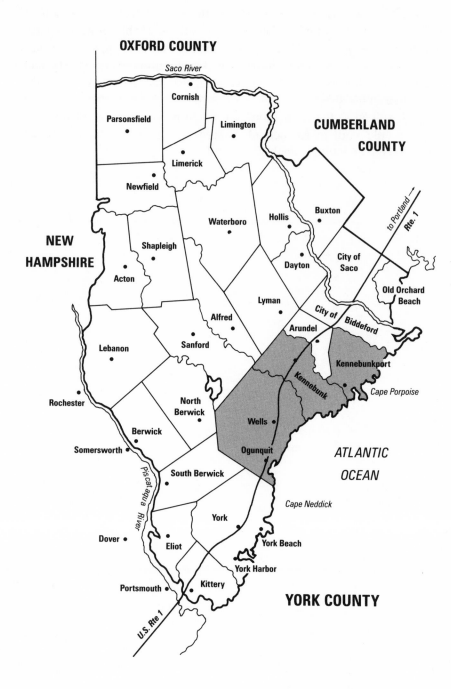

OXFORD COUNTY

Saco River

Cornish

Parsonsfield

Limington

CUMBERLAND
COUNTY

Limerick

Newfield

to Portland —

Rte. 1

NEW
HAMPSHIRE

Waterboro

Hollis

Buxton

Shapleigh

Acton

Dayton

City of
Saco

Lyman

Old Orchard
Beach

Alfred

City of

Arundel

Biddeford

Lebanon

Sanford

Kennebunk

Kennebunkport

Cape Porpoise

Rochester

North
Berwick

Wells

Berwick

ATLANTIC
OCEAN

Somersworth

Ogunquit

South Berwick

Cape Neddick

York

Piscataqua River

Dover

York Beach

Eliot

York Harbor

Portsmouth

Kittery

YORK COUNTY

U.S. Rte 1

★ 9 ★

A Wrecked School Principal, A Wrecked Ship

Immediately to Kennebunk's south, the 3,500-population town of Wells and its 1,000-population Village Corporation of Ogunquit lay in a media wasteland. From Ogunquit south, Mainers read mostly Boston and New Hampshire dailies. The Maine dailies circulating in York County, the *Portland Press-Herald* and the *Biddeford Journal,* placed no value on those southerners, who shopped and played in New Hampshire, and the small New Hampshire dailies stopped their northward coverage at York. Wells, about equidistant from Sanford, Biddeford, and Portsmouth, New Hampshire, scattered its shopping to those places and to Portland.

Our decision to extend *Star* coverage was unavoidable: a weekly that served only the Kennebunks was condemned to economic anemia. The direction of our extension was nearly unavoidable too, since the 8,000-circulation daily *Biddeford Journal* bordered Kennebunkport to our north, and the *Journal*'s corporate sister, the large weekly *Sanford Tribune* hunkered just to our west. Below Ogunquit on the coast were the Yorks and Kittery, and inland to our southwest were North and South Berwick, all four boasting their own tiny weeklies.

Without reserves, we had to establish our Wells-Ogunquit presence quickly. I did so by jumping into town and village affairs with all pens firing, creating issues by exploring the closet-grown nightshades of municipal government and school system, leavening my news with stories of natural event and human interest. I upbraided Ogunquit for its tourist overkill and conservative snobbery. I criticized Wells's headlong rush to honky-tonk and its deplorable shortage of ordinances, its desecration of God-given resources, for having no library and no center of town. I scolded the entrenched, self-serving municipal boards, the sloppy, one-man, elected police department. My first banner-headline story was based on an interview with a just-fired Wells town manager, a youngish man of brains and vitality who just couldn't believe the nasty intrigues he had encountered. I quoted him at length on the backbiting, feuding, favoritism, and general paleolithicity in Town Hall.

Wells was a tough town for newspapering. Its early readers only bought us to see what else they could get angry about. My skin was not as thick as a reporter's should be, but my phrenological bump of outrage was as sensitive as any. The entrenched, smugly unresponsive Wells officials — elected, appointed, or hired — resented all inquiry and all publicity, as well they might have. Their sloppiness and ineptitude, their catering to commercial interests, their insensitivity to uglification, stirred me to rash confrontations, and them to uncommunicative hostility. The merchants and business people preferred to hear nothing of their own plans and activities, and nothing but praise of their surroundings. All were livid at my editorial attitudes. I dreaded every meeting in Wells.

A coalition of vicious parent activists and dissatisfied schoolteachers was trying to get the School Board to fire Norman Holder, the high school principal, for starting a trial program of "ability grouping" in math and English. Hearing only the anger at its regular meetings, the School Board called a large public meeting, hoping to hear from Holder's supporters, but the anti-Holder coalition was well organized and so strident that the Holder supporters attending timidly held their tongues. At that meeting the bellwether anti-Holder teacher, an elderly spinster who had taught, and was revered by, most of the native parents, demonstrated her misunderstanding of both the purpose and the mechanics of the grouping experiment. The exercised parents hated grouping mainly because it hadn't flattered their own children. With slander and innuendo, the coalition diverted public attention from the initial complaint, loudly repeating a mess of extraneous rumor, gripe, and suspicion, and on the strength of it calling Holder a liar and a man of loose moral character.

I knew Holder as a man of natural modesty and admirable comportment whose educational goals I admired, and followed the unfolding developments with report and editorial in fascinated disbelief. But mine seemed to be almost the only such voice. The School Board timorously decided that the public ruckus was disruptive of the educational process and accepted Holder's resignation "for the good of the children."

In a long editorial I set down the picayune charges against Holder, in all instances unsubstantiated, that were aggressively asserted at another large public meeting before representatives of the Maine Teachers Association, concluding that in the judgment of most of those present at that revealing meeting, Holder had emerged from it untarnished and with dignity.

Without the exposure the paper had given this "War in Wells," few but the ax-grinders would have heard anything but gossip. Scant public knowledge would have developed scant public interest. An uninformed public would have interpreted Holder's resignation as an admission of guilt, taken note of the departure of one principal and the arrival of his replacement, then turned its attention to other things.

Not this time. Wells was suddenly overcome with such enlightened remorse that a group of hitherto dormant citizens and teachers blew up a second storm, forcing yet another public hearing. The whole town turned out for it. The absent principal was defended, even eulogized. The School Board responded happily to the nearly unanimous vote in favor of offering Holder his job back. After brief deliberation Holder declined — he was well out of Wells.

During the 1960 vernal equinox of the news doldrums we got busy making news happen again. Town meetings and local elections were over; school and town budgets were fixed; referendum questions were decided; winter sports were over, spring sports not yet begun; the annual crop of new summer-business hopefuls hadn't arrived yet; we were in mud time. Two stories fortuitously broke in March, two good-news happenings. More accurately, the *Star* broke them, and then rode them.

After the paper was out one Friday, photographer George Stevens, always on the qui vive for salable photo possibilities, called to say that he and a couple of his pals had been down on Dipsy Beach at low tide after a storm looking for beached clams and had seen the rib-tips of an old vessel poking up from the sand by the sea wall. Did we want a picture? George said a couple of other known wrecks lay under the sands and were occasionally seen when winter storms scoured away their cover, but he'd never seen this one before, and it was a big mother. The sand must be down four feet, he said, right up to the sea wall.

John jumped in his car and drove down to the beach, where George led him to the 65-foot outline of the massive rib-ends, obviously the lower-hull remains of a longer sailing vessel. John removed an inch-long diamond-shaped wedge and a six-inch treenail, a hard cylindrical wooden peg used by early shipwrights. He phoned Massachusetts marine historian Edward Rowe Snow, who drove up the next day with two associates.

By the time they arrived a tide had come and gone, and the sand had begun to wash back. Seeing the activity at low tide, crowds gathered. Some boys tried with shovels to uncover more of the timbers, but the wind was cold, and seawater filled the holes as they dug. John persuaded Fire Chief Coleman to send a hose truck and volunteers, who got enough of the stern showing to give the experts a good look at the crude construction. A piece of plank was hacked off for age analysis. Crowds were still gathering when the tide returned.

Snow took his story home to his local daily, which broke it next day. He thought the hull might be what remained of the old cargo packet *Industry,* which disappeared in 1790 with 13 aboard on a voyage from St. George, Maine, to Boston. He based his speculation partly on the rare diamond-shape wedge, used by early Irish shipbuilders. In the 1780s a small Irish colony had flourished briefly in St. George, and the *Industry* had been one of its creations. Some flotsam from the *Industry* had washed ashore near Kennebunk.

Next day four young men with shovels reached the keel, finding pottery shards, a piece of leather with triangular holes punched in it, chunks of a hard black substance, and half a lignum vitae pulley, which John sent to a Boston museum laboratory for analysis. A metal detector passed over the wreck revealed no trace of metal, reinforcing the surmise that it must be very old.

The wire services had picked up the story, and it was appearing on television and in Boston and Maine dailies. Wednesday more historical people arrived. Kennebunk cops were dispatched to the narrow beach road to handle traffic snarls. John got another band of high-schoolers down after school, and before dark they managed to gouge out the whole middle of the wreck with a makeshift, truck-hauled scoop. While three hundred freezing stragglers watched, accurate measurements were taken. The new digging uncovered an old leather boot, a bone, a china plate, and a brick, all with dubious *Industry* connections, but all featured prominently on the evening TV news.

Also exposed by the storm, outcroppings of a smaller vessel, not buried so deep and seen every several years, were bared farther down the beach. This sailing packet had been carrying pig iron in 1750 when it struck an offshore Kennebunk Beach ledge. Survivors had been brought ashore before the vessel broke up. Its construction was sufficiently more refined than that of the newly uncovered hull to give reason to suspect that our relic was older than Snow had thought.

"May Be Raised — Thousands View Vessel's Sandy Grave" was John's first headline on Thursday, by the luck of the weekly reporter nearly a week after the discovery. For a month afterward his sequels were sprinkled with laboratory reports, more quotations from experts, and interviews with local antiquarians, convincing readers that we had the most authoritative voice.

But that was all there ever was. For three decades since, no combination of winter wave and tidal drag has contrived to uncover the old wreck again.

The other doldrums story broke the same week. "Gold Rush On! Engineer Discovers Gold Dust and Nugget in Perkins Cove Gravel" was my headline.

The Monday after the old ribs had emerged I was at Perkins Cove, the man-made harbor basin in Ogunquit, to check the progress of a routine Army Corps of Engineers maintenance dredging project. I entered the Corps trailer, on-the-job office for supervisor Ervin Pickering. His dragline dredge was working by the outfall of the Josias River, source of the silt he was dredging. We chatted for a while before Pickering remarked off-handedly that he had something that might interest me. He stepped to a wall shelf and handed me a pickle jar of gravel flecked dimly with yellow, a small vial with about a thimbleful of yellow dust in it, and a nugget the size of an oat grain. He watched in amused silence while I inspected them, and then said, "Gold."

Where had he found it?

Pickering pointed out the window to where the rig was working.

No kidding? My reporter's antennae were quivering wildly.

Yes, Pickering said, he had been casually inspecting the mud being dumped to expand the parking area. In a bucketful inadvertently scooped from the alluvial gravel below project depth, he had noticed the flecks. He had borrowed a pan from a local rock-hound and separated about a quarter of an ounce. He called the gravel "rich in gold" — first quality — he could spread the nugget like butter. Most of it was down there below the silt, under six feet of salt water at low tide. Unfortunately, the Army's contract didn't permit him to dig deeper, into the gravel or to bedrock where most of the gold could be assumed to have settled.

It was Monday — we wouldn't hit the stands till Thursday night. Pickering assured me that no other reporters ever came around to see him. Unless someone tipped them off, we'd have the story first.

I returned to the office and wrote my story, holding it off the copy hook till Thursday morning. I carefully combed the other area papers. Nothing. I sensationalized a bit, ending with:

Meanwhile, Ogunquit has visions of regaining out of the Cove some of the gold, or its equivalent in legal tender, sunk into it this year. Also in prospect is a parking lot sparkling goldenly in the soft summer moonlight of 1960 — or as much of the lot as remains after the prospectors have finished with it.

When that stuff hit our fans they moved en masse to Perkins Cove, carrying pie pans, fry pans, basins of all descriptions. The parking lot underwent considerable hell. Everyone had tales to tell, but most were of fool's gold — iron pyrite present in more than usual quantities. It looked as if Pickering had panned out the only dragline scoopful with anything exciting in it.

The wire services and electronic media people picked up the gold story as they had the old vessel story, and had a field day with it. No more gold was found. By the time Thursday rolled around again the story was fizzling. *Star* readers had something, though. "Uranium Possibilities Abet Perkins Cove Gold Fever" was my headline.

Among the thousands of amateur gold-panners was a mineralogist whose excitement was pricked by a piece of rock he found in the parking lot. He pronounced it almost certainly pitchblende, the black oxide of uranium and chief source of radium. People with Geiger counters began tracking the cove environs, finding traces of lead but no more pitchblende.

In two weeks it was all over. No one found enough of anything to justify the effort of finding it. Maybe I had been conned, and had unwittingly conned others. A flash in the pan, maybe, but a gold rush anyway — Ogunquit and neighboring towns were sprinkled with gold equivalent. A Sunday cartoon in one Boston paper had the traffic backed up as far as the eye could see over the hills from Ogunquit south, cars full of prospecting gear and people in sourdough costumes. What with the old boat and the gold rush, our four towns were crawling with the jocular curious. Shops, eateries, and motels that had never opened in March and April before were doing a land-office business. The native tourist-trappers temporarily forgave us our editorial trespasses, everyone else was chortling, and *Star* circulation was booming.

★ 10 ★

A New "Star" Is Born

The people of the Kennebunks resented the dilution of their newspaper with Wells-Ogunquit news. Instead of changing their reading habits and skipping what didn't interest them, they now found themselves reading about Wells and Ogunquit and feeling shortchanged. We'd remind them that the paper was now much larger, with more of "their own" news in it, but they were not to be mollified. From Wells-Ogunquit readers we heard the other side of the complaint: the *Star* was not their paper, it was the "Kennebunk" paper.

Our third summer, with its impending ad and circulation increases, was coming on fast. I made what was for us a momentous decision: we would launch a Wells-Ogunquit *Star,* not a separate newspaper, but an edition with its own banner, a changed front page highlighting Wells-Ogunquit stories, and some inside changes of minor stories. All advertising and copy of general interest would appear in both editions.

The separation would mean more work for all of us — more stories to write and set, more photos, additional page make up, a split pressrun, and general confusion — but it made sense. We ran mostly 14 pages in both editions that summer, with news for 20. By summer's end we had nearly reached the same saturation readership in Wells and Ogunquit that we enjoyed in the Kennebunks.

Two years before, a man had arrived in Wells to start a summer "throw-away" tabloid, the *Tourist News,* offered free everywhere in Wells and Ogunquit, filled with restaurant, entertainment, and lodging advertisements at high rates, fleshed out with free promotional copy, tide tables, and coming events. The tourist-business owners had never bought *Star* advertising — their customers were not interested in local affairs. I started a slim summer magazine, *Clue,* with small ads and home-written copy about things to do and places to see, illustrated in ads and headings with my wife Anneke's drawings. The idea was to sell its ads and print it during the slack winter season to keep the Heidelberg press busy during the lean months before May. *Clue* didn't follow the script, however — advertisers wouldn't sign contracts till spring — so the big printing job swamped us at our busiest time of the year. But after the inevitable new-publication loss years, *Clue* eventually grew large enough to be profitable.

Clue, the new Wells-Ogunquit edition of the *Star,* and steady printing volume increases sustained hopes that helped compensate for the ceaseless drudgery and threadbare life that what I now called Star Press was inflicting on me and my family. John and his attractive wife, Cynthia, were close and cheering friends, but they and their two children were in similar straits, without resources other than John's salary. While John was not a partner in the business sense, he was a partner in personal commitment. Without equity, he saw no gleam at the end of our tunnel. As he lost faith in our future he resented his commitment, and a barrier began to grow between us.

One July morning, four months after our second *Star* anniversary, John called to ask me if I had time for a talk. The formality of the request itself was ominous. When we met he spoke carefully. Even leading the most spartan life, he couldn't make ends meet. He knew there was nothing in the treasury, but he needed assurance of more soon. Much as he loved the *Star* and what we were doing with it, he'd have to leave unless he could make more money. What did I foresee?

He knew the answers. More drudgery, I replied ruefully. Deeper debt. Growth in spite of it all, and eventually, maybe, better times. I thought I could foresee an $80,000 gross that third year, and not far beyond that maybe some profit, meaning merely several years of retiring the most oppressive parts of the debt. The trouble was that more growth meant more borrowing, not more cash to distribute. And I wasn't even sure we could pull through another winter.

Couldn't I just borrow about $60,000 privately, John suggested, to make things easier? Even if the investor wound up with majority ownership, at least I could save part of it.

Unlikely, I thought, that anyone would risk that much, even for outright ownership.

In that case, John said sadly, he couldn't stay. He had been offered a managing editorship at the *Brunswick Record,* the newspaper that would not long afterward overtake the *Sanford Tribune* and become Maine's largest weekly.

So our friends would leave, and my life would change. My stomach felt empty. With no one to share my work and fears and commitment, even my few compensating hopes, the bleakness of my future was numbing. Failure — bankruptcy, simply walking away from it all — haunted me but was unthinkable.

John left a lot of himself in the Kennebunks. From things he has written and said since, I know he feels grateful, as I do, for our early association and the budding newspaper career that made him one of Maine's most charismatic people. He would become editor of the *Record* and recruit Peter Cox, our first summer reporter, to edit the *Record*'s sister publication, the small daily *Bath Times.* Several years later publisher Campbell Niven merged the two papers into the daily *Bath-Brunswick Times-Record,* with John as editor and Peter managing editor. When influential and wealthy Oscar Cox, Peter's father, died, with Peter's inheritance he and John left the *Times-Record* to start the successful journal of news and opinion, *Maine Times,* with Peter as publisher and John editor.

After John left I was the only reporter for four towns. Fortunately, the summer printing rush was almost over, and most of our systems had been at least somewhat refined. I had already been working as hard and as long as I could — I could do no more. For a time I ignored detail and hung desperately on. The pile of memos on my desk reminding me of imperative things to do immediately, grew steadily deeper.

The winter after John left, my credit with bank and suppliers was stretched to the snapping point. Unwilling to throw good money after bad, Ocean National was insisting that I get up its March mortgage payment in full and on time. Willis Watson was there too, waiting. Fridays I sprinted up and down Main Street collecting overdue receivables to cover payroll, skipping my own paycheck every third week. I was making partial payments to suppliers as checks arrived in the mail, but all debit balances were growing. I never bounced a payroll check, but everyone worried.

I needed $3,500, minimum, for the mortgages. I talked to half the bankers in York County. The local banking dean looked at my books for two minutes, then laid an avuncular hand on my shoulder. "Son," he said, "my advice is, quit." Sell it if I could, he told me, but he couldn't see anyone buying it. "If you don't like bankruptcy as a way out, pay off your creditors when you find work."

I wrote to Oscar Cox, who summered with his family in the former Booth Tarkington mansion in Kennebunkport. The Coxes had been more than friendly to me and my family. Oscar responded quickly. He wanted to come up with his son, Warren, Peter's brother. He had a proposal to make to me.

I remember receiving Oscar and Warren in our little Summer Street rental one winter evening. My desperate hopes were high. The meeting began cordially. I knew Peter, of course — and here was Warren. Peter and Warren were looking for something to do. Oscar would invest the $3,500 I needed in return for 51 percent of Star Press, the business I had bought for $30,000 two and a half years before, and would be prepared to invest more as needed. I could remain as publisher. That I would really be working for Peter and Warren, my juniors by a dozen years, was unstated.

I continued civil, and as attentive as my insides permitted. When it was over I told Oscar I'd consider his offer and be back in touch. Desperate as I was, I couldn't bring myself to accept, for $3,500 or $35,000. Given my balance sheet the offer was fair enough, but at the time I was insulted by it. I'd struggle on till my last drop of lymph had been squeezed out. That evening I sat down and composed a letter: "Dear Oscar . . ." Thanks, but no thanks.

I called Henry Strater in Ogunquit, a wealthy elderly friend. I told him how things were, withholding nothing. How much did I need? At the last moment $3,500 seemed so outrageous a request that I couldn't bring myself to say it. "One thousand dollars," I blurted. Henry reached for his checkbook and wrote out a check. "Pay me back when you can."

Two days later Gene Kelly, a Portland banker and social friend, called me. He'd been unable to get his directors to consider a loan, but he'd found an anonymous lender of $2,500.

It took me three years to repay Strater and my anonymous benefactor. When I made the final payment to Kelly I coaxed him into telling me who had helped. It was Edith Lapirow, who lived in a grand antique home in Kennebunk and believed in what the *Star* was trying to do for the area. She probably never expected to get back anything at all.

★ 11 ★

Yellow Journalism?

Another Edith, Edith Barry, was a genteel old lady of considerable self-assurance, a prop of Kennebunk society. She had given the town a museum of local history in the handsome Main Street building once known as the Brick Store, source of her merchant-seamen ancestors' wealth. In the Brick Store Museum complex she encouraged the activities of local artists and craftspeople.

In my first feature tribute to Edith Barry's cultural efforts, I called her "Mrs. Barry" twice or thrice, assuming that the late architect William Barry had been her husband rather than her brother. The day after my story appeared, an aging, tweedy relative, mustache twitching, stormed through our office door to stand behind the counter loudly demanding to know who had written the blasphemy about his "maiden lady" relative, and what kind of muckraking yellow journalism did we think we were foisting on a nice little town like Kennebunk?

My nerves were raw with overwork. I circled the end of the counter while he, shaken, got the hell out the door before I counted to three, as I was urging him to do. Next week I amended with another short Brick Store piece in which "Miss Barry" was featured prominently.

The words "yellow journalism" came easily to the tongues of readers who felt wronged by the newspaper. Another incident that autumn taught me more about the strength of hometown reaction to the published word.

The high school principal in Kennebunk then was a man named Andrew Peterson, a tall, imposing, crew-cut man with a tight-throated voice and an austere demeanor. He ran a taut school, keeping his personal eye on conduct at the high school dances. The day after an October dance at which Peterson had taken disciplinary measures against some obstreperous young-bloods, an oafish teen-age boy entered the *Star* office. Would I dare publish his mother's letter anonymously? He handed me a brief hand-scrawled thing on lined paper, accompanied by a third-gradish drawing of a stick figure in a cage, labeled "student," and a couple of stick figures outside the cage with guns.

> The pupils of the Kennebunk High School under their present principal are treated as prisoners and have no freedom. . . . They can't do this or that. I say they should have a chance to live a little. . . . The dances are poorly attended as he is always making his rounds. Why does he have to attend when they have parents always at these dances and help out. . . . As a taxpayer I'd like to know what can be done to remove him from high office which he is not capable to handle. . . . Please withhold my name as I have a future pupil of KHS and I know he would make it hot for her.

I felt strongly that our letters column should be open to all, reflecting the thoughts of all the community, not just those of people satisfied enough with their literary styles or sure enough of the popularity of their expression to sign their letters. The letter at hand could hardly be taken seriously. It did, however, express a minority view. I felt its sentiment should be out in the open where it could either be defended or, as I reasoned it would be, scoffed down.

Out to the newsstands it went Thursday evening. When I returned from my post office delivery run I was alone in the office, rearranging the mess. The November night outside was dark and dank. I heard footsteps on the entrance stairs. The door opened to Principal Andrew Peterson and his wife, Phyllis, the pictures of righteous wrath. Peterson bluntly demanded to know if I had written the unsigned letter in the paper he threw on the counter between us.

Had I what?

If I hadn't written it, who had? What kind of yellow-journalism sheet did I think I was publishing anyway, that printed unsigned letters?

If I wouldn't tell him who had written that letter, maybe there were ways he could make me tell him.

As I had with Miss Barry's relative, I started around the counter menacingly, telling him to get out before I threw him out. He did, precipitously, his wife with him.

In the mail Monday were five letters demanding to be published. I was happy to comply. The only signed one of the five, measured and restrained, was from the superintendent of schools and all three members of the School Board, who were dismayed that such a letter should be permitted to appear. Another was from a student, addressed to the writer of the offending letter. Among other things, it said:

> . . . I'm also sure that Mr. Peterson would not hold your irrational statement against your daughter. He is more mature than that.

A third, signed only "A loyal member of KHS," called the offending letter an "article" and said in closing:

> . . . I just want to say I'm very proud of my school, my teachers, and most of all my principal.

Another was signed only "3 Senior Girls":

> As a few of the students of KHS we are writing an answer to last week's editorial [sic] about our principal Mr. Peterson. We feel that it is unfair and untrue. We do not think that anyone could find a principal more interested in each and every student as an individual.
>
> We feel that his presence at our dances and at lunch time is appreciated, he shows that he has interest in us and wants the school and pupils to be respected. He was very proud of our football team when we beat our rival Old Orchard Beach. Also, when we get on the honor roll, he is interested enough to write "Congratulations" on our rank cards.
>
> We can say for ourselves and others that we are proud to go to KHS and to have as fine a principal as Mr. Peterson.

The fifth, signed "Name Withheld," from an Athletic Boosters Club parent, defended the need for Peterson's form of discipline and urged the original letter writer to attend the next dance and meet the Petersons to find out "what a really fine, conscientious couple they are."

Ten more letters of similar sentiment, all unsigned, arrived and were published the following week, and a few more the next. I assumed they had been at least induced — perhaps at the angry parents' meeting on the subject, copiously attended, at which Peterson had been roundly applauded, Editor Brook roundly denounced, and reprisal measures discussed. What daily newspaper is rewarded with such instant reaction to so mild a replication? Peterson had not theretofore been notably popular, but for months afterward he had a phalanx of supporters.

There was only one letter, signed "Betty Joyce," that supported the newspaper:

> Will someone kindly tell me what the fuss is about? With all the things in this world to really get het up about, what is there in a letter written by a disgruntled parent to put everyone so on edge? I'm sure Mr. Peterson isn't excited about it. I imagine he took this quite unimportant gripe with equanimity, if indeed he paid any attention to it at all. . . .
>
> Also, it might be safe to assume that Mr. Peterson, as head of a democratic institution, would be horrified if this tempest in a teapot were to put the lid on further expressions of criticism in the *Star,* signed or unsigned.

But criticism persisted: publishing unsigned letters was simply immoral. Seven years later I felt compelled again to defend the practice that made possible a much livelier local involvement in community affairs. I called my editorial, "Sin Is Not Unsigned Letters."

> We publish letters from people who ask us to withhold their names provided the letters are signed, sound, sane, OR significant, the least important, often disregarded by us, being the first.
>
> The man on the street is not a polished writer. Too often he fears that what he has to say, his burning grievance or humorous parry, may sound ridiculous to the sophisticated, or may cause the Establishment to mark him out as a troublemaker. If he criticizes the fire department his house may be left to burn. If he criticizes government his taxes may go up. If he criticizes the schools his children may flunk. So he keeps still. The newspaper was his ombudsman, in the old days.
>
> The *Star* encourages the voice that dares speak out only in disguise. It tries, within its serious limitations of time and money, to be a forum for all public opinion, a true member of the Fourth Estate, the monitor — or the champion — of the other three. . . .
>
> Of what value is a signature, anyway? Why need a thought be signed to serve a purpose? Why arbitrarily impose the fetters of signature on freedom of expression? . . . Often the lack of a signature helps us look at the contents more objectively, and this is seldom bad. . . . Why do readers righteously wag their fingers? Sin

is not alcohol, or drugs, or sex, or candy, or money, or unsigned letters to the editor. Sin is mis-use of these things.

Two weeks before Andrew and Phyllis Peterson had stormed up the steps and through the porous old door in the *Star* office to vent their outrage at a childish anonymous complaint, I had written a brief front-page comment under the title "Can This Be Kennebunk?" accompanied by a photo of a black stuffed-leotard dummy suspended by the neck from a sort of gallows lamppost at the entrance to Kimball Lane in the rural section of Kennebunk known as Alewive.

Unpaved half-mile-long Kimball Lane had once, in horse-and-buggy days, been bordered by three or four farms. It had continued across the river into Arundel before the old stone bridge went out. Two of the farmhouses still stood, only one inhabited: the one at the end nearest the river, a large white house with enormous barn and outbuildings surrounded by fields, woods, and river. It was home for semiretired inventor and mechanical genius Herman Cohen, then in his early fifties, and his wife, Sallie. In Yankeeland Cohen was rather reclusive, resentful that the local Chamber of Commerce had once declined to help him pressure the owners of neighboring property to sell their land to him and advance his dream of building a large scientific research center on Kimball Lane.

Beneath the hanging dummy at the entrance to the lane was tacked a crudely painted sign: "Cohen." The effigy was probably the work of local deer hunters, against whose annual intentions Cohen had posted his extensive wild acreage. When he found them trespassing, Cohen made angry gestures. There were uglier implications, of course, substantive or otherwise. I had written my unlabeled editorial under the photo, thinking I had a shocker.

On the eve of national, state, and local elections when the grand old words on democracy and the American way rise proudly to the lips of our citizens, out in Alewive drivers along Route 35 on Monday and Tuesday, coming around a bend of the lovely farm-country road, passed, with an astonishment that curdled to mortification and a crawling sensation at the napes of their necks, the ugly reminder that even in America, even in Maine, even here among our neighbors, lives a man, or boy, or group of men or boys, capable of presenting them with the detestable sight of a fellow-citizen hanged in effigy.

The occasion was Halloween, a time of childish exuberance. . . . While mothers were stuffing old clothes with straw and painting faces on burlap in the spirit of our festive harvest season, someone else with malice in his brain was stuffing black leotards for his own warped purpose. While our little children were ringing doorbells and gathering treats as imaginary ransom against minor trickery, while they ran, laughing excitedly among the candle-lit pumpkin-faces, someone else was taking the trouble to climb a twenty-foot pole to dangle a black figure with a wire around its neck.

On the second week after the unsigned Peterson letter, when our letters column was again filled with defense for the principal and abomination for his critic, one of my editorials gave voice to my perplexity:

On November 4th we published a photo of a black mannequin hanging on a pole with the name "Cohen" tacked below it. Two weeks later we published a letter to the editor criticizing Principal Andrew Peterson for being too strict in his discipline at student dances. We received one letter about the Cohen effigy, deploring the impulse behind the act. At date of writing we have received fifteen letters in which ninety-four people participated, condemning the writer of the Peterson letter. . . .

The amount of public indignation aroused by the letter surprised us, we must admit. The fact that so much of the criticism was directed our way was less surprising. But the fact that one public act was greeted with uproar, the other with deafening quiet, astonished us.

We are gladdened to see the public rise against what it feels is injustice. We like the spirit and liveliness of Maine people who speak out quickly and candidly. But we have here a situation that is puzzling, and since it is our business to be inquisitive about things that puzzle us, we ask for enlightenment on this strange enigma.

Where, we wonder, was all the public indignation when the picture of the effigy and our comment on it appeared in the *Star*? . . . If mild criticism of the High School Principal could tap such a gusher of angry sentiment, why did the other act not do the same? Who heard the voice of the schools on that one? Who heard the voice of the Town, or the voices of the citizens? Who heard the voice of the clergy? We, as a newspaper, apparently shouted into a vacuum on November 4th and whispered into an amplifier on November 18th. Funny thing.

★ 12 ★

T.H.W.T.B.

Maine was a local-option state, meaning that each municipality decided for itself how much alcohol flowed in its commercial veins. Every other November, balloting on six referendum questions determined the local option for two years: (1) for a state-operated liquor store; (2) for sale of wine and spirits in hotels and clubs; (3) for the same in restaurants; (4) for beer and ale in restaurants; (5) for malt liquor in taverns; and (6) for beer and ale in markets.

In the four *Star* towns, Question 2, for wine and spirits in hotels and clubs, had been the only winner since Prohibition days — even the ladies of the Woman's Christian Temperance Union acknowledged the bottomline demands of the vacationer. Portsmouth, New Hampshire, and Biddeford had liquor stores, and there were a couple of licensed beer stores in York, but in the Kennebunks and Wells-Ogunquit, Listerine was the strongest thing you could buy in a bottle.

Most people bought their liquor once a week in Biddeford or Portsmouth, and saved the rest of their weekly shopping for those trips, as well. I figured Kennebunk needed a liquor store to help overcome its commercial handicaps, and decided to take on the dries with an editorial blitzkrieg. I pried some clandestine encouragement out of the merchants. Not one would let us quote him, let alone her, so we put together a full-page ad sponsored by "The Merchants of Kennebunk." A handful contributed about half of what we needed to run the ad twice, but we ran it twice anyway. None of the sponsors but Star Press had any real hope for it; during the preceding five votes the liquor store question had lost 468 to 841, 557 to 929, 630 to 764, 803 to 870, and 693 to 841, respectively.

On October 14 I wrote two editorials, "Tilting Against Gin-mills" and "Beauty and the Beast," with three more the following week, another the next, and a final the next, just before the voting. In them I wrote that the worthy anti-rum ladies were ruining downtown and thereby uglifying the town; that liquor had done as much good as harm to mankind; that all dryness did was cause highway accidents when people drove out to get liquor and then drove home with some of it inside. I argued that if Kennebunk had a state store more money would stay in town and the taxpayer would benefit along with the businessman. I got a statement committing the Maine Liquor Commission to a Kennebunk store if the vote were favorable, and then got Commission approval of an available Main Street site. Then I held my tainted breath for the returns.

When I heard the figures late Tuesday night I was jubilant. In Kennebunk the liquor store had won, 1,291 to 910. The dries had turned out in force, but 800 more wets had voted than in 1950, and nearly 600 more than in 1958, the last time around. Two hundred more locals voted on the liquor store question than on any of the other five, and never before, except during a couple of presidential elections, had so many Kennebunkers voted on any subject at all. They resoundingly turned down taverns, as I had urged them to do, 1,545 to 310.

In Kennebunkport, too small to attract a state store in any event, voters favored one for the first time ever, even voting wet on all the other questions but taverns. Arundel, with less chance for a store, no hotels, no restaurants, no wide place in the road, voted wet right down the line. Like Kennebunkport, Wells voted "Yes" for a liquor store for the first time in history.

I had the proof, all 86 of it. Next morning I walked across Garden Street and through the rear door of Murdock's Pharmacy. Proprietor Bill Berry was seated at the counter in animated conversation with another of our bashful merchant sponsors. As I entered they turned together with a certain hilarity. "By golly," Berry blurted, "I've heard a lot about the power of the press, but I've never been a believer till today."

On Saturdays I wrote stories I hadn't had time for during the week, or caught up on bookkeeping or correspondence, or set type and printed overdue job work. One winter Saturday I was in the back shop alone, feverishly setting type on the Ludlow. The office phone kept me running back and forth. Between calls I'd have to pick up my setting where I'd left off. Let's see . . . where was I? . . . Oh, yes. So . . . Then the phone would ring again, and back to the office I'd sprint. Usually it was someone asking the price of a subscription, or wondering if we were open to accept payment for a 50-cent classified, or wanting help composing one. That was fine — that was business. It was the requests for information about local events from people who hadn't bought the paper — and even more, the complaints — that got me down. Someone had failed to get that week's *Star* in the mail — had the subscription run out?

I'd go check . . . Minutes later: No, it hadn't run out.

My caller hadn't thought so . . . remembered paying for it just last month. Would I please check the files again for the exact date? . . . Did I think the fault might lie with the post office?

It might, but it could have been us — no way of knowing. I'd wrap one up, I'd tell my caller, put a stamp on it, and take it to the post office on my way home, or I'd send him a dime and he could pick one up at the corner store.

Which way did I go home? . . . Oh, well, I practically went right by their door! Instead of sending it in the mail, maybe I could drop it off for them on my way home.

The umpteenth time the phone rang I picked up the receiver to hear a frosty middle-aged female voice wanting to know who "this" was.

"Sandy Brook."

What did I do at the paper? . . . "Oh, then you're just the one I want to talk to!" She had gone through the paper that morning three times from front to back and hadn't found the item she had sent us, in plenty of time, about her pug winning best of breed at a Connecticut dog show. She was sure it wasn't there. What had happened to it?

"It apparently got left out," I said.

She waited for amplification, but I had finished.

Why? What was happening to the paper? She composed the notices herself; no one at the paper had to do a thing except print them. The Watsons had always been grateful to get them. Some allowances could be made for my newness in Kennebunk, but after all!

By now I recognized my caller as the woman who lived with a woman friend in the largest and most lavishly maintained estate in Kennebunk, hundreds of acres on the Mousam River, a huge stone mansion with several handsome outbuildings, a brook-fed pond, extensive lawns, and a large stone kennel building where she and the other lady raised small show dogs as a hobby. The whole estate lay behind half a mile of fence, with impressive iron gates at the entrance to the blue-stone driveway. There were many signs: No Trespassing, No Hunting, Beware of the Dogs, Keep Out.

Notices like hers, I told her, should be sent to the correspondent who was paid to gather them for her column. That way they were routinely set in type. It was chancy to send them in for separate handling. We were quite busy. We wrote the stories with the headlines ourselves.

But she had always done it this way! She didn't care to have her items included with all those others about club suppers and visiting relatives. She must say, she had liked the paper better when the Watsons owned it. Didn't I care what went on? Didn't I want the news? I wouldn't last long as a newspaperman if I didn't. It was quite an honor for her to have won best of breed!

"At what?" I asked her.

"What?"

"You were best of breed at what? I was best of bunch, bananawise," I told her, but hadn't made the paper myself last week. I hung up, fuming like a Nicaraguan burgundy, and stomped back to my work.

Let's see, where was I? . . . The phone rang again.

"Hello?"

Yes. Was I the one who had just been talking with Miss S.?

Yes, I was.

Well, this was Miss T., Miss S.'s friend. My conduct just now toward Miss S. had been perfectly outrageous. She and Miss S. had been subscribers for years and had never had anything but pleasant relations with the Watsons. She could show me a scrapbook full of clippings of things the Watsons had put in the paper for them. Now, it seemed, these items weren't good enough for the paper which had gone steadily downhill ever since it changed hands, and this telephone call would serve to inform me that they wanted their subscription cancelled at once.

I kept quiet.

"Hello? Hello?"

I dropped the phone in its cradle, walked across the room, found the card in the subscription file, found the right slug, and dropped it into the trash barrel. Curdled, I returned to the Ludlow.

The phone rang again. I hesitated, but couldn't pass up business.

Hello? Was this the *Kennebunk Star?* Well, this was Mrs. W. calling to cancel her subscription. It seemed that people at the newspaper made a practice of being rude to subscribers and ignoring news of importance to them. So, would I be so good as to see to it that she didn't receive the *Star* any more?

"I'll stop it right away," I said.

Before I had taken care of that cancellation the phone rang again. Another lady was cancelling. Once more I returned to the Ludlow and picked up the composing stick, muttering something. It sounded pretty good. I picked out the initials of what I had muttered, T.H.W.T.B., in our smallest gothic type, cast the line, and cut it into the front-page banner over "Price 10¢." When a couple of observant readers asked me later what the initials stood for, I told them.

The news of the *Star's* banner slogan sped around town with the speed of rumor. Some people got sore, others laughed, others didn't believe what they'd heard, wondering if the letters complied with some obscure postal regulation. To this day people take me aside to ask what the letters T.H.W.T.B. stood for. They think they know, but they want to hear it for themselves. My answer to them is: The Hard Way's The Best. But I smile when I say it.

One day that year a *Time* stringer called me. *Time* was doing a story on newspaper slogans, like "All The News That's Fit To Print," he said, and he was calling Maine papers. Did I have one?

No, I told him, nothing boosterish like that. But we did carry some initials on our banner which might be said to represent a slogan of sorts. They were T.H.W.T.B., and they meant one of two things, depending on the questioner. I told him the two.

In a couple of weeks local people were quick to call me with the news: the *Star* had made *Time*. In the "Press" section a playful article titled "Maxims and Moonshine" told of the *Toledo Blade* calling itself "One of America's Great Newspapers"; the *Los Angeles Times* was "One of the World's Great Newspapers"; and the *Chicago Tribune* was "The World's Greatest Newspaper."

"Rare is the U.S. paper," the story continued, "that forgoes the opportunity to nail a brag to its masthead . . . 'The Climate Capitol of the World' . . . 'Covers Dixie Like the Dew' . . . 'America's Farthest North Daily Paper' . . . 'The Best Newspaper Under the Sun' . . . 'Carolina's Most Outspoken Newspaper' . . . Masthead moonshine flows thickest through the Nation's weeklies," the writer continued, citing a couple, one in Maine whose slogan was "All the News That Fits We Print," before writing, "In another Maine weekly, the *Kennebunk Star,* the mysterious initials T.H.W.T.B. sprouted recently on Page One. Halfheartedly Publisher Alexander Brook explained that they stand for 'The Hard Way's The Best.' In fact, they represent the classic cry of exasperated newsmen everywhere: 'To Hell With The Bastards!' "

T.H.W.T.B. graced the *Star* banner for the rest of my time with it.

★ **III** ★

★ 13 ★

A Sheriff Sues

Libel suits are to small publishers what natural disasters are to small farmers — unpredictable and potentially ruinous. In 1960 the annual cost of libel insurance approximated my net worth. Like most other weekly publishers, I took my chances without.

Most libel suits are initiated either to punish the publisher or to make some extra money. The exception is the wholesome suit filed to gain just compensation for loss of reputation or opportunity. In the legal sense, libel is written defamatory statement, true or false. In court the judge and jury first inspect the truth or falsity of what was published. If they find it false, they turn their attention to the manner of, or motive for, publication. If they find that the publisher, or editor, or reporter knew that what was published was either untrue or reckless with the truth, malice is assumed. Untrue malicious libel is a fatal rap; even with dubious evidence of injury to the plaintiff a jury will usually reward him in high figures.

Only the truth or falsity of the published libel can be determined before trial. Relative malice, responsibility, and damage to the plaintiff all defy prior determination. For this reason it is blood rare that a Maine judge will dismiss even the most obviously opportunistic or vindictive libel suit before it goes to trial.

When I was publishing in Maine, and until the Supreme Court changed the rules in 1986, the publisher accused of libel was considered guilty until proven innocent, another way of saying that the burden was on him, first to prove truth, then lack of malice, then to demonstrate his responsibility. Criminal defense lawyers usually wait to see what tack the prosecution takes and then rely on counterpunching. The fact that in libel cases the burden of proof was on the defendant subtly reversed the roles of the attorneys. The inexperienced libel defense lawyer came to court poorly prepared.

I was threatened with libel suits more or less fortnightly, but was actually sued only five times. Most threats were empty — just irate news subjects letting off steam. They menaced me with lawyers to damage my peace of mind as they felt I had damaged theirs. Quite a few went so far as to consult lawyers, who then advised them to cool it.

Most libel suits are settled out of court. The publisher may be sure of what he published, and his conscience may be hound's-tooth clean of malice. He may be able to show that elaborate precautions were taken to preserve objectivity. Still, when he is served with a demand to defend himself against a libel charge, he can hardly shrug it off. By the end of the first exploratory meeting with his lawyer, the meter has already been running an hour, and letters and phone calls and cogitation good for a couple more have been generated.

I was sued for the first time in November of 1960. My desperate financial circumstances made me feel like an accident patient being beaten up by a hospital orderly. I remember it well, that pitch-dark Thursday evening. I had bagged the paper and tucked it into its post office bed, closed up shop for the day, driven home, and just finished supper. A car drove down the long driveway to our cottage. I held the door open while Chief Frank Stevens turned sideways to get through it, his expression pained and apologetic. He handed me a formal document, and I read it standing up.

"I don't like it," he said, "but I have to ask you to come up to the station."

I threw an old leather jacket over my sweaty khaki shirt. When Frank opened the police-station door and motioned me in ahead of him, bulbs flashed — the *Biddeford Journal* people had been tipped off, and their gleeful myopic photographer was waiting. My accuser wasn't there, but I had recognized his name on the legal document. He was Sheriff Harold Nason, running for reelection. In an editorial that day on the local candidates I had written only three sentences about Nason:

> Republican Fred Gowen is fighting for the office of Sheriff against incumbent Harold Nason. Nason looks like a loser this time because of talk of favoritism and corruption in his department. Gowen is an honest, candid man who has made himself a lot of friends and who is campaigning on a clean-up slogan.

That was all. I hadn't accused Nason of anything. I hadn't even said his *department* had been guilty of anything, only that there was *talk*. I had heard a lot of it, and Gowen was using it as a campaign weapon. Was it possible that my mild remark would cost me $50,000, the figure quoted in the document? How much would it cost me to defend myself? How could I prove the truth of what I'd written? I could hardly count on the memories of the people I had talked to, let alone their testimony against the county sheriff. The scuttlebutt had been about deputies being paid off, work done by prison inmates for favored people — nothing big, just the usual talk about the seamy side of small-time law enforcement. Would I have to prove not only that there had been talk, but also the truth of what I'd heard? My lawyer, Robert Winton, seemed to think so.

Winton hardly bothered with preparation. He was the defense attorney, so he'd counterpunch. I told him I knew people who might be brazen enough to testify about slot-machine payoffs or trusty labor, and he thought that would be fine, but didn't refer to it again. Elections were imminent, scheduled before the case would normally be heard in Kennebunk Municipal Court. Nason would have trouble proving damage if he won, and if he lost he wouldn't be sheriff any more, so we'd have an easier time finding witnesses.

To my astonishment, Winton agreed to an immediate hearing. Chester Cram, a youngish Kennebunk lawyer taking his turn on the local bench, presided. When Nason's lawyer asked for a continuance because the sheriff had been "unavoidably detained" I was unutterably relieved.

But Winton was on his feet, objecting, saying that ample notice had been given, that we had our case together and were ready to go, etc. I was too naive to understand the steps of the legal waltz. We had called no witnesses, taken no depositions. Everyone was flying by the seat of his pants. Judge Cram agreed to Nason's continuance, as I'm sure Winton knew he would. A week later Nason was reelected, and he dropped the case. I paid Winton $1,500, a third of my annual take-home pay.

★ 14 ★

Cape Porpoise Dream House

That February, 1961, almost three years after Anneke and I had put our New Jersey home on the market and moved to Maine, the place sold at last — a relief, not a boon. The Basking Ridge real estate market had been so badly crippled that there was no money left after we had repaid the bank and my mother's share of our down payment. She, meanwhile, was being forced out of her rent-controlled New York apartment and wanted us to use the money we returned to her as down payment on a Maine home for all of us. The modest Maine prices made things possible.

What we found in Cape Porpoise had the basics of our dream house: ample room, small barn, and three acres of grove, bush, lawn, and ledge on a private dirt road on Nunan's Cove. Cape Porpoise was a simple remnant community within Kennebunkport whose historic excuse for identity was a broad and busy fishing harbor protected by 7 of the cape's 13 inshore islands. It owed its scent to tidal rockweed, bayberry, salt spray, and lobster bait, and its flavor to proud but friendly native people and simplicity-seeking newcomers. The two aging spinsters who had used the house as a summer home accepted our $13,600 offer, and our mortgage included money for a well and central heat. For nine months of the year we would be alone beyond a short causeway over a creek empty-ing into the cove, isolated from all but wading traffic during storms and high tides. Anneke and I swapped the old $60 rent for $64 mortgage payments, hauled our belts in four notches, and started living again.

Shortly after we all moved in, Elaine Nedeau, my cheerful ad salesperson, told me she needed more time with her family. As so often before, a wave of desperation overtook me, modified but not dispersed by her agreement to stay on till I found her replacement. Elaine had been a quick study with a good eye for layout, who moved with a sportive air along an efficient sales route. Where could I find a comparable person for what I could afford to pay?

The small-town back-fence wireless got me a single response.

"Hi, Sandy! How goes the battle? A little bird told me you're looking for an ad manager — that right?" Bill Briddell took a direct approach. His normal voice was near shout, but there was always a smile in it — almost laughter — like the one perpetually on his face.

To his question I answered yes, and did he know a prospect? Himself, it turned out, and could he come down and talk? Over the phone it sounded to my eager ears like an amplified call to colors. Better in his office, I told him; there were only three walls to mine, and insufficient space to seat both of us at the same time.

Bill was about my age, by then nearing 40, like me a relative newcomer, but already a respected business luminary — president of the Chamber of Commerce, member and soon-to-be chairman of the Kennebunk Budget Board, Rotarian, mixer, master of quip and banter. After college he had worked for an investment bank, then sold for a large cable manufacturer, becoming manager of the Philadelphia office before he bought National Woodworking in West Kennebunk and moved to Maine. His attractive wife, Melanie, taught at the junior high school. Their two daughters were the same ages as ours.

Bill was shinily scrubbed and smartly groomed in sports jacket and gray flannels. His head was large and oblong, full under the chin, but otherwise sharp featured. From his sloping, not-broad shoulders hung overlong arms dangling with rather hairy hands. His torso was short and rotund, legs long and thin, like the Tin Woodsman's.

Talking to Bill, one was distracted by three arresting fidgets. The first was a jumping facial tic that reinforced the permanent smile and winked the crinkles around his eyes. The second was that with the side of one forefinger he kept brushing up and down the profile of his sharp nose, as though he were rolling a bead on it. The third was that while he talked and laughed he was forever grasping his left sleeve above the elbow between the first two overturned fingers of his right hand and drawing the fingers gently downward along it, as though he were cleaning out sweat.

I drove out to rural West Kennebunk, where the general store and post office were the whole downtown. Bill had bought the good will, some woodworking machines, and the diminutive cement-block plant from National Woodworking's native founder. He employed six or eight men fashioning boxes, tripods, furniture and fireworks parts, toys and games. Orders were small and contracts short-lived.

We talked in his plain, windowless office. Soon after he had bought the business, Bill told me, he knew it wasn't all he'd been led to think. To raise money he had sold a partnership, but it was soon plain that the business wouldn't support two executives, so the partner had arranged to buy his remaining interest. Bill and his family had grown to like Kennebunk, and his job inquiry was part of his effort to stay put.

That might be, but really and truly, what was he doing applying for a job at little old, struggling old, Star Press? The answer, Bill told me in his fully packed voice, was that he thought we were going places. I couldn't believe my good fortune. I offered him the same salary, $5,000, that I was trying to take regularly, and the same increases as we grew. With Melanie's salary and the money he'd get from selling his partnership, he allowed as how he thought that could get him by for the time being, and surprised me by accepting.

Bill jumped on the job fresh as a daisy and was soon leaving our customers smiling in his wake. For a couple of months as summer came on I was buoyed by the advertising response. Once the summer pattern had been established, however, it was plain that Bill was having trouble engaging gears. He wasn't getting around to nearly enough customers each week, and was spending too much time with those he did see. He couldn't seem to say good-bye. "Well, OK, yes . . . OK, sure — shall we leave it like that? Fine. OK. Well, don't take any wooden nickels. I'll see you around. So long . . . Oh, by the way . . ." The complaints began to come in from neglected advertisers. When summer was over, ad volume began to drop below the corresponding inch totals of the year before, an alarming state of affairs for a business that predicated its ability to pay off loans and meet expenses on a steady increase in billings.

Hard at it by 6 A.M. and oblivious to others' routines, I took at face value Bill's time-saving schedule of driving out directly from home on his sales rounds in the mornings and arriving at the office around 11 with the bulging briefcase he took home. He'd spend an hour or so paper-shuffling and talking with the compositor, and then an hour at lunch before setting out again.

It slowly dawned on me that Bill wasn't getting out at all until after lunch, that he was spending inordinate amounts of time with a selected few customers, and that his other actions — driving, walking, or his compulsive exchanges of pleasantries on the street, were inefficient to the point of peculiarity. Although they all liked Bill, my puzzled employees began bringing me anecdotes and aping Bill's street manner-isms. One of them told me about letting himself into the plant after supper and being startled to find Bill sitting motionless and alone by his desk, hands hanging at his sides, just staring into the center of the room in the dark. I interpreted all this as symptomatic of massive temporary self-doubt, and hadn't the heart to come down heavily on him. In the world of chance encounters, Bill was the picture of bushy-tailed self-confidence.

Autumn turned into winter, and then late winter, while ad sales dwindled and customer complaints multiplied. Town meetings were approaching, with the attendant printing frenzy. We were printing Town Report books, the annual municipal reports, and were running late with the Kennebunkport book. Bezo, working all day and overtime at the Heidelberg, suffered a collapsed lung and was hospitalized. I was the only backup for anything, so I simply picked up the job less efficiently and settled in by the press for the duration. I cut paper, made up pages, locked up chases between pressruns, and lugged stock, running wide open. People would bring me sandwiches for all meals. For three days and nights solid, I stood there on blistered feet, sweat-soaked, stinking, unshaven, red-eyed. At about 1 A.M. the third night, with the town hushed in snowfall and its homes dark, the press overheated, and the hydraulic cylinder with sliding piston that drove the flywheel expanded and locked. Photographer George Stevens, cruising late in his battered Buick, saw the shop lights on and dropped in with a beer. He found me with the press apart, trying to free the piston with penetrating oil. George took charge.

He bullied awake a mechanic friend and harassed him into getting dressed and driving down to let us into Greene's Garage. George and I sweated grimly over a machinist's press to force the piston out of the cylinder. Back in the shop we oiled up the parts, got the press back together by 3 A.M., and away I went again till Anneke brought me my breakfast sandwich.

When I had finished the final pressrun and folded the final section, while Rita Welch was gathering sections and gluing covers, I at last drove home for a bath and a few hours of sleep. When I took my socks off most of the outer skin peeled off with them.

Next morning I loaded a station wagon and, limping, carried enough cartons of reports to the Kennebunkport Town Offices to cover household distribution before Town Meeting, but three days beyond our delivery deadline. The clerical lady who had ordered the reports on our low bid had helped to make us late by violating her own copy deadline, but she was the customer. She gave me hell for being late, and punished me for many years afterward by refusing to let us bid for town work. The selectmen, sore at me for past editorial criticisms, happily spread the word of Star Press unreliability.

Soon after the Town Meetings in March, with advertising at a low ebb, printing in its seasonal doldrums, and bills mounting, I had a frantic call from one of our biggest retail advertisers, about to hold an important sale. His patience had been frayed by a dubious freight delivery schedule for some of his major sale items. The delivery delay superimposed alternative sale items and last-minute pricing on an already difficult and crowded two-page ad design, or double-truck.

It was Wednesday; our shop ad deadline was early that afternoon. Bill Briddell was scheduled to pick up the double-trucker's late copy and changes at 10 A.M. and show him final proofs before the section went to press that afternoon.

At 10:30 the advertiser called: Where the hell was Bill?

I didn't know — Jesus! — I'd check and get back to him.

Wednesday was to the ad salesman what intermission is to the hot-dog seller — each minute was precious. With a sense of foreboding I called Bill's home — no answer. I called Melanie at the junior high school; she said Bill had been getting up when she left for work at eight. I called their home again. I called other advertisers on Bill's Wednesday list. No one had seen him.

I drove to the double-trucker's, wasting his time because all the instructions he had given to Bill now had to be explained to me. I picked up a few more ads from Bill's call list, dropped them off at the shop, and at nearly noon, with stories still to write, I drove to the Briddell home. I ran up the steps to the rear door and knocked wildly. A deathly quiet reigned inside. I let myself in; I was in the kitchen. The breakfast table was set for one. On it was a glass of orange juice, a plate of bacon strips, two fried eggs, sunny side up, buttered toast, cream in a creamer, coffee in a mug, all stone cold. I will not forget the eggs, underdone for my taste, or the opacity of the bacon.

"Bill!" I called. No answer. I walked quickly to the bottom of the stairs. "Bill!"

Upstairs there was a muffled, cloth-induced noise, then a thud. I started running up the stairs. The bedroom door was open, and I could see motion through it — Bill, in his pajamas, starting up from the edge of the bed, rubbing sleep from his eyes. What time was it?

I told him.

He summoned up his confident, booming voice, asking how I was doing, and saying he'd be at the office in a jiffy. I left him, returned to the shop, and got back to work. I let it slide — there was too much else to do on Wednesdays. Bill got himself on the road; I had a meeting to report that night; next day was paper day — no time to talk then, and I wouldn't be done till late at night. Two days later, with Bill suitably wound up and sufficiently contrite, there seemed no point in bringing it up at all.

But the same thing happened again, in different form. And again. Bill knew we couldn't go on that way. One day, after what was to have been my final warning, he gave me his notice, a year almost to the day after he had arrived. He had found a job upstate that required not much more than a speaker and good fellow.

Bill left a lot of friends in the Kennebunks, and I was one of them. I trust that he recovered from whatever it was that was sapping his effectiveness. If he did, I'm sure he became an attractive and valuable member of whatever he joined. But I have no way of knowing: I never heard from him again.

★ 15 ★

Acquisition

When Bill Briddell left, I delayed finding a replacement, opting instead to save a few months of sales salary by spending part of my own week on the road. But selling made me resentful. At the least snub or the merest questioning of the value of what I was selling, I bristled. Peg and Art Hendrick had become our closest friends, and when she heard my lament about sales duties, Peg offered to give sales a try part-time when her four children were out of school in June.

Exuberant and more than handsome, Peg had a quality employers prize: she was good at whatever she did but afraid she wouldn't excel at it. In three bustling days a week she covered half again as much ground as Bill had covered, building ad volume and pushing us into extra pages, all accomplished between calls, reading proof, billing subscribers, and even becoming the liveliest inspiration at our Thursday get-out-the-paper hullabaloo. I was elated — so there really *was* more advertising out there!

With summer printing on the flood, two expanding editions to fill, *Clue* to produce, and accounts proliferating, I had hired another printing trainee, but soon found that wasn't enough. I couldn't afford a circulation manager, or a business manager, or a janitor, so I hired the first reporter who had ever knocked on the door. Crosby Day was a young journalism graduate who had settled in Ogunquit with wife and baby, eager to launch his career. He was loose-jointed and long-legged, flaxen-haired, with mild manner and brown fawn's eyes, altogether an unlikely young man, it seemed to me, to have been an Olympics-class middle-distance runner.

Crosby was a typical product of the early sixties. He wrote in the self-conscious, stilted manner usually associated with undergraduate job-seeking letters. I rewrote almost every sentence, sometimes taking time out to explain my editing process. Puzzled and unconvinced that I was doing more than stroking my own editorial ego, Crosby tolerated my little exercises without petulance or dismay. Having covered Wells-Ogunquit for three years, I was able to help him navigate the territory without making dangerous errors in fact or interpretation. He was receptive and unresentful, capable of gathering the sense of what he observed. By the time he left us a year and a half later, he had gained a reputation for competence that helped him land a job with the *Portland Press-Herald.*

I had particularly needed reporting help when I hired Crosby because that June I had bought another newspaper.

In early March, a couple of weeks before my fourth *Star* anniversary, as the deep Maine frost was collapsing to mud, I had a phone call from Horace Mitchell of Kittery, then in his early fifties. Horace and his wife owned and operated a one-and-a-half-person job printery and weekly newspaper. The *Kittery Press* was that town's equivalent of the Watsons' *Kennebunk Star.* Horace ran the business in their leaky barn on degenerating equipment with occasional help from his wife and teenage daughters. Mrs. Mitchell's teaching salary, not the *Press,* was the mainstay of their livelihood. Horace was gauntly lean, ravaged by work and worry, with strange, maniacal eyes, but lively and Maine-flavorful.

Kittery's population was larger than that of the combined Kennebunks, but only because it was a bedroom community for employees of the nearby submarine base and a rural suburb for Portsmouth, New Hampshire, across the Piscataqua River. Commercial downtown was vestigial — residents shopped in Portsmouth and read its small daily *Herald.* The once-proud town of mid-seventeenth century origins was now disconnected from its past, populated mostly by transients without loyalty to the town or its newspaper.

Only loyalty could have explained a favorable response to the quaint and atrociously manufactured little tabloid disseminator of small-town doings. As part of a last-ditch effort to salvage his life-support system, Horace had recently hired a young man named Frank Soule to sell advertising, write some news copy, and distribute the paper to a few stands, while Horace himself set copy at the Linotype, then filled the chases and printed on a rotting little flatbed.

None of this was known to me when Horace phoned. He had run out of newsprint, he said, and couldn't get delivery in time for that week's edition. I concluded sympathetically that his credit was shot. He had about half the sheets he needed — he'd bring them and his chases with him, ready to print. Could we do it for him that week? Sure, I said, we'd run it off for him.

Horace published Fridays. Late Thursday afternoon he drove up in his old heap and hung around watching the *Star* come off the press. When the last run was off we transferred his metal to our chases and ran the *Press* off on our own sheets, print and turn.

Horace's *Press* wasn't due on the stands till next morning, so after I had made my post office drop I returned to the plant to talk. The talk was mostly just hard times. Horace was fascinated by what he'd seen. I think he saw it as an indictment of his career. My dismal nonprofit picture was worth only a shrug — he took that for granted. But how had I managed to quadruple gross in four years? How could I do it with payables always at least twice receivables, and long-term debt doubled, while employment had grown from 4 to 11 and payroll quadrupled? How had I done it without venture capital, even my own? In four years I had paid my major suppliers only about twice as much as my current debt to them; how come I could still buy on credit? When did I write?

We talked and talked, while an image took form in my mind of a man who had started proudly to be an old-fashioned country editor, cherishing his satisfactions with a few story sales to outdoor magazines and his local reputation for scraping together a livelihood as his own man — the only one of his kind in town.

Our talk pulled these defenses away from him. He was groping for a solution, but saw my answers only in terms of sweat and drive, too much of both for a man so long ravaged by the business, burned out by it, without resources, fighting creditors. We made a deal to print his *Press* every week.

I think he carried his newspapers home that night dull with discouragement and a yearning to sell out, quit his hopeless struggle, do what job printing he and his family could handle, and trust to fate to throw him a rope.

Before I was in any sense ready for him, in early June, he told me his plan. Did I want his newspaper? Frank Soule would stay on — Horace had asked him. Frank would bring me the copy, Horace said — ads and releases and mail culls, along with a quick, home-written story or two. We'd set type and print, and Frank would deliver. That was the size of it. My extra expenses would be one salary, some extra newsprint, postage, shop time, and odds and ends. If I could transfer some of the *Star* magic to Kittery, maybe the *Press* would make a profit some day. He wasn't thinking beyond that. He wanted $2,500 for his good will, meaning his subscription list, but he'd need all of it right away to pay off his creditors.

I needed another newspaper like a hole in the head, but being a sailor, I rationalized that a hole was not a bad thing to have in the head. I took the proposition to the bank. Bob Stinson shook his head in disbelief. I argued that I had managed by then to pay off exactly $2,500 of the original $5,000 bank mortgage and to reduce my debt to the Watsons by $8,000, and no one had taken a machine back.

Bob was dubious. Maybe the directors could be persuaded; he'd give her a whirl. He did, they were, and I bought the *Kittery Press*. A month before its last issue passed over into local legend I was able to tell *Press* readers and mine to expect a *Kittery-Eliot Star*. On July 27 the first issue burst on the people of Kittery and its neighboring town of Eliot. Burst? "Borscht" may be a better word.

I sent Crosby Day down to help Frank Soule with reporting and added Crosby's Wells reporting duties to mine, with the Kennebunks. Editorial-page copy, mostly about our old area, ran in all three *Stars*. So did the features and the catchier stories from all six towns. We offered combination ad rates at very modest markups, and Peg got a few takers. Few enough of our advertisers could expect an areawide response. As advertising bait to give the new *Star* the bulk it needed, we sprinkled a few ads gratis in all three editions, hoping for measurable customer response.

The *Kittery-Eliot Star* began life with eight broadsheet pages, twice its former size. I maintained the stingy Mitchell ad rates temporarily, and by guaranteeing triple the former circulation of 500, Frank Soule was able to attract a few small Portsmouth advertisers.

We were able to do this — guarantee triple the paid circulation — by making a species of deal I think I originated. The only large food market in the area was Dan's Star Market, the focal store in a developing shopping center near downtown Kittery, where Dan also owned a small-ish department store. The food market did a thriving business, the department store just so-so. I made a date with Dan, and he liked my proposal.

How could he turn it down? I offered him a weekly quarter-page ad for the department store, to run in all three *Stars,* if he would pay me 3 cents apiece for 1,000 copies of the 10-cent *Kittery-Eliot Star* and have his check-out clerks drop one copy per customer in shopping bags until all were gone. For $30 he got a large ad and a gift for a thousand customers each week. In this way we tripled the paid circulation, saved our second-class postal permit, saved postage in the bargain, and saved delivery time and mileage with one big newsstand drop, while overnight gaining a salable medium.

We did, in fact, double our space sales in short order, but we also doubled expenses. My bookkeeping system wasn't sophisticated enough to tell me whether or not the *Kittery-Eliot Star* ever turned a profit during its three years in that dormant life-stage — I think not. We picked up a couple hundred readers in 3,000-population Eliot, a farm and bedroom town without advertisers. Beyond Dan's thousand, we gained another hundred or so in Kittery. But there we stagnated.

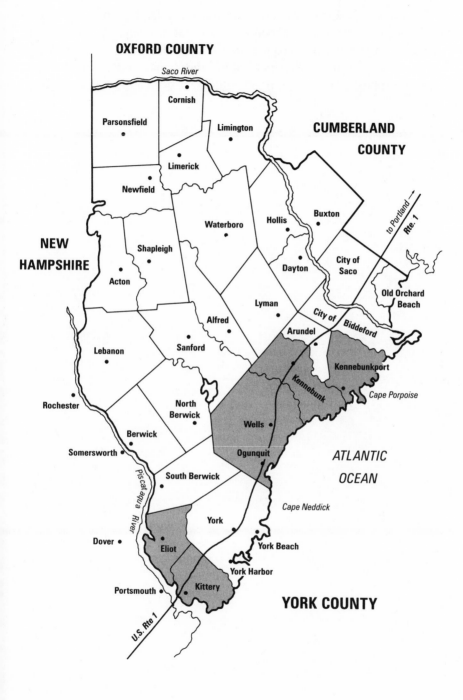

OXFORD COUNTY

Saco River

Cornish

Parsonsfield

Limington

CUMBERLAND COUNTY

Limerick

Newfield

Waterboro

Hollis

Buxton

to Portland — Rte. 1

NEW HAMPSHIRE

Shapleigh

Acton

Dayton

City of Saco

Old Orchard Beach

Lyman

Alfred

City of Biddeford

Lebanon

Sanford

Arundel

Kennebunk

Kennebunkport

Cape Porpoise

Rochester

North Berwick

Wells

Berwick

Somersworth

Piscataqua River

South Berwick

Ogunquit

ATLANTIC OCEAN

Cape Neddick

York

York Beach

Dover

Eliot

York Harbor

Portsmouth

Kittery

YORK COUNTY

U.S. Rte 1

Buying the *Kittery Press* caused me a frightening, unplanned diffusion of my already oversapped energies and produced an uninspiring, stop-gap, chrysalis-like product that nevertheless served its main purpose of keeping the newspaper out of other hands until it could win its metamorphosis. Without it, there could have been no *York County Coast Star*.

★ 16 ★

A Rising Political Force

The year 1962 was significant to me for its expanding local awareness of the vitality of the newspaper. After a year of vituperative dissension, the Kennebunk Planning Board adopted a comprehensive town plan, prelude to a zoning ordinance proposal, and then, with the *Star*'s continuing support, voted — by only 15 votes, to be sure — for its ordinance, the first in York County. Federal and state funding were allocated to dredge the estuary harbor portion of the Kennebunk River, border between the Kennebunks. As member and sometime chairman of the Harbor Committee, I helped defeat the antidredging forces and brought in favorable votes to raise the local share of the money. Years before the whole-word-recognition method of teaching reading — along with Dick and Jane, Spot and Puff — drained the hell out of American schools with a great gurgle, my editorial shouting match with school officials bore fruit with a return to phonics teaching in the Kennebunks. After years of spoiling the chances of attractive candidates for local office by endorsing them, the *Star* was becoming a positive political force; even in Kennebunkport the stand-up comics abandoned their kiss-of-death jokes and sat down. Within three years it would become virtually impossible to gain local office without *Star* backing.

I was growing surer of my positions and more confident of the newspaper's lung power, and was campaigning on several fronts each week. My editorial emphasis was changing. At first unemployment and decay had been the most obvious ills, but the tide was turning. The sixties were upon us, with the Vietnam War and black turmoil in the cities. Disillusioned young people were dropping out of college and off the jobs ladder, and old people were retiring earlier. Poor, relatively crime-free Maine was a compelling attraction. As York County's economy improved, "in-migrant" pressures developed, spreading the viruses of suburbia and foreign tastes. It was the local landscape and quality of life that were now endangered.

As a brand-newcomer in 1958, I had written my first editorial paean to the salt marshes. Now, in 1962, marsh lovers were still contrary eccentrics and prudently silent. The marshes were useless breeding grounds for stinging insects, inhibitors of tourism thereby. Developers were encouraged to fill them to build taxable summer cottages.

The bulk of the Town of Wells was a landmass of sparsely populated woods and fields. Most residents, and all tourism and commerce, clustered around Route 1 and the beaches. Between the highway and the five-mile barrier beach stretched a magnificent emptiness of salt marsh around the Webhannet and Merriland Rivers, which converged in the marshes and emptied together into the Atlantic between Drakes Island and Wells Beach. The small rivers meandered through the marshes, their waters having little effect on the ebbing and flooding of the ten-foot tides rushing in and out through the gap in the barrier beach.

For three years I had been attending all meetings of the Wells Harbor Committee. By virtue of insights gained during the similar effort in the Kennebunks, I had acted in some respects as consultant without portfolio, and supported the Wells dredging effort, there almost universally popular. That year federal and state funds had also been allocated to Wells, to dredge what would be a totally new harbor. Accompanied by sustained cheering from the Wells commercial establishment, the Town of Wells voted its own share.

The harbor would be a scooped-out section of marsh at the confluence of the two small rivers. The gap in the barrier beach would be lined with riprap and extended with jetties. Dredged material, or spoil, would be dumped onto 15 more acres of marsh, a tiny fraction of the whole, where harborside enterprise was expected to flourish. More dredged spoil would build a connecting roadbase across more marsh inland to Route 1.

For centerless Wells I had visions of a pleasant village green on the uplands overlooking the harbor, away from tawdry Route 1, and was urging town officials to refine and develop a new center I had designed in outline form. Fractious Wells could be made whole. So when the dredge started pumping sand and muck onto the assigned sections of the lovely marsh, I held my editorial tongue.

As the harbor entranceway was widened and lined with stone and the basin scooped out, slowly it penetrated the consciousness of the contract dredger, the Army Corps of Engineers, and Wells officials, that Mother Nature was establishing a new equilibrium. As fast as the dredge sucked out the marsh mud, the big Maine tides rushing in and out between the jetties were dragging sand up the entrance funnel from the miles of beach on either side. Each day the engineers recorded the number of cubic yards of muck deposited on the marsh, and each day that much more filled in behind the dredge. The beaches on either side of the entrance jetties were being carved away; patches of rubble, once covered with sand, were appearing in front of the rows of beachside cottages.

The first dredger went bankrupt trying to reach contract depth. He could no more dig to design depth than "seven maids and seven mops, sweeping for half a year." The engineers huddled and decided to extend the jetties out into the ocean to a depth where the sand didn't swirl. They dipped into their Corps slush fund for the money, and after more months of jetty work, a new dredger resumed pumping.

First results were encouraging, but the official euphoria was short-lived. It was apparent that the beach was building up in crescents on either side of the lengthened jetties until it reached the ends, when it began again to pour back up the entrance funnel. The second dredger too went broke. Instead of a quarter of a million dollars, nearly a million had been spent. The chagrined Army engineers decided to double the length of the already-extended jetties, and tried to get Wells to pony up part of the new money required. But the selectmen, with *Star* urging, resisted. A monumental boo-boo was in the works.

The dredge filled the prescribed marsh area by the harbor, then the roadbase, but there was plenty more spoil to come. The long discharge pipeline was shifted briefly to the ocean beach, where its effluent was obviously simply making the round-trip back up between the jetties. The dredger's contract-completion deadline was coming on fast, with penalties behind it.

The dredger went to the selectmen: All right, gentlemen, I can't keep going without another spoil site — any suggestions? How about the Drakes Island marshes on the north side? Make a nice little parking lot . . .

The selectmen saw their opportunity. OK, they said, but let's get it going before the Drakes Islanders get their act together.

Drakes Island, really part of the barrier beach, with its own road-way inland across the marshes, bordered the harbor entrance channel to the north. The islanders were almost all summer residents and non-voters, severely taxed, who made few demands on town services and none on the school system. They maintained their summer idyll free of commercialism and the bustle of Route 1 and the other beaches. I had seen several island representatives defensively monitoring the Harbor Committee meetings to assure themselves that the harbor plans would not affect their lives any more than they could prevent. Particularly offensive to them was the recurring commercial pressure to make more tourist parking available at the tranquil Drakes Island beaches, notably those nearest the harbor.

One spring morning the weekending island homeowners who over-looked the marshes awakened to the same old sounds from the dredge. Only this time the business end of the discharge pipe was pointing at them, spewing its stream of silt and water inside a bulldozed ring of marsh clods. They thought they recognized the makings of a parking lot.

The islanders met hurriedly and called the selectmen. They stated their fears, tactfully at first, as discretion dictated. The selectmen said, Oh, no, that was just a sand stockpile to be removed when a new spoil site was found. But the islanders had the wind up, and their speech quickened. The selectmen told them there was nothing to fear, but they'd get the dredger to switch his pipe.

They didn't — the dredging continued without interruption. The islanders consulted among themselves, and called me. Would I come down for a look?

I had been unaware of the selectmen's decision, apparently taken in closed session. Alarmed, I responded to the phone call quickly. It was Sunday morning, but the dredge was working. When I arrived at the cottage nearest the outfall end of the pipe I was ushered into a sunny room with harbor exposure to find a group of seven or eight islanders waiting. The noise of the dredge was in the background as we talked.

How could they stop it? First get a temporary injunction, was my suggestion. Which lawyer? I recommended my old friend in York, Dave Strater. By Tuesday Strater had the injunction.

During the next few weeks, in long lead articles, I reviewed the complete history of harbor affairs from memory and earlier *Star* reports, sprinkling them with quoted official reassurances that no Drakes Island parking lot by the harbor would be considered. Until the case was heard ten months later, I reported weekly developments and editorialized repeatedly on the duplicity of the selectmen, town manager, and town counsel, quoting all of them and the Harbor Committee members and noting the discrepancies between their past promises and present ac-tions. I met frequently with the more than friendly islanders and at-tended every meeting of town government.

No evidence of growing support came from the people of Wells, not even grudging sympathy with my views. Most resented the islanders for being rich and aloof. They continued to read the *Star* as before, but punished us by curtailing their advertising and taking their printing custom elsewhere. The hostility of officials and commercial people at the weekly selectmen's meetings and over the telephone gave me my most unpleasant reporting experiences to date. My Drakes Island friends were a warm and rewarding minority, but one that had no occasion to buy anything I sold but 10-cent newspapers.

At last, in Superior Court of Alfred, the county seat, Justice Cecil Siddall heard the Drakes Islanders' suit for a permanent injunction against the selectmen and the Town of Wells. Except for the promises I had quoted and the improbable and unlawyerly sympathy of the court for maintaining an uncluttered view, Strater and Drakes Island hadn't much of a case. After three days of testimony, during which Strater argued against a high-powered municipal attorney, Justice Siddall found everything precisely as we wished, even expressing himself cynically in his written summary regarding the sworn testimony of Wells officials. If we had lost, I could easily have been sued for what I had been writing. Justice Siddall ordered the town to remove every one of the 8,000 cubic yards of silt deposited on the marshes before the temporary injunction had taken effect.

The language of Justice Siddall's verdict thrilled me. In it was evidence, some of the earliest on record, that even in the austere court-room, blind justice acknowledged the measurable injustice that loss of natural beauty could inflict on people who cherished it. The verdict further served to put local officials on notice that they departed from the truth and from evenhanded treatment of their constituents at their peril.

My closing editorial was euphoric:

Justice Siddall's decision does not specifically deal with conserva-tion, but underlying it must be a growing public awareness of its principles as they relate to the salt marshes, those immensely fertile spawning grounds for the species of life that preserve the fertility of our ocean bays. Behind the text is a clear vision for the grandeur of the marshes, and the growing need to preserve natural beauty in a nation seemingly hell-bent on cicatrizing its own countenance.

More subtly, perhaps, the Siddall decision seems to recognize a change in the whole concept of private property, a change which must take place, whether we wish it or not, because the population of the earth is rapidly filling and choking every inhabitable place on it. Inherent in the decision is a new awareness that private property must be viewed, not as man's individual kingdom to spoil or beautify, degrade or sanctify, according to his whim or desire for private gain, but as property held in the public trust. Man can no longer be permitted a dictatorship over his land. He holds it in fee simple to his town, his state, his country, and his countrymen.

A portion of the marshland, at least, had been saved. The people of four *Star* towns had been exposed to the concept of marshes as magnifi-cent assets, not liabilities. And justice had triumphed. The corrobora-tion of the accuracy of *Star* reporting and the vindication of its sense of values gained us further enmity from our Wells customers, but a new respect as well — the *Star* might be paltry of size and shabby of purse, but in defense of the public weal it was big poison.

When I had first hung out my little shingle on the least hovel of the Fourth Estate, I had seen it as a license to live where I wanted to live and earn a living from my writing. Now I began to see the *Star* as a rallying point in the crusade for quality and integrity.

★ 17 ★

Fifth Anniversary

My state of mind during the frazzling early weeks of the *Kittery-Eliot Star* were about what you'd expect of someone who doubtless was the most strung out, impecunious three-newspaper-owner in America. Frank Soule lasted only three months in Kittery. He excused himself with the obvious: we were treading water there, and he couldn't foresee improvement. Bob Roffler volunteered to be Frank's replacement as reporter-salesman. Bob brought to the job no training but an enthusiasm for local news and a huge sales optimism. With doubled ad revenue he could see himself making nearly as much money doing something that excited him as he had been making as traveling salesman for a pharmaceutical manufacturer. And why not? The other *Stars* were at 16 pages, and the potential in Kittery and Eliot seemed as great. He had observed the people of our other integrated communities snapping up the paper eagerly each week and reacting vigorously to everything in it.

But soon Bob, too, lost heart. The day-to-day local activities Bob loved to discuss fell without vibration on the plump eardrums of his new audience in rural suburbia. What's more, Bob found his advertisers apathetic. He was losing as many as he was gaining, and the heart went out of him. He stayed on through the autumn and winter, but in early March he told me he had decided to return to selling pharmaceuticals.

I needed a professional. I picked three responders to my trade magazine ad and scheduled the likeliest last, to be able to make him my best offer on the spot. He was Jerome Robinson: about 26, good-humored, trim and lively, married to a honey-haired fellow employee at the respected trade journal *American Press,* published by his father. After Dartmouth Jerry had worked in both editorial and sales departments at two giant New Jersey weeklies and now wanted to shed New Jersey for Maine country living. I offered him the combination job at Kittery and the salary I had recently awarded myself, $5,500, with prospects of part ownership.

Jerry and Jane Robinson drove home to arrange their move to Maine with two young daughters. A few days before Jerry was to start work, an auto accident hospitalized Jane and put Jerry's leg in a cast. When he finally arrived he couldn't yet drive, so I kept him busy editing and doing whatever telephone reporting and selling he could do from the Kennebunk office. Jerry was good at whatever he did.

March 17 was my fifth anniversary date, the legendary financial watershed for small-business owners. I proposed a humorous anniversary issue, and ad manager Peg Hendrick suggested delaying it a couple of weeks and filling it with April Fool spoofery. Jerry's immobility would be no handicap. We'd write almost-believable copy under the "A.F. Wire Service" (April Fool) dateline and persuade our advertisers to join the fun.

We culled photos from other publications and ran them off on our newly purchased Scan-a-Graver. Peg sold an ad to Dora's Beauty Studio in which a photo of an old female orangutan, labeled "Before", was flanked by another of a fashion model labeled "After", with the slogan "Let Us Bring Out the Loveliness." For the Kennebunk Systems Store we found a primitive witch doctor with his tongue out and had him exhorting customers to "Get It Out of Your Systems." A fish market advertised an end-of-winter clearance sale to make room for new merchandise, and Ocean National ran a sale on dollar bills. There were scandalous ads too, for fictitious stores and services.

Our A.F. Wire Service stories began plausibly enough but degenerated into farce, like the one about the winter hunting party whose members swore they'd seen a herd of elk, theretofore unknown in eastern states. In the final sentence one of the hunters was quoted on the depth of the cold that evening, and the party's efforts to keep warm with Sterno, internally. In another story the water and sewer districts announced a merger to save money on their mains. There was a story about Police Chief Stevens pinching a starlet on Route 1, another in which a Planning Board meeting slowly soured into a member brawl, another in which a Wells selectman notoriously antagonistic to Drakes Islanders, heroically saved their storm-threatened stone groin by jamming his knee into it. We wrote phony letters to the editor and announced some funny weddings.

In another story by *Clue* manager Peter Agrafiotis, who was selling advertising part-time, a French-Canadian boy had died in a highway accident while his family was vacationing in York County. While still an infant this same boy had been lost from a Canadian farm and adopted by wolves. At nine he had been seen running with the wolf pack and was elaborately captured and returned to his parents, who taught him to speak and trained him back to apparent normalcy. In the final sentence Peter told our readers how the boy had died: he had been caught up in the front wheel of a car he'd been chasing and yapping at. Years later, a Canadian film director heard the story from someone else and wrote me to find out more details. He was planning a documentary of the wolf-boy story.

From time to time, under a "Pretty, But Not Correct" logo, I had been publishing the funniest of the typographical errors we caught as we read proof. Typos of the sort generated by worn-out machines like ours will not be seen again on this earth. It was mechanical idiosyncrasy, not human error, that caused most of them — the dropping of wrong matrices or spacers, or matrices dropped in the wrong sequences. In the spirit of April Foolery we reproduced about a hundred of them, complete with my one-line comments. Here is a sampling:

. . . will discuss the requirements of a good art program, its costs and advantages. There will be a display o fart by his students. Founders Day will also be observed.
As an anticlimax.

The Dec. 4th meeting will be at the York Beach grammar school and will feature a talk on the dangers of child molesting by a State Trooper.
An ever-present danger.

The Kennebunkport Town Meeting Saturday was small, not particularly cantankerous, and far from controversial. But it lasted $3^1/_2$ sours.
After $3^1/_2$ the controversy just melts away.

Currently the Langsford and Ward Roads are served by 8-inch and 10-inch mains fed by an 8-inch man traveling down School Street, across Buttonwood, down the Wildes District Road, and across Nunan's Creek.
They don't make them like that any more.

Among his many writings on scientific subjects is his "Field Manual of Biology" published in 1935 and revised in 1956, now a widely-used college and university teet.
Bless my soul!

Mrs. Delmar Rowe was deceived into membership of the First
Congregational Church on Sunday.
But once she gets to know people she ought to enjoy it.

. . . inoculated for babies . . .
That's all there is to it, children.

Suction V is called "Government."
Tell us something we don't know.

Hundley, 31, has attended a number of police training schools,
where he took classes in photography, fingerpainting, and narcotics.
*The fingerpainting sounds useful, but why should we send them
to school to do narcotics?*

The Planning Board finds itself in some such predicament with the
developers. The developershit the roof when the subdivision was
proposed.
Better him than us.

The firemen put up Christmas lights in town last week. They make
the Squire look quite festive.
Maybe he was lit when they got there.

Indeed, they had gone all out to put the tissue to the citizens of
Kennebunk on the basis of trust and confidence in the Directors.
Right where it would do the most good.

The bride carried a bouquet of white sweetheart roses, ivy, and
papy's breath.
What had Papy been drinking?

Daniel, 11, likes to be with his dad on the delivery truck, or fooling
around the worehouse. He may join his father in business when he's
older, but there's time for a lot of career ideas to spark and die
before then.
*Well, if you want to make money, there aren't too many ways you
can do it these days without a substantial investment.*

I called the edition a wild success, but reader reaction was mixed.
Half loved it; the rest either missed the humor or weren't amused by it.
Some objected to the George Stevens photos accompanying my long
story of recent *Star* history, of employees at work with beer or pint
whiskey bottles propped at their elbows, or were offended by our
homespun ribaldry. We heard the disapproval for our 16-page joke
louder than the approval. The issue reflected just the sort of rude

depravity expected of a man who promoted liquor stores and was forever calling attention to local eyesores and official wrong-thinking.

My editorial that week was called "Our Second Fifth."

Five short long years. That's how we think of them. Long in that so much has happened in so many hammer-head hours of so many hammer-and-tongs days of so many sledgehammer weeks of so many trip-hammer months of each of them. Short in that we hardly knew where they went. Bong, they went, as Spring rolled in each year — bong, like the end of one round or the beginning of the next. Sometimes the bong sounded like the end of an act in the old Major Bowes Amateur Hour.

We figured on having the primary opponent, Financial Failure, on the ropes in Round 5, too groggy to come out for the next bell. And that's the way we feel today — a bit pooped, but a hell of a lot stronger than Failure.

If the humor irritates you, we're sorry. If you don't think it's humor, we're sorrier. If the odd raw note offends you, we can only add that we ourselves don't care how funny a joke is, so long as it's dirty. . . .

The end of the fifth year, the paper anniversary, is the magical date that everyone calls The Hump for small-business owners, and we are cheered at being over it. So here we are, over the hump, and there it is, right in front of us — another hump. But we're conditioned to the altitude, and we've got our climbing legs. The next hump isn't that far above us, anyway, and we've found the climb exhilarating.

The weekly's small world isn't filled with the cataclysmic and glamorous happenings of the full globe available by wire service to the dailies. You have to spike things up with what you can find nearest to hand.

★ 18 ★

Protecting the Land

The daily newspaper takes its mission seriously. Humor is found only in comics, cartoons, and syndications — you will find no "A.F. Wire Service" or "Pretty, But Not Correct" homegrown irreverence. The daily editor feels the cold stare of the public and the hot breath of the shareholders over his shoulder. The weekly owner may take his mission just as seriously, but he doesn't have to take *himself* seriously.

Neither of the Kennebunks was zoned, but both were considering it. A rare subtlety of understanding was required on both sides of the argument. Generally speaking, the native thought of zoning as a device whereby the wealthy newcomer could mold the community to his liking. He resented laws that would restrict him from doing any damn thing he pleased with his ancestral land. He liked things the way they were, but with more money, and he saw zoning as change and a restraint on his opportunities. He didn't quite understand zoning, but he knew suburbia was zoned, and he didn't like suburbia.

The newcomer had come to Maine because he liked what was there. His former community had been ruined for him by overgrowth and commercialism, so he wanted to restrict both in his adopted town. He often misjudged the native objections to land-use controls as products of backwoods ignorance. He overlooked the dangers to community spirit, civil rights infringements, and questions of constitutionality. He spoke scathingly of tar paper shacks and pig farms, neither of them generically ugly to the native as they were certainly not to me. I preferred both to the sterility of mass-produced homes, or even to expensive developments. The shack on its stony acre was a beginning home for a native working family, and the pig farm represented local enterprise and a life from the land. I tried to distance myself from the newcomers' attitudes while promoting the mild and sensible ordinances being fashioned by the planning boards. As zoning was eventually adopted in one *Star*-area town after another, the natives discovered that it was neither burdensome nor distasteful but their own protection against change and the newcomers, and became zoning's most dedicated champions.

But in 1963, although the seamier faces of growth were beginning to alarm some native Mainers, for most of them resentment of the newcomer had mushroomed into a dark pall of hatred directed against zoning, the loosely applied, despised name for property regulation of all kinds, and against me, who promoted it. The opposition was taunting me with anonymous phone calls, even snatching my notes from my hands at meetings. Things were getting personal.

To alert people to the hazards of living without land-use controls, one week I wrote a couple of phony stories, both ending with "(See editorial)." The first told of plans for a jazzed-up motel-restaurant, the "Gum-Drop Inn," on Kennebunk's lovely old residential Summer Street. I wrote that a New Jersey man had bought the old Bonser Mansion (fictitious) and was going to replace it with a motel. A prominent feature would be the big, winking gum-drop sign. The other story told of an amusement park about to go up on a piece of undeveloped riverfront land in historic Kennebunkport Village, the same site that would later become the source of one of my most strenuous editorial campaigns when my hoax story nearly came true.

My two shock-therapy stories sent citizens scurrying to their telephones before they read the editorial that explained them. I was practicing improper journalism, of course. I defended the stories by saying they caused no harm but did make people think.

One morning soon after Jerry Robinson came aboard, George Stevens dropped in with a flash photo he'd taken at night of a fat raccoon squatting high in a crotch between the upreaching arms of a huge roadside elm. Only the head and shoulders of the raccoon were visible. The big trunk and branches were grey, the background sky black, the coon's face bright. Could I use it? The snap was a corker, George insisted — make a hell of a spot. My best reason to use it was to appease George and keep him solvent. So I said OK, I'd try to find some way of sneaking it in.

I did — top center, Page One. Under it I described how intrepid photographer Stevens, prowling the woods at night, had been startled by a threatening noise, whirled, snapped the shutter, and fled. He had, I announced, been lucky to get a shot of the rare — and even more rarely photographed — deadly, tree-climbing orock, one of the first ever photographed in Maine.

Reaction was explosive. Our phone jangled busily for three days, local and long distance. Everyone wanted more information. Some said they had seen similar creatures they now identified as orocks. One woman said she'd have called it a raccoon, but the ears were too far apart. Some had heard orocks and described their cries. Others had looked for "orock" in reference books. Two had called the American Museum of Natural History in New York and were shocked to learn that the museum officials had never even heard of orocks. Most were incredulous — what on earth was an orock? But others were super-cilious — why all the fuss? They'd seen plenty of them.

Next week I turned the photo upside down, drew a couple of minor lines on it, trimmed the background until the reversed raccoon became the face of a turbaned, barbel-chinned witch in a black cloak, with trunk and branches the new background. Sorry, I wrote, we'd gotten it upside down the first time. Jerry and I collaborated on a long, hammy story of the obscure orock origins in early settlement times, and how the beast had been named. Everyone in six towns heard the story — the *Star* was at it again.

As a member of a discussion panel of fellow editors at a press association convention, I once recommended advocacy journalism. I meant mainly on the editorial page, but didn't stop there. Pure reporting objectivity is a myth, a "eunuchorn," I argued. Certainly, the reporter is morally obliged to set down all important information and present conflicting views. But objectivity pursued too rigidly deprives the weekly journalist in the thick of community affairs of the involvement required for insight.

To attain *pure* objectivity the reporter must set down every word and detail, however meaningless, in the sequence he hears it. Each story will be many times as long as it can afford to be. As soon as the reporter chooses whom to quote, or what part to repeat, or decides to delete what he considers extraneous detail, he is exercising subjective judgment.

The reporter is the outgrowth of the unique combination of genes, background, and experience that give him his biases. The condition of his mind and body during reporting activity sends his biases off in loosely predictable directions. He jots down only those impressions that seem important to record. The questions he asks are those that his biases tell him to ask; he has usually reached some conclusions already. The answers he gets reflect the biases of his interviewees. What the reporter learns becomes his story, and what he doesn't learn gets left out. His readers absorb his stories with a sense that an unstated judgment has been made. And so it always has.

Even were he to attain the pristine objectivity he seeks, what reaches the reporter's readers will not be pure, because behind him are his editors. Editors decide which stories are used, how they are cut or amplified, how big their headlines will be and what pages they appear on, whether or not they are illustrated. The editor may give a story added emphasis by assigning a sequel to it, or a series, or a feature that illustrates a point of view he has formed from the story. He highlights or lowlights according to his subjective perceptions.

The weekly reporter self-assigns most of his stories, following his interests, ignoring stories he finds difficult to research or that require interviews with people he dislikes. Whole subjects that bore him are downplayed. For the public, what goes unreported never happened.

Someone once said that a newspaperman should approach the world the way a mosquito approaches a nudist colony. I like the phrase, but not the philosophy. Certainly he must be skeptical — unlike the minister, the newspaperman should not approach the world with a determination to see only what's good in it, or even mainly what's good. He should reflect the world with honesty, but that is not the same as objectivity.

A man who spends his life writing about education may be assumed to prefer good education to bad. The crime reporter may be assumed to be against it. The writer on environmental subjects may be assumed to dislike pollution. Subjectivity is assumed by the reader. Pure objectivity may be a worthy if unattainable goal for the daily reporter or electronic newscaster, but for the weekly reporter, professions of objectivity are just bad jokes.

Like most newspapers, the *Star* contained mostly informational news that occasioned no stands or grandstands, and in which objectivity was the rule. But whenever someone did something unselfish for the common good, we hailed it subjectively. When we saw things going wrong, we wrote about them too, without biting our tongue.

I was forever being asked why there wasn't more good news in the paper, why the *Star* was so negative. Why give the towns a bad name, when there was so much good in them that went unnoticed? The fact was that we avoided whole categories of bad news, like the juicy tidbits of divorce, petty crime, and misdemeanor. Again we were criticised — why not report them? Shouldn't a self-respecting newspaper record these things, hold them up to public view as lessons to others? I didn't think so. I'm not sure the divorce rate would have been lower, or the accidents fewer, if we had inflicted publicity. The authorities and fate administered adequate punishment.

Besides, there wasn't time to do a proper job on all these stories, by which is meant a thorough job. There wasn't time to learn why people were divorcing, or what flaw in the social structure had led to a theft, or whose fault the accident was. We had no time, nor does any newspaper, to find out whether the speeding motorist was on a mercy mission or an adrenaline high. Unadorned facts of crime and personal misfortune can be brutal, but they are the only ones a newspaper can safely report. What is on the public record is fair game, so newspapers may safely and sanctimoniously copy the police blotter.

Bizarre crimes can't be overlooked, but in our rural communities these were rare. North Berwick, population and settlement dates both about 1700, with ambience to match, nestled with its three historic manufacturing plants around the Boston & Maine Railroad. Its central square was lined with make-do shops and dominated by a small branch bank.

In the rustic quiet and sunny bucolicity of an October morning, North Berwick shopkeepers are entering their shops. Next door to the bank, the local barber is draping his first customer. Two long black limousines with Massachusetts plates, carrying four swarthy men, are observed by all the Anglo-Saxon Yankee townspeople astir in the square. Six times the limousines circle the block with the bank on it, then roll across the B & M tracks and make a U-turn outside the Hussey Manufacturing Company's engineering offices. From the Hussey windows, four young draftsmen preparing for work watch the cars with casual amusement. The first car swings too wide and drops its front wheel in a drainage ditch. The four swarthy types jump from both cars in trench coats and fedoras. They hurriedly lift the errant wheel back onto the road and scramble back into their cars at just about five minutes to nine, leaving a great mess of footprints and tire tracks in the mud. The engineers joke among themselves that the men look like a bunch of bank robbers. One of them even jots down the license numbers.

The limousines recross the tracks toward the square and park in front of the bank, the town's precise focal point. Three of the four men get out carrying suitcases and enter the bank. A passing freight train blocks the engineers' view, but others, too, are observing this burlesque.

The three robbers in the bank herd the middle-aged branch manager and his two elderly lady cashiers into the vault at gunpoint. They try to lock the vault on their way out, but the heavy door jams ajar on a portable ramp. They grab what money they can find quickly and skedaddle, zooming away in the two limousines, their course well noted. Seconds later a local minister enters the still bank, to be greeted by the detainees emerging cautiously from the vault. Immediately behind the minister comes a swarm of suspicious locals, the barber among them. Within 15 minutes the square is alive with local and state police and sheriff's department men, and within 30 minutes four FBI men are on the scene. Roadblocks are set up all over the place, radios are sizzling with the news. Ten newspaper people, one from the *Star,* are there within the hour. How could the stumblebum amateur bank robbers have fared worse? By taking a lot of new, marked bills? They did!

If W. C. Fields as the Bank Dick couldn't have captured those four clowns single-handed by stumbling over a mop pail of water on his flight out the rear window and leaving the robbers to pile up behind him, put to sleep by the ammonia in the mop water, he isn't half the comedian I remember. But there was no W. C. Fields in North Berwick that morning, and no trace of the robbers, cars, or money has ever been found.

I wrote the story as a humorous short story, in reverse pyramid. Our readers had read all the bald facts before we went to press three days later. From the *Star* they got the feel of the town waking up, the weather, thumbnail sketches of the people involved, atmospheric detail, afterthought quotations, and a sense of the comic. Our story was six times as long as the others, which were all basically identical, but ours was alive. The liveliness was in the subjective.

I am reminded of another incident involving the police. A seedy-looking middle-aged man was apprehended while trying to pass a bum check in a Kennebunk drug store. It turned out that he was wanted for similar offenses all over Maine. There was only one colorful detail to the story, but it had no bearing on the police action and didn't appear on the blotter. There was no journalistic excuse to report it, any more than there was to report that the man had entered the police cruiser through its door, or that when he walked into the police station he did so by placing his feet, alternately, one in front of the other. To report this one detail was to include a relevant aside — to editorialize, in fact. As the check-forger was waiting in the station for his detention papers to be processed, he was observed to take off his shoes and socks, pull a deodorant bottle from his coat pocket, and spray meticulously between his toes.

★ 19 ★

Growing Pains

Not long after that fifth anniversary April Fool edition, our Main Street job printing competition, Frank and Althea Beard, decided they wanted a change. They had come to me as the logical chief salivator to offer their Arundel Print Shop for $10,000. They told me that their employees, Vic and Bunny Sampson, and Roger Edgerly, all experienced in their craft and respected citizens, were willing to stay on.

There was nothing I coveted more than eliminating the only significant job printing competitor in our *Star* area, more than doubling our printing volume and gaining the respect that eluded me for quality jobs. There were other long-range benefits, too, that Bob Stinson at Ocean National was quick to acknowledge. He remade and extended our notes to include the whole purchase price without overly bloating quarterly payments. I hadn't felt so buoyed in years. Anneke and I threw a hooker into our weekly budget and celebrated with our first restaurant meal of any kind since moving to Maine.

For five years I had worked in desperation; now the summits were coming on like peaks on a meringue. The graph of weekly circulation figures showed that each week we had been exceeding the same weeks of preceding years in steady progression, with the winter lows and summer highs farther and farther apart, until the graph reminded me of a conical shell, with its point down to the left, where I'd started, and the growing animal building each year a more stately mansion.

When Crosby Day left us for the *Press-Herald*, I hired a young man named Harris Dulany, a trained writer, to take his place in Wells-Ogunquit. With Harris there and Jerry Robinson in Kittery-Eliot, I could concentrate my own reporting efforts in the Kennebunks for the first time. Peg Hendrick managed to find enough advertising after Labor Day to keep us almost at our summer average. I was raising salaries and wages as high and as often as I dared. Every few weeks someone opened a pay envelope to find a little note in it sprinkled with appreciative messages and apologies for the undeniable fact that the increase didn't begin to equal what was deserved, or what could be expected with the same talents elsewhere. "But we're gaining on it," was the theme.

The old shop was insufferable in the summertime. All machinery went at top speed. Most of the windows were rotted shut and would have fallen apart if we had forced them. Garden Street was sheltered from breezes in all directions. The molten lead in the typesetting casting pots could never be shut off, so the place was an oven, even at eight in the morning. Then there was the gas-fired lead pot in the mat-caster, and the steam from too many hustling, deadline-ridden people working in too little space.

I can remember standing on the Premier newspaper press platform in my undershirt, with my head about a foot below the ceiling where the heat hung heaviest, flicking and guiding the sheets of newsprint from the feedboard into the cylinder grippers, the old flatbed screeching and racking back and forth under me, the whole shop shuddering, when receptionist-bookkeeper Beryl Oswell took a phone call in the front office and came out back to shout up at me what sounded in the din like, "It's Leighton Powell!"

Now, who the heck was he? I knew a Leighton Perry and knew of a Lawton Powers, but who cared? Beryl knew enough not to get me off the press for a phone call — the run was late enough as it was. "I'll call him back!" I yelled down at her.

Beryl returned to the office and picked up the receiver, but in a minute she was back, looking harried.

"He says, do you want him to pull the switch?"

"What! Who did you say?"

She cupped her hands to her mouth. "George Noiles."

Noiles, big and dour, was the longtime manager of the local Light and Power district. My foot hit the impression plunger and my hand reached for the power toggle. "Oh, my God!" Light and Power. I jumped down from my platform. Yes, I told George, I'd have a check in the mail that afternoon. I knew it was very late. I could take care of a month of it now, and I'd try to clear up April, too, in a week or so. There was a paper supplier's salesman in the office listening, and he was after money too.

The Garden Street quarters were too cramped to absorb three more people and the Arundel machinery, supplies, and appurtenances, so I settled temporarily for a split operation. Vic Sampson became printing manager, with Fern Loranger as his foreman at Garden Street. But carrying dual inventories and separate bookkeeping, production, and delivery at the two shops was wasteful, so I began looking for a new home — not looking hard, because I had no idea how to swing it, just looking, the way people scan real estate sections, dreaming. The zoning ordinance I had worked so hard to promote was restricting my choices. The manufacturing zones were small and scattered, with the smallest, the one close to Main Street, which I was loath to leave, almost completely covered with shops and residences. Of all the real estate people around, only one turned himself loose on my problem.

"Got a minute to look at something with me?" Jon Milligan had a hushed, autochthonous style. Why sure, I said dubiously. Jon led me to the confluence of Route 1 and High Street, at the top of the rise looking down Main Street. We stood before 1 High Street, the former Unitarian parsonage, a big white clapboard house converted recently into four apartments. "$12,500," Jon said.

Fantastic, I allowed. But I'd have to have a concrete base for the machinery, or we'd all wind up in the cellar.

Jon pointed to 3 High Street next door, almost the ex-parsonage's twin, also now converted to four apartments. That one was built in 1799, Jon told me, one year before the other one. By coincidence, it too had just come on the market. $13,500 was its price. He let that sink in for a minute. "Do you see it?"

Then it hit me. With the combined lots the ordinance would permit me to connect the two handsome old homes with an 80-foot shop. We did some pacing. I'd need only 35 feet in width, and the jogs in the twin buildings suited that perfectly. We could use one of the four-room apartments downstairs in the parsonage and rent the other seven apartments to carry the mortgage.

Jon even had the answer to my money needs — Warren Cochrane, a leathery, loping Boston man, semiretired to Kennebunk, who had supplied venture capital for some of Jon's own schemes. With a $14,000 Cochrane investment as down payment, Jon was sure the bank would take a first mortgage on the two old buildings and remake our notes for the new construction. Without our two current rents to pay, and with income from seven apartments, I should be able to cover bank payments and taxes. Paying off the Cochrane notes would depend on consolidation efficiencies and growth. As we expanded I could simply take over another apartment, and another. That both buildings were available simultaneously was a phenomenal stroke of luck. How else could I possibly swing it?

I drew plans and elevations and took them to Peg's contractor husband, Art Hendrick. No friendly charity, I told him, but no extras. He refined my plans and gave me a ridiculously low figure for the shop and a few office alterations, even including a reinforced pit for a Model A Duplex newspaper press — no sense in moving the old Premier.

Back to Ocean National I went. By now president of the little privately owned bank, Bob Stinson had another opportunity to exercise his dry wit. What was this — a little bank takeover attempt? Well, I said, I wanted to remake my notes to include a $4,000 used Duplex press and, after subtracting the Cochrane notes, a $26,000 mortgage loan to buy two old buildings and connect them with a 35-by-80-foot shop on a concrete slab. I presented the safeguard hedge for the bank. That was true enough — they were in Star Press too deep to stop now. The directors cogitated. Maybe. They scrutinized my figures for expected savings from consolidation. They inspected my plans and drove over to look at the two old buildings. And did some more thinking. And met again. In the end they agreed, and Round 7 was joined.

★ 20 ★

First Profits, First Prizes

At year's end our accountant, grinning conspiratorially, told me that Star Press had made its first calendar-year profit, all of $2,000 and change. Of course, that handsome figure was buried under mounting receivables and debt service. I called it a "paper" profit, convulsing the accountant.

But it was a profit and all the excuse I needed to blow about fifty dollars on an initial membership in the New England Press Association and the privilege of sending entries to its annual Better Newspaper contest. Most states (but not Maine) had their own press associations and held similar contests. There were two or three other regional associations too, and in a more rarefied atmosphere there was also the National Newspaper Association for all newspapers, not only weeklies and community dailies.

The New England contest was unique in the professionalism of its judges, who were not the usual random group of publishers and editors from other states' press associations but the ten Nieman Fellows of Harvard, all youngish journalists whose unusual promise was being rewarded with a paid year of study at the university, under Nieman Foundation Curator Louis Lyons. The contest judging was an annual exercise on the Lyons agenda.

There were contest categories for typography, sports, photos, and advertising — the numerical bulk of the awards — in which the *Star* presented no threat to anyone. I entered all five writing categories — news story, editorial, feature, local column, and community service — and the two that were broken down into five sections each by newspaper circulation size — under 2,000; 2,000 to 3,500 (ours); 3,500 to 5,000; 5,000 to 6,500; and more than 6,500. Best Editorial Page was one of these two; the other was the plum of the prizes, General Excellence. One of the five General Excellence winners, almost invariably the winner in the largest circulation class, was awarded the plaque for Best Weekly in New England.

When January came around I got a form letter from the New England Press Association (NEPA) saying that the *Star* had won something, so I splurged on eight tickets to the awards banquet in Boston. Anneke and I asked Peg and Art Hendrick, Jerry and Jane Robinson, and Harris and Barry Dulany to come with us to see what went on under the big top, and what sorts of people were doing weekly newspapers.

By then we were all good friends, and merry ones. The ladies were, I thought, the four liveliest and best-looking of the five-hundred-plus banqueters in the hotel ballroom. We were all feeling festive from the free drinks at the preprandial reception, and we dallied when the bell rang for dinner. By the time we entered the ballroom all tables were filled, so we found a table outside and levitated it in, to the amusement or otherwise of our dignified audience. A waiter brought us a dinner bottle I commissioned him to find.

Over coffee laced with bourbon we listened half-heartedly to the speaker of the evening. When he had resumed his seat at the long table reserved for dignitaries on the ballroom stage, NEPA President Bennett rose. Before announcing the usual awards, Bennett said, he had an unprecedented announcement to make. "Will Alexander Brook of the *Kennebunk Star* please come forward?"

Anneke nudged me. The other *Star* revelers leaned across the table to repeat it to me. I rose unsteadily, wondering if this might have to do with the table levitation, and made my way through the maze of banqueters. When I was standing below him, looking up in glazed puzzlement, Bennett began to read this letter from the Nieman Fellows:

To the New England Press Association:

The Nieman Fellows, as judges of the annual newspaper contest . . . have no authority to confer awards. They can only select newspapers to receive awards. We, the Nieman Fellows of 1963, have done that. We have chosen winners for all the assigned categories, and now, having paid our respects to solemn professionalism and to what we are pleased to call progress, we find that we have still not dealt to our satisfaction with one newspaper. Therefore, we wish through this letter to call special attention to the *Kennebunk Star* and its alter-edition, the *Wells-Ogunquit Star*. We commend its peculiar excellence to all who love weekly newspapers.

The *Star* is unique in the . . . journalism submitted to our judgment. It does not fit comfortably into any of the contest categories. After severe contemplation, we have concluded that the trouble with the *Star* is that it is more than a newspaper. It does not merely offer a selection of current events, in the manner of respectable journalism, permitting the reader to pick and choose as he would in a supermarket. The *Star* demands to be read entirely. It does not accept a ten-minute allotment between *Newsweek* and the *Christian Science Monitor*, and it declines to be skimmed. . . .

The Kennebunk *Star* is published by a person who loves good writing, and it is produced for people who have the time and taste to read it. It is possible that the *Star*, like an amber sherry glass, would have been more at home in an earlier century. We are glad that it lives in this one, and we wish it well.

When he had finished reading Bennett passed me the letter with one hand and reached down with the other, his jowly face beaming, to press my own sweating palm. The banqueters, few of them until then aware that there was a *Kennebunk Star*, rose to a noisy ovation. I wobbled back to my table and sat down.

Seven more times the *Star* was called, once for each of the categories in which we had submitted an entry, while Jerry tripped back and forth to the speaker's platform to collect certificates, more than any other newspaper that year, including first prizes for Community Service, and Best Editorial Page and General Excellence in Class 2. I learned that two of the Fellows had voted to give us the All–New England plaque, but had been outvoted by their more realistic colleagues, who pointed out our inadequacies of size, typography, reproduction, makeup, layout, illustration, sports coverage, and the rest. I had been plucked from the deepest professional uncertainty to greatest elation, all in the space of an evening.

★ IV ★

★ 21 ★

A New Press, A New Home

The daily *Biddeford Journal,* 8 miles to our northeast, covered primarily the small cities of Biddeford and Saco. It was one of six links in a small newspaper chain known as the Alta Group. Alta's other members were two community dailies in Massachusetts and New York, and three weeklies on our periphery. One of these sister weeklies was the 8,000-circulation *Sanford Tribune,* 11 miles to our west. The *Tribune*'s southern area dribbled out to meet that of another Alta member, the 7,000-circulation weekly *Courier* in Rochester, New Hampshire, just across the state border. The third Alta weekly, the *Somersworth (New Hampshire) Free Press*, was a tabloid with less than half the circulation of the *Courier* and situated only 8 miles from it, directly across the border from Berwick, Maine. Together with the small independent dailies in Dover and Portsmouth, New Hampshire, the four Alta newspapers closed a tight half-ring around what I thought of as potential *Star* territory.

By 1964 three graphics companies were making web-offset presses that small dailies and the largest weeklies were beginning to buy to replace their old letterpresses, most of them Duplexes. Offset, the process of printing from thin metal plates with type "burned" onto them through large photographic negatives, rather than printing from heavy plates of cast lead type, was a much faster process than anything we were used to for the newspaper — although our job department was equipped with some offset presses. The printed results were much sharper, particularly the halftone reproduction. The 16-by-20-inch negatives, taken of full pasted-up pages, were shot with a large, complicated camera, and the page images were then burned onto the metal plates. These thin plates were then clamped around the press cylinders, and a continuous "web" of newsprint from thousand-pound rolls was run through the press and printed as it went over the turning cylinders.

The Alta Group had decided to buy a web-offset press for Rochester and to consolidate the printing of the *Courier, Tribune,* and *Free*

Press there. Because the revised operation would require closer manufacturing coordination between the three papers, Alta had decided to
give the publisher of the *Sanford Tribune,* Bud Wright, top titular
authority.

Bud was a year or two my senior. He spoke in the confidential
manner of the large-town community leader. At the *Tribune* he did
some selling and overseeing, and attended all the club affairs and civic
occasions, a business overseer rather than a journalist. He left the
production end of things, including job printing, to his plant manager,
and the editorial end to his long-time editor, Elizabeth Mitchell, who
shared an office with her assistant. The only other member of the
editorial team was a free-lance photographer who also reported sports,
a puckish fellow who happened to be a drinking buddy of our photographer, George Stevens.

The two editorial women, pleasant and sedentary, reported
matter-of-factly on important official decisions, but for the most part
were content to fill a third of the large weekly's news-hole with
correspondence from ladies in the surrounding communities, and most
of the rest with every release that came in the mail. In this way the
Tribune saved itself the money it might have paid reporters. The short
Mitchell editorials praised the efforts of the civic-minded, supported
the decisions of established authorities, urged contributions to worthy
causes, and promoted spectator support for the local high school
teams. Vandalism was deplored.

Sanford was the central dominant town of York County's interior,
the isolated shopping hub for its rural satellite communities. The *Tribune*
acknowledged these satellites by reproducing their correspondents'
social news. The *Tribune* enjoyed the largest circulation, greatest ad
linage, and greatest bulk (about 32 broadsheet pages) of any weekly in
Maine. Writ large on its banner was "Maine's Greatest Weekly."

The *Tribune*'s ad rates were more than double ours, and it ran 60
percent ads to our 50, giving it nearly three times as much revenue per
page. All debt had been retired long before. The well-heeled Alta Group
was there behind it, and a long string of profitable years. Sanford's
commercial center, insulated from competition by miles of rural boon-
docks, was condensed and easy to serve by toll-free call and shoe
leather, assuring heavy production per salesman. With no greater sales
and less editorial expense than ours, nearly five times our revenue, no
debt, efficient quarters, and better equipment, the inland *Tribune* was,
further, blissfully unaffected by seasonal business fluctuations. *That*
was the plush way to run a weekly.

And so it happened that while Art Hendrick was completing the work on our new High Street quarters, with its concrete maintenance pit for a Model A Duplex press, the Alta Group would be selling or scrapping two Model A's. I called Bud Wright. I could have either press for $3,500, he told me. He'd be making up a Rotary luncheon in Kennebunk that very day and could drop by and take me for a look.

Our trip was to Rochester. Driving along in his big new car, Bud held forth about Alta's plans and his newly inflated administrative responsibilities. The headaches! — decisions, decisions. Which equipment to buy? How to manage the installation? (If you could only do it the way you wanted and get done with it, but you had to hold everybody's hand.) One good thing, though, he confided: he was going to get the production monkey off his back — delegate a lot of authority. That's what you had to do when you got big. One man couldn't do it all, but even if he could, that wasn't the smart way. The top man needed time for planning.

Gliding over the surface of the black road to Rochester, I won't forget Bud turning to glance at me for my reaction, shaking his head gravely at the thought of all the weight he was carrying. "Never get big," he told me.

At the spacious Rochester plant, electricians, technicians, sales reps, and installers outnumbered the regular work force. The 12-foot offset camera was being installed, and partitions were going up around it. The darkrooms, with their new pastel sinks, thermostats, conditioners, and underlighted glass surfaces, were almost ready. The floor had been prepared to receive the shiny press and folder units, already sitting in crates in the yard outside. Practice sessions were being conducted on the electronic typesetting equipment upstairs.

The squat, soon-to-be-surplus Duplex, knobby and gear-ridden over its ink-soaked maintenance pit, looked like Stonehenge. I stood by, marveling, while a pressman demonstrated it for me. Newsprint was fed from thousand-pound rolls at one end. Not counting stoppages, eight-page sections came off the press folded, 3,000 per hour. Twice as many pages per run, at twice our Premier's effective speed, and no folding time: one-eighth the man-hours per edition. Maybe even, some day, when those early web-offset presses too were glutting the market — but no, never mind that. "I'll take it."

Good; that was a load off Bud's crowded mind.

In our July 23 edition of all three *Stars,* my lead story began:

This is the story of the people who moved two print shops and a newspaper shop from their ancestral homes to new quarters in five days during their busiest season, and then had two days to get a newspaper out.

How can a man say what's in his heart, even when he's sober? The best I can do is try to set down an appreciation of the people who worked with me. But it would embarrass them if I did it anything like justice. . . .

It is past midnight. I have just seen the first eight pages come off the press. . . .

As soon as the last run had come off the Premier at Garden Street the week before, we had started. Next morning cartons and cases, small equipment and furniture, all with Star Press people underneath, had begun moving out the doors into a borrowed pickup and the same rusty six-wheeler George Stevens had commandeered for us when we wrecked the Whitlock. In the morning the Duplex arrived at High Street on a flatbed. A three-bruiser trucking team worked all morning getting the bulk of it through the garage doors and over the pit. There the setup man took charge, with Bezo and Larry as his assistant assemblers. Electricians were on tap to energize and illuminate. After they had positioned the Duplex, the truckers took the heaviest Arundel Print Shop equipment out through the roof of the Main Street quarters with a tall crane, while some of the rest of us skidded the smaller pieces down the wooden outside stairway onto the pickup, making many trips. Star Press shop and office people were emptying the Garden Street plant, load after load, and then unload after unload at High Street, with more lugging into place. Long into Friday night, all day Saturday, half of Sunday, and on through Monday and Tuesday we labored. Some of the job shop was operational Monday, and the typesetting by Tuesday. The Duplex was rolling late Wednesday, with barely enough time the next day to rumble through four other pressruns. The little market just up High Street from us almost ran out of beer, and on the hottest week of the summer.

Even ignoring the smudges, the newspaper we printed that week had a new look. Each page was an inch and a half wider, and the borders were narrower, giving us an eight-column format instead of the old seven. Now a 16-page paper would give us the equivalent, in words and advertising, of 18 in the old *Star*. Page layout became more flexible, and somehow grander.

George Stevens had used his muscle with excited abandon during the move, but hadn't neglected his Speed-Graphic. At the top of Page One was a shot of the Duplex going in through the overhead door, looking too big to make it; below it a jubilant group photo in front of the press after installation; and at the bottom an exterior shot of contractor Art Hendrick and me serving as foreground props for the new shop facade. George had yelled at Art to "point at something," so Art had pointed vaguely upward to the junction of roof and trim. My photo caption was:

> "That is the roof." Contractor Arthur Hendrick points out the roof to Publisher Brook. According to Hendrick, the roof is of great advantage in Maine, because it helps keep heat from leaking out.

Sharp in my memory is the celebration that first paper night, and the triumphant faces of my fellow sufferers, and the smiles on the faces of the people who dropped in off the street to see what the hullabaloo was all about and stayed to contribute to it.

The new quarters did more than save money and make things easier — and add to the debt. They gave us all a pride in our surroundings and an unstated feeling that better quality was expected, infusing us with an exciting sense of upward mobility. They moderated the frictions of too many people in too small a space. Instead of one office and a walk-through closet, we had separate offices for editorial, advertising, and reception-bookkeeping, each large enough to keep swept, and a brighter outlook from all the windows. The Arundel Print Shop crew gained a sense of being integrated into the mainstream at last, and the Star shop's job printers gained by emerging from tail-of-the-dog status in the shadow of the newspaper.

But the issue of July 23 had its sad aspect for everyone, me not the least of all. It was ad manager Peg Hendrick's last week — she had decided not to make the move with us to High Street. I found her replacement in Kai Suhr, middle-aged son of a Danish banker, a broad and portly man of considerable worldwide experience and what appeared to be overqualifications for our job. He had been selling advertising for the small Biddeford radio station, WIDE, and wanted a change. The business community joined me in thinking him a find, someone who would convey a light-hearted respectability to our customers. But it was with a real sense of loss that I bade so long to Peg.

Kai had the most luxurious quarters in the new building by virtue of the fact that he occupied the smallest of the three offices alone. None of it was luxury except in the sense that it was a far cry from Garden Street. And in the literal sense, it was only a far cry. From High Street, within days of our move, we could hear the far cries of the wreckers and the thudding of timbers as the old Star tenement came down. Almena Greene, owner of Greene's Garage next door, had bought it from Willis Watson for a used-car lot, an improvement any way you looked at it.

In a way moving was sad too — brings a lump to my throat, anyway — the way the end of anything you've struggled with, even so lowly and rotting away, is sad, the way hard times come through memory as nostalgia after enough years have rolled away.

★ 22 ★

Circulation Race

Which newspaper has most readers where is the recurring question asked of any paper's advertising salespeople. While we never had reason to quarrel with the claims of the Portland, Portsmouth, or Dover newspapers, the circulation boasts of the *Sanford Tribune* and the *Biddeford Journal* made book on the gullibility of our mutual advertisers.

In bold type below "Maine's Greatest Weekly" on the *Tribune*'s banner was its claim of readership, a figure usually between 28,000 and 30,000, followed by the word "Readers". The figure was always specific, perhaps "29,837 Readers." To give the figure the force of greater reality, it kept changing. Our advertisers, as a genus not awesomely analytical, assumed that 29,837 was the *Tribune*'s claim to paid circulation the week before. But even much later, when our circulation was higher than theirs, the *Tribune*'s "Readers" figure dwarfed our claim. *Tribune* Publisher Bud Wright got his Readers total by multiplying paid circulation by something between 3.5, the average American household membership, and 4.5. Who was to say that the Sanford family wasn't larger than the national average, or that every *Tribune* copy sold wasn't read by every member, tots and seniles alike? Bud violated the provable truth only in the number's specificity.

The *Biddeford Journal,* which had changed its name to the *Biddeford-Saco Journal,* observed our local merchants growing increasingly comfortable with advertising and began trying, with some success, to sell advertising in our area. My salespeople began repeating to me the canards that the salespeople of the "B.S." *Journal,* as we could now legitimately call it, were claiming for circulation in the Kennebunks. Particularly irksome was their claim that the *Journal* "sold more papers in the Kennebunks than the *Star*." Our advertisers assumed that the *Journal* wouldn't dare make an outrageously false statement — they didn't suspect sleight of mouth. The *Journal* published six days a week to our one; what they were really saying was that they were selling more than one-sixth as many copies per issue as we did in the Kennebunks. The *Journal* ad rates were higher than ours, so the unwary advertisers who fell for the semantics and bought *Journal* ads paid at least eight times as much to reach each reader in the Kennebunks. My salespeople, whose grasp of circulation figures was uncertain, had been caught with their mouths open in the presence of their customers. It couldn't be true, could it, they would ask me later, that the *Journal* was selling more papers in the Kennebunks than we were?

The postmaster in a weekly's hometown is the only official who in any sense monitors the newspaper's claims to circulation, or its qualification for a second-class postal permit. The difference in postage charges between second class and the alternative may exceed the weekly publisher's salary. Since the postmaster's salary is tied to the volume of mail his office handles, and the publisher is a heavy source of custom for the postmaster, the two carry on a sometimes strained, always symbiotic, relationship.

Before he will dispatch the publisher's mailbags each week, the postmaster must have in his possession a completed form signed by the publisher and attached to a marked copy of that week's issue. Among the things the postmaster learns from both are weight per copy and total weight by postal zone, from which he computes that week's mailing charges. He also learns what percentage of the paper's image area that week is devoted to advertising, as well as other things that will assure the Postmaster General that second-class privileges, conferred to help perpetuate robust American freedom of expression, are deserved.

Unless the publisher pays unceasing attention to his record keeping, the figures on the forms keep getting further and further out of whack, until the postmaster responsible for enforcing their accuracy is driven far enough up the wall to be able to leap from it, carrying the heavy book of postal regulations under his arm, over to the publisher's office without touching the ground. The expression on the postmaster's face as he greets the publisher is pained. The *postmaster* is a nice guy. He knows the *publisher* is a nice guy, and means no harm. He's sure that the *individual who makes out the forms* isn't consciously trying to break the law or to get *him*, the postmaster, fired or thrown into jail. But can't the publisher *please* get himself a better system?

Kennebunk Postmaster Lewis Burr was the pleasantest of men, roly-poly and cigar-chomping. He had the softest job imaginable, one that gave him next to nothing to do but worry, and the *Star* was his biggest source of worry, as it was his biggest customer. Our aberrations, exclusively noncriminal in intent, he was sure, resulted from what he accurately diagnosed as a too-casual attitude toward postal law and departmental difficulties.

I always feigned concern and promised to do better, but Lewie knew he couldn't count on it. Every now and then he'd have our mail sacks weighed individually, finding discrepancies. Our totals were often accurate within normal tolerances — it was the breakdowns that were haywire. I'd get a call from Lewie, and it would be either, Did I know how much I was getting away with? or, Did I know how much I was losing by overpaying him? Who was filling out the forms now? Couldn't I work out a better system? He'd send Bob Spofford down to go over things with us. The records, for Christ's sake, had to be accurate, or his tit would be in the wringer.

With the forms we delivered, Kennebunk Postmaster Lewis Burr could check the approximate accuracy of the "average copies mailed" figures on our annual, sworn October statements. Neither he nor anyone else checked our figures for newsstand sales. While I didn't keep track of the subscribers' postal zone changes, I did keep my own meticulous sales records, and each October published figures accurate to the nearest digit. Each year I was able to report higher totals, because each year we grew. When circulation is falling, the temptation to fudge is powerful. Most weekly publishers fudge their newsstand sales somewhat, and some indulge in bald-faced perjury. Declining circulation is not only an embarrassment but also an economic threat, because circulation is the newspaper's bedrock advertising sales tool.

It is advertising that puts meat on the publisher's table. At least three-fourths of his revenue comes from it. The success of the circulation manager and the justification for having one, lie in the logic that advertising rates and volume rise hand in hand with circulation. Ad rates can't be raised arithmetically with circulation, because the potential response to a store's ad disperses geographically as circulation rises. So if you charge $1 an inch with 3,000 circulation, you might get away with $1.60 with 6,000. What you charge for the ad has nothing to do with your cost of selling, composing, or printing it. If you break even at $1 an inch, you make 60 cents at $1.60.

No matter how successful the weekly's circulation manager is at his job, his salary will never be matched by any increase in profit from paper sales. The 16-page community daily or the skinny large-circulation weekly that sold for 25 cents in 1964 could skim a modest profit from circulation. But if your paper sold for 10 cents, as ours did, and the blank newsprint cost 9 cents, and you had to give either the newsstand or the post office 2 cents, and 10 percent of all copies were unsold or in make-ready or press overruns, and you factor in the cost of ink, delivery, bad debts, collection efforts, and billing costs — as one old-time comedian said to another, "You can't make money that way."

★ 23 ★

The Ad Business

Selling advertising for the *Star* mostly amounted to visiting advertisers, offering banter and suggestions, and helping them compose their messages. Not much actual selling went on. In high-powered metropolitan zones advertisers pick and choose among many media possibilities, assessing the demographic and distribution assets of each. Their ads set them back hundreds, even thousands, of dollars per inch or per minute. In our area we were the cheap, logical choice.

Most of our advertisers had no idea what our circulation was. Intuition was their guide. None kept analytical records, or would have been able to tell whether good or bad response was caused by the medium, themselves, their prices, or the weather. Without convictions, they were forever finding excuses not to spend their money. Some advertised from habit, others in self-defense, afraid that when the urge came to buy, the public might remember only their competition. When the self-defense advertiser saw his competitor stop advertising, he often breathed a sigh of relief and stopped too.

Another merchant might advertise with marked success for a while but be unable to see clearly cause and effect. With business humming, he would be tempted to stop advertising and test his momentum. Because the good effects of advertising wear off gradually, he would be encouraged at first to think he could ignore it. For months business would go on pretty much as before, with unattributable dips and spurts. Maybe business looked better when the advertising money stayed in his cash register. Little by little, however, the public would forget him. New residents overlooked his store; old customers moved on. Pretty soon a heavily advertising competitor would be on the upswing at his expense. At first he would find other reasons for the decline in his volume — he had already satisfied himself that ignoring advertising hadn't hurt him. Things would keep sliding until advertising became a financial hardship, too great a gamble. Optimism gone, he would retrench to the subsistence level of meager stock, low markup, and "poor-neighbor" traffic. Or he would sell the business, or it would die. In my memory the pattern is repeated over and over, like a wall papered with old *Stars*.

Everything offered in the weekly is available at a familiar place of business to every reader with the money to buy it. Every article in the classified section, every want ad, is of potential interest to that reader. Every house for sale can be compared with his own, every entertainment is within range when he feels like a night out. For many reasons he prefers to buy near home. He checks the city prices in the daily to keep his home store honest, and then responds to the ad in the weekly. He is, by the way, about half of America.

Budweiser can advertise anywhere, choosing the most expensive media. Joe's Pub serves Budweiser, but Joe doesn't advertise Budweiser. He advertises his pub, a nice, friendly place to go get drunk. Joe's Pub and Bob's Shirt Store are lucky. The corner New York City haberdasher is not so lucky. The smallest practical ad in the *New York Times* will cost him $300, and it's gone in one day. Only residents and workers within a seven-block radius will buy at his store. That may be the equivalent of the total population of Kennebunkport, but only a fifth of them read the *Times,* and only one in three hundred readers will notice his little ad for shirts. Of those two people — because that's how many we're down to — one may even go to that store to buy a shirt. The advertiser has sold one shirt for a dollar over cost, and he's spent $300 to do it. Bob, of Bob's Shirt Store, Kennebunk, spent $6 for a larger ad in the *Star*. Two thousand people in town and three thousand in neighboring towns noticed it, and Bob had the only shirt sale around. For $6 he could sell out his whole inventory. One of my filler ads read: "If you can't sell it in the *Star,* you ain't got what they want."

In the early sixties our typical local businessman thought about advertising hardly at all, and never advertised if he felt he could avoid it. He bought wholesale and sold retail. Apart from rent, taxes, and utilities, the difference between the buy price and the sell price went into his pocket. Gambling part of his profit on advertising offended his Yankee sensibilities.

But insidiously, each week, a genial *Star* salesperson reminded him that it was that time of the week again. If he didn't happen to be waiting on a customer or talking with a crony, he might give this week's advertising nonsense a moment of his attention. He might deliver his instructions verbally ("Yes, let's see — why not give me two columns four. Gloves and shirts — make it raincoats and shirts. With my logo. And somewhere, 'Open til 8 P.M. Thursdays.' "). Or he might scribble some prices on a piece of brown wrapping paper, or even rough something out on a piece of *white* paper. Later on, when he got more used to advertising, he might clip an ad that took his fancy and tell us to give him something like that.

There were the sophisticates, too. One restaurateur wrote funny letters about what was going on in his restaurant, or what happened to him on vacation trips — gossipy stuff, some of it mildly risqué. The complaints reinforced his conviction that he was on the right track.

A youngish couple, Tom and Dottie, opened a bookstore in Kennebunkport that soon became a casual meeting place for errand-goers who thought a lot about reading, nuclear waste, and keeping in touch with the right people. At the cozy oasis customers could bump into friends and fill a cup from the coffeepot always on the wood stove. Socially, Tom and Dottie were charmingly relaxed, but in business hard as flint.

Dottie handled their advertising. Format was static, but interior copy changed weekly. It took the form of refined correspondence, intimate and chatty, about new books, flatteringly describing people who dropped in carrying doughnuts to go with their coffee, saying what fun it was to be there in Dock Square, and how many interesting things were going on for those with the perceptions to notice. Dottie had a warm feeling about her literary style — more than once she told me that many people she knew read the paper primarily for her ads. She was very tall, with severe black hair, and the long, tranquil face of a Renaissance beauty. Her expression, when she delivered her creations, was queenly, but alert. She discussed her ad in precisest detail with someone who scurried out of the advertising office to help her. She demanded proofs and studied them critically, sometimes making author's alterations and demanding new proofs.

Twice Dottie and Tom made formal appointments with me to discuss their frustrations about the sort of attention they were getting from the *Star*. They wanted Page Three, Section One, upper right, reserved for their ad each week (the advertising manuals were calling this the preferred spot). We usually placed it there, but not always. Why not? I'd explain that our process prevented us from guaranteeing it. They would press angrily, but I'd remain firm, and the next complaint would be raised: the *Star* didn't seem to think their shop party for the author who autographed his books was newsworthy enough to deserve a reporter — why was this? They spent a lot of money with us. And another thing: they shouldn't be charged for an ad if we erred typographically or in interpretation, or failed to follow Dottie's instructions precisely.

Our people dreaded Dottie's weekly visits and made nervous efforts to avoid unpleasantness, meaning special handling all the way. During our appointed discussions, Tom and Dottie would hint that if we didn't shape up they might stop advertising altogether. Each time I said I would miss them.

Other merchants and tradespeople continued to advertise desultorily, even though they couldn't see that it did them any good. They were destined never to catch fire, but at least the public didn't forget them. At every opportunity they'd tell us they didn't know why they kept it up — never got any results from advertising. The list is etched deep in my memory. One was a real estate man who had never, to his knowledge, ever sold anything through a *Star* ad. Earlier the very week he last said that to me, he had sold the single property he'd just advertised to a man who told me he'd gone to *that* agent to see *that* house because of *that Star* ad. The agent spent about $15 a week with us and made $2,500 on that one sale.

All I know is that the merchants who advertised a lot and kept it up usually became the most successful business people in their fields, but whether it was because of the advertising or the adrenalin drive that caused them to advertise, I don't know, and no one else does, either.

But I remember Bill Berry, who had decided at age 60 to quit whatever he'd been doing, leave his Massachusetts home, and come to Kennebunk to buy old Burton Murdock's drugstore. There were two other senior druggists in town, at least one too many for the population. Eschewing discount and bargain, each of the three old druggists had accumulated his own loyal clientele.

Newcomer Bill Berry's hair was silver, going on white. His chin receded, and he was growing a discreet potbelly. He leaned forward when he walked, arms bent like a kangaroo's. Bill was going to get on the rail early by advertising with us, something his competitors had never seriously considered, and with free coffee and effusive customer greetings — all very pleasant, because Bill was a good-hearted man. He was one of our hottest early advertisers, gimmicky and promotional. He gave a lot of things away, and the giveaways were focal to his advertising. But they were minor items without drugstore significance, like plush bunnies at Easter. The store alterations he made were cosmetic rearrangements. When old Burton Murdock's customers came in for the freebies and to get a look at the new man and his store, they found all the old inventory at the same prices, or maybe a bit higher to cover advertsing and freebie costs. Released from their former loyalties, they claimed their plush bunnies and drifted over to the other drugstores where things were being run in familiar ways.

In his youth Bill must have observed his own druggist forebear leading a secure small-town life, much as the old three in Kennebunk had done. It makes me sad now to think of Bill Berry, one of the few merchants on whom our advertising worked a reverse English. After a few encouraging months it was all downhill for Bill. Shortly after he sold his doomed business, Bill Berry died. I'm sure his death was hastened by worry and disappointment, but even more fundamentally, perhaps, Bill was a victim of misapplied enthusiasms inspired by some obscure pharmaceutical recidivism.

I recall a local banker who channeled his advertising through a local ad agent. The banker leaned on the agent to get some free bank publicity in the *Star*. I exercised my editorial judgment and told the agent that the fact that the bank had sent a teller to a weekend banking seminar wasn't newsworthy enough. The agent fumed. Was that gratitude? The bank spent a lot of money with us.

Well, I told him to tell the banker, space was what we sold, money was what the bank sold. The *Star* had given the bank a lot of business too. When we got our freebies, he would get his freebies. Neither of them could see any logic in that.

In ad-rate cost per thousand readers, most metropolitan daily newspapers seem to beat the weeklies hands down. But you have to analyze it. How many of their readers live within normal shopping distance of the advertiser? Do they read only parts of the paper, or do they read it cover to cover? How many minutes do they spend per page? Where are they when they read it — at home in an easy chair, or at a lunch counter? How many family members see each copy? Is one of them the one who spends most of the family paycheck? Where is the paper next day — in the trash, or on the coffee table? Is the paper read only for news, or is it read also for buying opportunities? The weekly is read for both, and that is why the humblest ad in it, the one that tells the price of haddock at the local fish market, is effective. It is why so many otherwise worthless weekly newspapers continue not to die.

The median income level of the readership has an even greater influence on the ad rates a newspaper can charge than circulation does. The median income of the Kennebunk family then was about a sixth that in Darien, Connecticut, meaning that there might have been one-thirtieth the amount of discretionary purchasing power around. Reader income level has little to do with a paper's production costs, however. Newsprint, machinery, telephone rates are all pretty much the same all over America. So are the costs of insurance, fuel oil, transportation, postage, power, water, sewer service, finance charges, and office and shop supplies. Newspaper salaries vary with geography, but only moderately. Local median income levels reflect the *kinds* of work the readers do — a high median doesn't mean that the pressman in Darien makes six times as much, or even half again as much, as the pressman in Kennebunk.

Because *Star* circulation became increasingly strung out geographically, our circulation increases were only marginally translatable into higher ad rates. The most fortunate weekly publishers are the ones who operate in condensed, isolated, competition-free, high-income areas. When I was breaking even at $1 an inch and 10 cents a copy, one of those fortunates could charge perhaps $3.75 an inch and 20 cents per copy. Of that, $2.60 and 10 cents could theoretically have been the publisher's profit — $230,000 a year — if he operated with the same circulation and ad linage, the same equipment, the same debt, in similar quarters, and with the same number of people as I did.

In reality, of course, when a publisher starts making money he hires 20 people to do the jobs 10 *Star* people were doing. He curtails his own operational activities and hires others to do what he has been doing. He builds comfortable quarters, loosens up on efficiencies, hires janitors and cleaning women and grounds keepers, throws away his pencil stubs when they get down to six inches, and takes a lousy $90,000 a year.

Even by raising ad rates consistently after 1967, and with a year-round average circulation that would reach 14,000 by 1976, we still worked average rates up to only about $2.25. If, in 1976, we could have charged $6.00 an inch, as newspapers of our size and circulation in higher income areas did, our annual profit would have been more than a million dollars.

★ 24 ★

Power Company Power Play

In 1964, a young couple named Witherell had bought a vacant piece of land at Cleaves Cove, Kennebunkport, but couldn't afford to build. They liked old things, so they decided to look around upcountry, where old buildings were available at very low prices, for a house to move onto their land.

The Witherells had overlooked a critical detail. It involved the lords of the rights of way, Central Maine Power and New England Telephone, whose wires crisscrossed back and forth across the roadways over the miles between whatever the Witherells found and their Kennebunkport shore property. The utilities resisted extracurricular nuisances like the Witherells, who were asking for linesmen to ride along on top of an old house, lifting wires over the roofpeak, occasionally cutting and re-splicing before and behind. To discourage such requests the utilities assigned prohibitively high values to their work, making it more costly to move an old house than to build one from scratch.

If the Witherells had consulted me beforehand they could have saved themselves some bother: I too had made inquiries when fine old structures were being demolished to make room for filling stations or fast-food eateries. If, instead, the utilities had gone underground, America might still be unqualifiedly The Beautiful. The dividend no one could have foreseen would have been the preservation of much of our architectural heritage. As progress overtook them, all the movable old structures could have been transplanted out of harm's way.

Faced with the utilities' stonewalling, the Witherells persevered with commendable ingenuity. In midsummer they learned that the Camden-Rockland Water Company had bought the old Wilson place in West Rockport to protect the watershed of Mirror Lake, and was offering the cottage to anyone who would remove it whole or in pieces. The cottage was a story-and-a-half Cape Cod, distinguished more by being one of Knox County's oldest homes than by its refinement. It had sat since before the American Revolution down a steep, rutted driveway off a country road in the shadow of Ragged Mountain. The Witherells drove the hundred miles to West Rockport, saw the cottage, and bought it for a sum equal to the value of its timbers. They hired house-mover James Merry to haul it out of its steep hollow and down to a Rockland pier. There the old house, still on Merry's lowbed, would board a barge to be towed down the coast to Cleaves Cove.

The house was insured for its ocean passage by a rather sporting insurance company. There were hazards in jacking up its brittle body, getting it to and aboard the barge, carrying it on a long sea voyage, and finally dragging it up the rubble beach and onto a foundation at Cleaves. *Star* photographer George Stevens would record the hauling process to the pier, and then, himself constituting another kind of hazard, would accompany the Merry Men and tugboat crew on the rolling sea.

Merry busted an axle getting the house onto skids and out of its gully, and his cable parted three times before he got the building on his lowbed. George was excited about being our official representative. He telephoned me repeatedly as event followed event, assuring me that he was frightening off all other photographers and reporters to give us an exclusive. When the house was at last on its barge and ready for sea, the weather report was favorable.

But my story on August 13 began:

> The house itself was unprepossessing, a workaday old man of a house, crotchety, set in its ways, suspicious. It had sat at the bottom of a hill in the shadow of Ragged Mountain for 185 years, used to its own people and its own view down the gully across the trees and open spaces to Mirror Lake. Understandably, as those involved in the transplanting think back on it now, it didn't want to move.
>
> The house seemed to object right from the start. Like an old man uprooted from his land and memories to begin life anew in a foreign place with a new family, it sat down and kicked, unaware that it was doomed if it stayed, and that the transplanting was a labor of compassion. In the end, during heavy weather in the dead of night, it slipped from the grasp of its benefactors on a long sea voyage and sank in sixty-five fathoms.

What do you do about such losses? The road trip would have been easy. How could the utilities be persuaded to do the job at cost? My editorial that week referred to the squalid maze of poles and overhead wiring along the streets and byways of America, and the loss of our heritage, chunk by chunk. Perhaps, I wrote, the buildings at least might be preserved. Supposing a nonprofit historical society were formed whose ultimate goal would be saving *all* the old meritorious homes, not necessarily historic or outstanding, in a town or a few towns or a county? Or the *country?* The usual building conservation society either saved one or two special landmarks in place as museums, or resurrected dilapidated city neighborhoods. Maintenance forced the societies into the never-ending rounds of fund-raising activities my society would avoid.

"Homesteader Society" volunteers would compile records and site data for all old local buildings and undeveloped land. Each building would be catalogued and photographed, and old photos sought. Complete pedigrees would be developed and dates for additions noted, as well as brief biographies of former owners. The production of historical data and pamphlets would qualify the Homesteader Society as a tax-exempt educational institution.

The first homes to be studied would be those most immediately endangered. When one was threatened the Homesteaders would be ready. They would first approach the utilities people. Sensitive to public criticism, I reasoned, the utilities would prefer favorable publicity to confrontation, and would agree to raise wires at cost. The Society would acquire the building for its timber value and move it temporarily to a vacant lot, or permanently to a parcel of Society-owned land already occupied by one or more saved homes. With its experienced volunteer membership of lawyers, realtors, construction people, and public officials, the Society could immediately publicize the move and put the old building on the market, proceeding meanwhile with on-site preparation and restoration plans. The buyer could have it installed, or in any stage of restoration, at a bargain price that would modestly exceed the Society's costs. Everyone would be happy. If the local chapter were successful, it would have imitators.

I called for volunteers. Among the first was a retired New York bank vice president named Thompson, who agreed to serve as our first chairman. By February we were a tax-free corporation. But we never got off the ground. Thompson kept thinking in terms of fund drives, precisely what I wanted to avoid. Two or three project opportunities came and went while the Homesteaders drifted uncertainly. When Thompson's term ended, we made an attempt at resurrection, but by then most of the directors had lost enthusiasm, and so the resurrection was not to vigorous life but to senility, and we finally died of hardened arteries.

Most of the *Star*'s editorial campaigns started this way, as events that would have been forgotten with last week's news if they hadn't fired the newspaper's imagination. We kept stories alive, hammered into the local awareness, until they became what people were discussing and forming opinions about. We kept several campaigns going all the time, giving the paper constant motion and continuity, its most important qualities.

★ 25 ★

The Politics of Prizes

When January came again in 1965 I learned that we had again won something in the annual New England Press Association contest. By then Harris Dulany, the reporter who had succeeded Crosby Day in Wells-Ogunquit, had left the *Star* to write a novel, so he and his wife, Barry, would not be accompanying us to Boston. And our former one-person advertising sales department, Peg Hendrick, had left to take care of her family. So only Managing Editor Jerry Robinson and his wife, Jane, accompanied the Brooks this year to the awards banquet. We called Peg and Art Hendrick to say we were on our way — too bad we couldn't repeat last year's wild festivities together — and set out in a blizzard from Cape Porpoise. Our way took us by the Hendrick home, where Peg was at the roadside flagging us down. She passed a bottle of champagne through the car window and pressed a sealed envelope into my hand. I stuck it in the glove compartment for later.

We arrived in time for the reception and awards ceremony. The *Star* was called to the podium eight times, all for editorial awards, including first prize for General Excellence, Class 3. I hadn't let myself think about the big one, the All–New England plaque. But the Nieman judges, nice Fellows, gave it to us, the smallest newspaper ever to have won it. Was I imagining a reserve in the customary ovation?

After dinner Jane and Anneke repaired to the powder room. When they returned they reported on the crush there, and that from what they had overheard, people were pretty sore about the All–New England award. At one of the hotel bars we learned that it was worse than that. Already a furious meeting was being held in *Sanford Tribune* Publisher Bud Wright's hotel suite. A standing-room-only nest of disappointed publishers was there, calling for a termination of the Nieman Fellows' judging tenure.

In defending their choice at a convention breakfast next morning, Nieman judging chairman Ray Jenkins said that each Fellow had taken a couple of categories, selecting the ten best entries in each for review by the full panel, which then selected the prizewinners together. The *Star* had cropped up in every major category. "The looks of the *Star* could have been improved," one Fellow noted, "but in the end it came down to the fact that we had to give it to the *Star*."

At first, they said, they had been "thrown off by the *Star*'s style," which they called "controversial," "narrative," and "featuristic," one that violated the usual newspaper precepts. But maybe, they theorized, a weekly shouldn't try to be like a daily. "Maybe there was time on weeklies to polish and produce literary pieces." At this point my dander didn't know whether to get up howling, or to lie down. The danders in the audience, however, propelled several publishers to their feet. Maybe the *Star* had time to polish, they retorted testily, but not many others did.

Judging had winnowed out two finalists, Jenkins said, the *Star* and a Connecticut paper, which was more professional looking. But the *Star* was "much stronger in its editorials, followed up its stories more aggressively, had special charm, and a conscientiousness in the presentation of a story that always made you understand exactly what it was all about."

When Jenkins turned the meeting over to his audience, bitterness was universal. It was all very well for the *Star,* one man said, this "conversational" style, but his own audience was pretty sophisticated, and folksiness didn't go down well with it. There was more in this vein, but most criticized our reproduction and typography, shortcomings attributable to a shortage of help and proper equipment. At the NEPA business meeting that day the directors voted to fire off a protest to Nieman Curator Louis Lyons, who felt constrained to defend the choice of the *Star* on radio next evening. The following year the Nieman Fellows were restricted to judging only a few editorial categories, not including General Excellence, and the year after, they were phased out of the judging altogether.

In next week's issue I told of the awards evening, saving comment on the furor for one of my editorials. I called it "In Nieman's Land."

In the weekly newspaper field one of the sweetest plums is the plaque awarded each year to the newspaper judged to be the best weekly in New England, regardless of size. To one who started on the bottom rung of the ladder less than seven years ago, the plum looked inaccessible. There were so many larger, better-equipped, conscientious papers that made themselves handsomely complete, that the *Star* seemed to have climbed at best only a third of the way.

Last Friday evening in Boston, that was how I felt. Next moment the plum was popped into my open mouth. My jaws closed: the sweet juice spurted. The sound of five hundred applauding fellow-newspapermen rang in my ears.

For every elation there is deflation. The rumble of indignation and disbelief that followed when the disappointed contestants compared their own handsome newspapers to the journalistic rats-nest of the *Star* displayed on the winner's table reached my ears, and, like the others, I felt that the judges had made an inexplicable mistake.

The judges explained their choice next day, saying many things that pleased me, partially restoring my shaken self-confidence. But the rumblings of discontent continued, creating in me a hollowness that food wouldn't fill, that persisted until I entered the car for the ride home late Saturday night in driving snow.

The windshield was frosty; I opened the glove compartment to find the scraper. My hand closed on a sealed envelope that had been thrust into it as I drove off for the fateful Press Association weekend. It was addressed only to "Alexander." Inside it was a clipping from *Life*:

SMITE 'EM, ALEXANDER

★ 26 ★

Environmental War

Heavy with symbolism it is for me, in retrospect, that week after our Boston Press Association banquet. My editorial subjects were two Englishmen of vastly different weights on my judgment scales. The first editorial eulogized Winston Churchill, who had just died. The second was inspired by a man who had come to Maine via Canada, a man of medium height and heavy body, with a liquid, clerical manner of speech, loris-like locomotion, a greengrocer's face, and acquisitive tendencies. He went by the appropriately melifluous moniker of Llewellyn Lloyd-Davies.

I had met Lloyd-Davies before, when reporting his several area hostelry efforts, last as the owner of a Kennebunkport summer inn known as The House on the Hill, whose outlook was across Ocean Avenue over the only stretch of the mile-long harbor portion of the Kennebunk River still undeveloped on both sides. River and tidal flats pressed in close on the House on the Hill side, and from the road the southbound traveler looked upriver toward the bridge, and downriver toward the jetty entrance. One came to this stretch refreshed by a prospect open in three directions — black fir and gray rock on the opposite shore, boats moored in the stream, piers and wharves along the banks, an expanse of stately African grass — scenes stirred by soaring gulls and salted by a whiff of the sea. In the foreground nearest the road, an irregular narrow acre of marshy wetland above the tideline went with the inn property, along with riparian, or underwater, rights to the mud flats that were covered at high tide. These flats extended 200 feet beyond the marshy acre to the "thread of the river." Lloyd-Davies's innkeeping experience of two summers may have been disappointing, because in 1961 he had sold The House on the Hill. Ominously, he withheld the marsh and riparian land across the road.

In January 1962, Lloyd-Davies dumped several loads of gravel fill on the marsh. At the Town Offices I learned that the three selectmen had granted Lloyd-Davies a building permit to construct a bulkhead around the marsh and perhaps an acre and a half of the mud flats and build a two-story, 34-unit motel on the filled land. When I asked the selectmen why they had issued a permit without holding a public hearing, they said his plans complied with the state plumbing code and he had approval from the Water Improvement Commission. We have no zoning, they said — we couldn't stop him if we wanted to. How can we refuse it?

I saw things otherwise. Lloyd-Davies owned the acre above mean high water, but it was too small and fragile to support a motel. He also owned riparian rights to — but didn't own — the mud flats. Riparian right merely gave him the right to *ask permission* from the town to construct things on the flats, effectively turning them into private property. I argued that the selectmen had had no business giving away the citizens' rights without first asking their permission.

My lead story, and three impassioned editorial pleas to Lloyd-Davies to desist, encouraged three summer residents to offer Lloyd-Davies $16,000 for the little marsh plot, pledging to give it to the town for a public park. Lloyd-Davies countered with a demand for $20,000, which they called blackmail. The selectmen were surprised and embarrassed by the public outcry, and furious at my impudence.

For reasons of his own, Lloyd-Davies stopped filling the marsh. Two years went by; the motel and bulkheading permit lapsed from disuse. But nearly three years later, on the first week of 1965, Lloyd-Davies resumed his filling.

A week later, in my editorial, I condemned what I pointed out was illegal — working with a lapsed permit to fill marsh property and riparian land, without the newly required consent of the Army Corps of Engineers and the Town of Kennebunk, and without even an updated permit from the Water Improvement Commission. Certainly this time the public should demand a review.

Most natives, resentful of land-use restrictions and in precarious economic circumstances, bridled at what they saw as an effete attitude from me and the wealthy people in the fashionable riverside part of town. But support for my editorial made the selectmen agree to a Saturday morning on-site inspection followed by a public hearing. Next week and the next I blew my bugle for a show of objector strength. The bulkhead would reduce the size of the tidal basin where young sailors raced their dinghys — a minor matter, but significant in terms of rights. Conservationists would object to the wetlands filling, environmentalists to the outfall of the motel's septic effluent into the river above the beaches. The open space was one of the Port's unique attractions. I addressed the selectmen: "A delay is all we ask today. But a delay will be a minor victory for common sense and posterity."

Earlier that week I had arranged a meeting with the three summer residents who had pledged the money in 1962 to buy the marsh. I had also invited a fourth man, not known to me or the others except by his name, McKinnon — wealthier, younger, and more flamboyant than the others — who had volunteered his concern. I had persuaded each of the four to a strategy: the only public access to the harbor on either side of the river was at the town-owned Government Wharf, used exclusively by working fishermen. The recent dredging had tripled the harbor's mooring space and deepened the channel, so another public landing was needed for local and visiting yachtsmen. No other suitable land remained, which provided sufficient legal justification for eminent domain proceedings. Lloyd-Davies was now refusing to entertain his earlier asking price, but he would have a price. If the wind headed him during the public hearing, he might be persuaded to change tack and settle.

The low end of any eminent domain award had been established by the earlier $16,000 offer, but because the courts were likely to be generous with such awards, the new offer had to be higher — say $35,000. Supposing we raised that much privately and gave it to the town to buy the marsh? With taxes unaffected, some of our opposition might vote with us to take the land. If the selectmen heard the support for eminent domain loud and clear, and the opposition was weak, they might take their easy way out by calling for a referendum vote to decide the question for them.

When a town votes to take property by eminent domain, the final cost of settlement remains in doubt. First the land is taken, then its value is appraised by a panel of professionals. The landowner can only appeal the appraisal figure. I reasoned that neither the appraisal figure nor a court award would exceed $35,000.

When the five of us got together, I was thinking of a public fund-raising effort. We speculated about local sentiment and possible contributors, observing that our time was short. After mostly listening to the others, McKinnon made his grand gesture. Gentlemen, he said in effect, let's get down to business — maybe we can settle things first and raise the money at our leisure. He would pledge $20,000 immediately if each of the others would pledge $5,000, to be repaid from whatever could be raised through public appeal.

There was a pregnant silence before one said, OK, count him in, and that broke it — the others could do no less. Before the public hearing I was able to announce the news.

Most local people at the hearing had expected to be members of a vociferous majority supporting Lloyd-Davies. They were shaken by the size and composition of the crowd. Summer residents, retirees, professional people, conservationists — some having driven great distances in the dead of winter — turned out in unprecedented droves. Expression for taking the land was robust.

Understandably, I wrote that week, the selectmen might still question the true voice of the town. In any case, they had the choice of heeding the sentiment they heard, or ignoring it and rewarding the man who had violated the local law. At no public expense, here was a last chance to gain a second access to a harbor dredged at great public expense.

Next week the three selectmen backed off and denied Lloyd-Davies a renewal of his permit on the shaky grounds that his plan's specifications were unclear. I wrote that week:

The most thoughtful of the arguments in favor of granting Lloyd-Davies his permit are that others have been permitted similar projects, and he is being singled out unfairly. It seems to us that the time has come to redefine the principles of public and private rights.

Precedents have been set, but they are precedents for the past. One must look today at "building" not just as structure made by man, but as building for a certain use. When the building was surrounded by wilderness these specifics were unimportant. Today one must know. There must be protection from spreading fire. There are cellars and wells and septic fields of neighboring structures to consider. There are traffic, and health, and nuisance, and safety considerations. There is also the question of beauty.

In the old days there was vast natural beauty in America, more than enough to go around. Natural beauty could hardly be tarnished by one person or one project. There it was all around us. The protection of beauty, unlike wealth or health, was not, and still is not, a function of law. Law cannot define beauty and so cannot specify that beauty must be preserved.

There is so little natural beauty left that the handsome animal that once stretched from the Atlantic to the Pacific is now riddled with flea-bite and infection. We are the fleas on its back, and we fleas on the coast of York County are among the few that inhabit a section of the pelt only half besmirched. . . . When the big body was sparsely inhabited, only rudimentary laws prohibiting one flea from biting another were required in the flea community. Things have changed. Natural beauty, and wealth and health, and existence itself, have overflowed one another's concept boundaries, and the beauty of the pelt has become a factor of survival.

If inaction that helps a few to exploit and grow rich is preferable to action, forceful action, to save our towns from ultimate poverty of body and spirit — if we must bow to almighty precedent and the obsolete concept of private rights to spoil or destroy property as a private toy — then let us revert to the older laws, and get rid of the weak and each take what he can. Let private rights be supreme, and public rights be damned. . . . Either we advance to higher ground or revert to lower. It is this middle ground, once a flowery field, that has gone to muck with the marching, the slogging, of too many feet.

Two weeks passed uneventfully. In March Lloyd-Davies was granted a hearing to present a modified bulkheading plan, to keep the marsh from "eroding," he said, something it hadn't done in living memory. I withheld comment until the week before the hearing, when I reiterated former objections, adding more. I was whistling in the dark when I wrote:

> We think times are changing, and have the feeling that the world is ready to listen to the people who are screaming, "Woodsman, spare that tree!" There is growing awareness that we have done to our towns and cities and open land what the seagulls have done to Bumpkin Island.
>
> The Chairman of the Board of Selectmen, C. R. Butts, has scoffed at our crusade, and belittled the feelings of those who are pained by the motel plans. We do not ask Mr. Butts to feel as we do. We ask him to be generous, to acknowledge the feelings we claim. . . .

At that second bulkhead hearing Lloyd-Davies, low-key as always, but acerbic, spoke at length. He had reduced the area of mud flats to be enclosed, he said, and so was meeting the objectors "more than halfway." All he was trying to do was to protect his land from erosion — others had done similar things. The selectmen, however, prudently agreed to honor any legally correct petition calling for an article in the next town-meeting warrant a month away, to consider a referendum vote on eminent domain.

That week the four men who had pledged $35,000 offered it to Lloyd-Davies, who told them imperiously that his land was not for sale. Money was pouring into the trust fund at Ocean National Bank. Before the week was out, with validated petitions in their hands, the selectmen reluctantly announced a special vote on eminent domain.

In another editorial that week I defended the suspect morality of eminent domain. To safeguard the rights of individuals, I wrote, the laws governing eminent domain were rigid, and the process demanding. The rights of an individual to use his property were conflicting with the rights of others to maintain the attractiveness of their community and their inherited rights of access to the flats. If the land were taken from him, Lloyd-Davies would be rewarded with a substantial profit. How low do you bow to individual rights before you say those rights cease? Where do you draw the line on individual rights to sell impure food, for example, or to distribute pornography, or to drive an automobile, or to carry a gun?

Take any law you please, I wrote. Each one represents an attempt to define the limits of public and private rights. In this case, either the public's rights to riparian land would be forfeited to Lloyd-Davies without compensating the public, or Lloyd-Davies's private rights would be forfeited to the public with ample compensation to him.

I knew that my fixation and prolixity on the motel subject were getting on my readers' nerves, but two weeks before the vote I wrote three more editorials on it. The first had more to say on eminent domain. The second readdressed the economic interests: Kennebunkport held just two economic high cards. One was the water that supported the lobster; the other was the water's attraction for people who liked to live in view of it, who liked traditional surroundings and a sense of space. To jeopardize an economy that relied so heavily on charm was foolish.

The following week I learned that Lloyd-Davies was himself circulating a counterpetition, busily traveling house to house in Cape Porpoise and other outlying sections of town where most of his sympathizers lived. He had also sent a printed ad hominem letter to all Port residents, in it characterizing himself as a poor individual struggling to make a living with land he had bought. He raised the specter of rampant eminent domain. He claimed extravagantly to have $20,000 invested in the land. "I actually bought NOTHING!" he wrote. "Not even the right to build a house on it and enjoy the view myself! I must yield my property to a group of people whose 'rights' to the tidewater exceed my rights as purchaser of the land itself!" There was more in this vein, as well as references to persecution by the Star.

In a letter to the editor that week, Chairman Butts of the Board of Selectmen replied to a previous week's letter-writer who had questioned his position. He said he was sorry he had no control over what was printed in the Star. The letter punked my short fuse. An editorial called "Ifs, Ands, and Butts" said what was on my mind.

We haven't criticized Mr. Butts publicly for hiding behind the barrier to thoughtful action he has erected for himself. There's no reason to expect strong, fearless action from the Selectmen, or efficiency either, or sensitive attention to detail, or conscientious effort, or foresight, since the Selectmen don't seem to feel accountable to the public. . . .

Mr. Butts and the other Selectmen had plenty of opportunity to refuse the bulkhead request. Why did they make so many people waste so much time attending the hearings if they had no choice but to grant the permit? When we asked Mr. Butts our question, he said he didn't like the idea of a motel there himself, but what could he do? He and the others had no choice, he said.

All it took was guts, and all we got was Butts.

My second editorial that week was also an angry one. Man was blighting the globe, ruining it for all other creatures. In 30 years there would be six-and-a-half billion of us.

Thirty years from now, unless we act with vigor and intelligence, you will hardly be able to recognize coastal York County. We must take steps to save our trees, our streams, our woods, our marshes, portions of our shores. We should be restricting development in ways that would shock even many died-in-the-wool conservationists, ways so far-fetched as to be unmentionable now, before we take our first tottering infant steps with zoning and plumbing codes. . . .

The megalopolis that spreads from Washington to Boston is traveling northward at about five miles per year. It will be in New Hampshire within a decade. If you don't like suburbia, you can always move farther east.

Unless you wake up. You! Wake up! If you won't help do the job yourself, at least stop making it difficult for others to do it for you. The days when we could afford to be fat, dumb, and happy are gone. The spread of man's blight is getting out of hand.

Those *Star* readers who weren't fed up with me were beginning to wonder about my head. My single-minded pursuit of the motel subject might be hardening Lloyd-Davies's support, but I couldn't die in the stretch. I kept writing, adding new wrinkles to my argument, trying to keep the public attention focused.

Following the brief second hearing, I devoted the whole editorial page to the motel subject. Four of my five editorials reargued the practical matters. The fifth was simply a final appeal for saving the beauty of the river, the strongest influence all along, the issue that had no legal or practical weight and could be raised only at risk:

What we should like to talk about in this next-to-last week before the vote on the taking of the marsh, is the spiritual meaning of that empty piece of land. We should like to call back somehow into your imaginations the way the river was in the time of Captain Huff, how the settlement men took the bright salmon out of it in the spring to eat smoked with their round bread, how they took their buttered rum and hot lobsters on its banks in the fall, what the wooded bend looked like against the gun-colored water when a canoe slipped into view around it, how the crows plucked at the fishbones on the scud-strewn estuary beach when the first snow fell, how sweet and fat the clams were in the flats by the wild-cranberry bog, and how the land looked, land and river and sea looked, waiting for their people.

The riverbank and the seashore are so changed now that it is nearly impossible to stand on either one and see it with the eyes of the early trapper, squatting quietly by the trunk of a tree, drinking in the dangerous beauty, an ear cocked for the snap of a twig, or the bird-call that might not be a bird, feasting with eyes that swept restlessly all the while. It is almost impossible to imagine this now, or to feel the deep pride in the land, land we fought for, land we love. There are too many people on it. It is cut up too small. There is hardly any majesty left to it.

Mainers have changed since we knew them first, nearly thirty years ago. It must be the old ones we remember, the dead ones, who used to talk about the America we grew up with as though they loved it. Except for a quiet handful who keep our own faith alive, there's hardly a native Mainer left in Kennebunkport with enough pride in the land to tickle the corner of your eye. . . .

So there seems no point in talking further of pride, or majesty, or beauty. The people who could have been affected by such talk are already with us, ready to vote to take the land and pay the price — for a principle — just as our ancestors were ready to do at Bunker Hill.

I gave the subject a rest on June 10. Then, on the 17th, four days before the referendum, I merely asked the people to vote with conviction:

Do not think we exaggerate: Monday will be one of the most important days in Kennebunkport's long, lively history. It will be remembered during the remainder of 1965 with mixed emotions, no matter how the vote goes, for or against eminent domain purchase of the Lloyd-Davies strip of riverbank. We feel certain that ten years, or fifteen years, from now, after time has worn the edges smooth, there will be nearly total unanimity of attitude toward the Town's decision. If the decision is "yes," to make a park and boat landing for public access to the river, fifteen years from now you will all say the decision was right. If "no," wrong.

If you vote yes you will have the way along Ocean Avenue as it is now, with the sudden sense, after a long drive home, that you face a freshness, the end of the land. You will still have the sight, half a mile downriver, of a beach, then nothing but sea and sky. Across the river you will still see the prow of the monastery land. On the river you will see the boats, the sails, the river life, the channel buoys straining, the circling gulls, the brightness of water and air and grass.

What you will see instead, if you vote "no" to eminent domain, will be a long, two-story oblong of masonry, paint, and glass, rows of cars, vacationers in shorts and hats, dark glasses and sun-tan lotions. Take your choice.

One will permit you to retain your identity as a Maine seacoast village: the other will help you become one with all other seaside resorts and watering-places from Massachusetts to Florida, the same, but colder, with a shorter season of unpredictable weather; the same, only not so well-off, a second-rate watering-place.

This is no time to vote off-handedly. Unless you feel strongly one way or the other, your vote will be a frivolous thing that may deeply wound a great many people. Vote with conviction or not at all, we ask. Just to dislike us or the people who have supported our stand is not enough reason to vote "no." Nor should you vote "yes" if your only reason is to spite the opposition. Make your decision for Kennebunkport, and make it for her alone.

Six hundred fifty-eight votes were cast, a staggering number in Kennebunkport for a single-issue meeting, more than were normally cast on annual Town Meeting day. When they were all counted, Lloyd-Davies had won by 30 votes, 344 to 314. If 16 people who had voted for him had instead voted for eminent domain — and town officials and their families accounted for that many — we would have won. I wrote my report wrung out, with a heavy heart. After six months, innumerable stories, and about forty editorials, I had failed. I had thought of my crusade as a turning point in local understanding, one to preserve the simple beauty of my hometown and set an example for the future. Was I responsible for the failure? Perhaps. But I was also responsible for the attempt.

The Friday before the vote, the *Star*'s social correspondent in Wells, Louise Taylor, had delivered her weekly copy to me with her usual mirthful greetings and commentary. In her middle fifties, Louise was one of my favorite correspondents, a self-proclaimed "battle-ax" who paid not much attention to her appearance, tough but gentle, full of good-humored iconoclasm. She and her husband, a Navy Yard foreman, had bought a little hunting camp deep in Waldo County, where they spent weekends and vacations. Up there, Louise dabbled in real estate in her spare time. When she delivered her column that week she dropped an envelope on top of it in front of me.

"How much do you think they want for this?" she challenged.

From the envelope I withdrew a typed property description and a couple of snapshots. "In Freedom, Maine — 7-room farmhouse, large connected dairy barn, good well, on public dirt road, 100 acres, 20 in fields, remainder hardwood." Behind the barn, Louise declared, was the biggest manure pile she'd ever seen. And the barn was gigantic — the hand-hewn timbers alone were worth plenty. Two brooks converged on the property; taxes were $46 a year — you should be able to cover taxes with selective cutting rights to four or five acres a year; there were other outbuildings. Of course, the old place could use some work, and the road was really ruts, but passable. How much did I think?

I cut my guess in half, but I wasn't even close. "$1,750!" There was a bunch of property up there in the deep country for sale at ridiculous prices, but this was exceptional. "If I had the money," Louise said, "I'd buy it tomorrow."

Anneke and I drove up with the kids that weekend, just before the eminent domain vote. I went to the bank on Monday for a $1,750 personal loan. I had no idea how I'd pay it back.

So after the close vote went against us, my editorial was "A Town Called Freedom."

There were tears shed Monday night, a few of them ours. But the vote, 344 against taking the land, 314 for an open space, as always before, at the river's edge, came as a surprise only to the people who had expected an overwhelming victory for the man who won by such a narrow margin.

We must write this tonight with the news still open like a wound in the side of Kennebunkport, a self-inflicted, senseless wound. There must be sensible comment here in this column which has dealt at such length with this subject. We must try to interpret the vote.

The fact is that 344 people in town felt strongly enough to vote to permit Mr. Lloyd-Davies to build his motel. It is our conviction that if the Selectmen and Planning Board had taken a position against the motel instead of against those who pledged upwards of thirty-five thousand dollars to give the marsh to the Town, the vote would have gone the other way. The motel, if it is built, will be a monument to official conviction, just as lack of zoning remains a trophy of official conviction of 1962.

There is only one other significant comment to be made now. It is that the "auslanders," as they now call themselves, interpret the vote as a spite against themselves, and us. Let them take heart in the knowledge that while fewer than seventy of them have the privilege of the local vote, 314 people voted their way. It is fair to assume that at least forty-five percent of all permanent residents are with us on a matter that has stirred up more partisan feelings in town than all but a handful of questions since Kennebunkport ceased to be a British outpost settlement.

There is a town called "Freedom," not far from Liberty, not very far from Union, in the hilly timber and farm country in Waldo County. There is a road in Freedom about three miles long that was once, in very early times, a highway, dirt then, as now. It was grander then than the present overgrown, branch-barred way between two other country roads, and half a dozen farmhouses lived and breathed along its edges. Only one house and its barn remain; the others are known by the stones of their foundations, and the small clearings returning to brush.

That one house has been preserved, lived in by family after family, finally going to auslanders after many sales, one made through the guardian for the last heir, unsound of mind, and two through the tax-lien process. Twenty of the hundred acres that surround the farm are in fields, grown with untended hay and covered with strawberries.

The paper on the old plaster is peeling in broad patches. Porcupines have gnawed holes in the privy walls. A spring-fed brook gurgles audibly down the field behind the alder thicket, and the chipmunks and woodchucks are curious and unafraid. The male ruffed grouse waddles at the intruder threateningly, then moans and sneaks lamely off, away from the nest. Beyond the brook the land rises to a ridge. Across the road in the other direction, beyond deep former pasture land with its clumps now of evergreens, lie the deep woods. Over it all, house and barn and fields and woods, deep beyond other human habitation, drone the stillness of the country and the stirrings of fresh, scented airs.

There, after a relatively insignificant sum, as these things go, changes hands, the Brook family will go for six or seven weekends a year to retreat from the commercialism and modern growth with which humanity is wrapping itself round. There a small boy will take his wilderness lessons from the brook, and two young girls in the open fields will drink in the solitude they may never find again. There their parents, denied one by one the vistas they returned to Maine to find, will refresh themselves and become whole once more.

★ **V** ★

★ 27 ★

A Weekly Editor's Vision

The overriding job of any weekly editor is to navigate, meaning that he chooses course, speed, and altitude. Each editor brings his own visions to his job. One is astigmatic, another farsighted, another cross-eyed. For one, quality means crisp typography, reproduction, and design; for another it lies in friendly folksiness. One emphasizes community service; another courts the approval of his fellow Rotarians; another clutches the banner of the iconoclast to his bosom. Leadership for one means extolling good works, for another the chronicling of local history. The editor decides what emphasis is placed on crime, or sex, or art, or sport, or commerce, or people.

Whatever his emphasis, if he is to succeed, the editor of the community weekly of record must cover the waterfront, reporting what appeals to the thoughtless as well as the thoughtful of all ages. His advertisers demand saturation readership, or near it, in his restricted bailiwick. A sense of community is critical, so his reporters must be given incentives to stay on after they acquire one. The best young reporters will accept modest salaries if the newspaper is vital and their coworkers compatible. If the editor is solicitous of the commercial interests of his advertisers, timorously ignores his community's blemishes, gushes over mediocre accomplishment, is severe only when dealing with drunk driving or inferior road repair, or extols the excited ministrations of Little League organizers, then he won't keep the kind of writers he needs, no matter how well he pays them.

Most daily editors encourage writing to accepted journalistic formulas that were developed to please the reader looking for a quick information fix. They see the reader as a busy skimmer bird, and trap him with salacious headlines and lurid leads. With his sensory apparatus quivering, this imaginary reader runs headlong into a pyramided story that leaves him disappointed and confused. His innate literary sense is neglected, and he becomes what the editor thought he was, a reader only of headlines and leads.

Like daily editors, the weekly one decides what stories are followed and which get biggest treatment. There the similarity stops. An associate of mine once described the methods of his former editor at a large, national publication, much admired. The editor, he said, never changed copy himself, he merely scribbled "rewrite" in the margin and sent it back to the reporter. The weekly editor can't afford such luxury. His young reporters are not professionals until he makes them so. When I hired reporters, until I was comfortable with their language I discussed it at length. I rewrote sentences and told them why. At first most were dumbfounded, looking on me as a man doing time after being convicted of semantics.

I look on writing news stories as a craft of a high order. Writing a good one requires a sure grasp of the basic tools, the elements that keep the reader on track. Beyond technique, there are savvy and judgment.

The most important element of savvy is the ability to answer all questions, or else to note the absence of explanation. For this the reporter must have a clear understanding of the subject and be quick to ask the right questions. He or she should only quote to improve the reader's understanding. When the language of the people being quoted is ambiguous, the reporter should make the clarification. The reader mustn't stagger as he goes, forced to reread a paragraph or refer to an earlier sentence to understand a later one. He must never be puzzled by the absence of facts that support the explanation, or receive these facts too early or too late.

The most important element of judgment is a sense of what is important and legitimate. The good reporter learns to question the motives and accuracy of the people he interviews and to leave out or label whatever he doubts. He assumes that the reader knows nothing about an event before reading the story. The reporter reconstructs background in sequel stories and makes judgments about the state of mind of the people interviewed and the comparative weights given to the different elements of the narrative.

If the news pages of the paper are its flesh and bones, the editorial page is its spirit. Without news you have a wraith, without editorials a robot. The weekly's editorial is most often used to call attention to worthy effort. Recognizing good work will encourage more of the same, but when bouquets are cheap, impact grows dear. Espousing popular causes may endear the editor to his audience, but he won't change much that way — the popular causes will win without him. There's no point in jousting with the enemies of motherhood and apple pie, or in exhorting people to carry on as they are. The true crusade urges a course of action or thought that is worthy but unpopular.

The only people who can initiate worthy projects at will are those who hold public positions or who have the public's attention. The rest of us need a way of moving reluctant officials and complacent mentalities. The newspaper is that way. It's up to the newspaper to goad the public figure into taking worthy but unpopular action. Either the official must be prodded unmercifully before he'll join a crusade, or the newspaper must convert the public and arouse it enough to rub the official's nose in the new consensus.

One of my later Christmas editorials was a defense against the recurring charge that the *Star* saw only what was bad about the county. Why didn't we have more *good* things to say? I called it "An Eye on Men and Wooden Chips":

> Good will is called for this week — good will toward men. Our good will toward men has been legitimately questioned. Men, the bums, are in constant need of correction, and editorial writing is one of the terms in large print on the job-outline we agreed to follow when we signed our contract with public affairs and joined the Fourth Estate.
>
> If you think about it, though, when our pen is most bloody, our venom most dripping, and our eye most wild, our will is most good, most good toward men. The well-being of the people who read the *Star* sits heavily upon us. When we see men (the genera, Homunculus York Countiensis) threatened by bad government, insufficient protection, poverty, danger, indifference, laziness, spiritual paucity, flabbiness of mind and body, corruption, ugliness, sin, drought, pomposity, bumbosity, storm, dinginess, disease, hunger, worms, sadness, debility, dilapidation, fleabite, spoilure, soilure, headache or neuralgia, we go into our red alert. . . .
>
> Privately, we don't like rigidity. We don't enjoy making enemies. We do so because it is our editorial duty to do what we can to protect the public from damage, self-inflicted or otherwise.
>
> In this Christmas season we promise our readers, old and new, a rededication to good will toward men, let the chips fall where they may.

The preservation of what's good, the elimination of what's bad, and the change in what can be better — these are the editorial writer's most compelling drives. The successful weekly editor isn't a one-shot thinker like the essayist, but a practical political activist. If a specific unpopular change is his passion, he can never persuade with a single editorial. It isn't enough for him merely to offer a point of view. He must repeat it and press it in as many ways as make logic. If he keeps hammering away at his subject, refuting and routing the opposition, the public intelligence — keener than you'd think — with all the facts familiar and all argument before it, will finally have the courage to think beyond the thoughts it was conditioned to think, and will render its judgment.

Editing a weekly is lonely, often frustrating work. The editor is always bedeviled by the thought that he may be engaging in propaganda. I would have worried more if I had thought my readers were like Germans in the thirties, lock-stepped, goose-stepped, gestepped on, and steppeward bound. Most Americans like to think independently, so even if the editor hammers away, he only wins some of his battles. But if he's right, and stays with it, he wins the war without anyone really knowing he's won it. Little by little, the officials grow more careful. They listen harder and work harder, because they know they'll be asked why not if they don't. Little by little, the public becomes more interested in itself and thus more knowledgeable and more active. Little by little, the things the editor championed when they were unpopular are adopted because the arguments against them have been exhausted. The editor begins to hear his own thoughts coming back to him, and he knows he's over the hump.

I never thought of social service as my newspaper's special destiny, although we did a lot of support work for the disadvantaged. I preferred more universal goals — good government, stopping pollution, conservation, better education, better use of tax money. I used the paper to expose corruption, hypocrisy, privilege unfairly used, and authority unwisely squandered. I wasn't a champion of the "working man," whoever he is, or the "elderly" or the "poor," whoever they are, or even the handicapped, much though I might sympathize.

I was often accused of prolixity in my editorials and reports, simply because of their length. But to be long isn't necessarily to be long-winded. Often it is merely to be complete. The weekly man must exhaust his subject, because his next chance to explain is a week away. If he wants to persuade people, against their will, to a subtle point of view unfamiliar to them, he simply has to write long.

The *Star* was often, but not primarily, a gadfly. To be consistently a gadfly seemed to me not only silly, but counterproductive. I didn't want to browbeat, or call people to arms against a magnified enemy. I hated trendiness. My goal was to express myself fairly, admitting fallibility and recognizing the strong points of opposing views. In this way, when I took a position my readers felt confident of my convictions. When the editor consistently espouses the views of any particular social, political, or economic group, his readers discount much of what he writes. To publicize without labeling it publicity, or to infer stupidity or degeneracy in my opposition, was unworthy. No group, no class or gender, is always right, or even right much more than half the time.

If it is worth its salt as a semipublic property, the weekly newspaper is a harsh commander. It tolerates no idleness, there is no slack season. There can be no sloppiness, no letting down the guard. There is constant drill. The public is always looking the editor up and down to see if his shoes are shined, his collar buttoned, and his fly zipped. Each week the bugle calls CHARGE! again, and he stumbles forward.

★ 28 ★

Three Stars Come Together

Anneke was doing our classified billing and record keeping at home, making a few dollars from the occasional sale of one of her paintings, taking care of the kids and the household, even doing the home maintenance chores I was hardly ever home long enough to do. We never had more than twenty dollars to our names the day before payday. The sixties were tough times for bringing up kids, too, and the grind was taking its toll.

Working alone weekends during summer and fall, I had patched, papered, painted, and otherwise prepared all seven extra apartments in the two Star Press buildings, renting them one by one as I completed them. There was no money to pay anyone else to do it, and the Cochrane notes and expanded bank payments lowered menacingly over the operation.

In off-hours Jerry Robinson and I had shoveled dirt out of half the basement at 3 High Street, lowering the floor about 18 inches. We laid a cheap floor, raised partitions, installed electric heat, and plumbed in water. When we were done we had a photography darkroom and studio. The idea was to pry photographer George Stevens loose from the anarchy of his decaying home and induce payroll status and security on him. Having George on the premises would give us access to, and some control over, his hours and production, whose waywardness were driving me berserk. Many hours of each week were spent in unsatisfactory telephone communication with him, or in trying to track him down so that some sort of communication could begin. Sour and restive, George watched the cellar work progressing. He didn't want a schedule. When the work was finished he erupted in a geyser of imagined persecutions, and we all simply went on crazily as before, while the new darkroom gathered dust.

By the end of a summer shoveling dirt and ledge by the basketful out of cellar windows and then into and out of trucks, lugging things up and down cellar stairs, bent over like apes in the unlowered area around the furnace, an 18-year-old lumbar problem hospitalized me for removal of a degenerated disk. For two weeks in late October the cloud shadows raced across my ward window while I lay on my stomach, writing on a stool perched beside my bed, signing checks and documents brought to me, fretting unnecessarily while my friends back on High Street rolled out the print jobs and the newspaper without me.

Meanwhile, Kennebunk was bubbling with rumors of its first shopping center, destined for Route 1 outside of town. Some of my hospital time I spent developing an elaborate alternative to what I saw as a swapping of Kennebunk's traditional commercial fiber for the pulpy tissue of Everywhere Else. I proposed an ambitious urban renewal project, which fortuitous circumstances had made possible with zero town funding participation, got a groundwork Chamber of Commerce subcommittee together, and campaigned strenuously. The plan involved leading Route 1 in a divided circular pattern around downtown instead of through it, and turning the bypassed section of roadbed into a pedestrian mall. Our main themes were revival of town spirit, strengthened commerce, removal of eyesores by the river, resuscitation of the tax base, graceful river parks at the approach to town, and the rare opportunity to have it all for nothing. Everything came together beautifully — even the dubious selectmen at last joined hands. My committee was confident of the outcome of the referendum vote scheduled for January 1966. But when the ballots were counted, I was stunned — we had lost by just six votes.

There was good news too. After two years of work, our Chamber of Commerce Industrial Committee was host to a ground-breaking ceremony for the plastics molding plant that today remains Kennebunk's major employer. In Wells, a three-year feud between the *Star* and a testy, secretive, ingrown government had finally been solved with a totally new, *Star*-supported, five-man reform Board of Selectmen, a new town manager, new treasurer, and new town counsel. Instead of the tight-lipped antagonism we had learned to accept in Wells, we now had the friendly cooperation of the reform group. In Kennebunkport, after years of inveighing on the sewer issue, we overcame official obstructionism and helped force a favorable vote on the sewer, the largest Port municipal project ever undertaken. The newspaper's relations with Town Hall, ragged before, were now in tatters. But who cared? They all had to run for reelection, while the newspaper was permanent, and stronger.

The Drakes Island and Lloyd-Davies campaigns had raised the level of county appreciation for its salt marshes. Washington took note and decided to buy or take by eminent domain 2,000 acres of marshland stretching from Kittery to Biddeford to be set aside as a National Wildlife Refuge to protect the migratory flyway — eventually expanding the project to 7,500 acres — and a portion was fragmented off into the Rachel Carson National Wildlife Refuge, which bordered high ground I had already persuaded the Maine parks commissioner to buy from its development-minded owners and leave untouched. We weren't winning them all, but we were the only ones around who seemed to be winning any at all.

Ever since Harris Dulany had left in July, I had been covering Wells-Ogunquit as well as the Kennebunks. Jerry Robinson was working harder than any employer had the right to expect, doing everything alone at the *Kittery-Eliot Star*. While that *Star* was not setting, it wasn't rising either. Nor, it dawned on me slowly, as the panic flush spread to my ears, were the Kennebunk and Wells-Ogunquit *Stars*. An advertising plateau seemed to have been reached, just when expansion was most crucial. I set about comparing ad linage per issue, week by week, for all prior years. Had we simply tapped all the bungs in the business? It became apparent that while ad manager Kai Suhr was conscientiously busy, he was finding no time for the missionary work without which there is gradual erosion.

I had several times broached the subject of incorporation to Jerry Robinson, offering him shares in the business for a commitment to it, but Jerry was young and understandably reluctant. He did, however, want to end his grinding commute to Kittery and transfer his attention to matters in the northern area, where he lived and where reaction to the newspaper was most gratifying. With summer coming we needed more editorial help. Credit exhausted, bank balance inconsequential, and cash flow dwindling, I had to decide between retrenchment and boldness, and opted for boldness. First I found two graphics teachers looking for summer jobs. I then hired an unemployed car salesman to sell advertising in Kittery and to take over Kai's Wells-Ogunquit sales route. Next I found an inexperienced sports enthusiast to cover sports for all three papers. Then I persuaded our Ogunquit correspondent, Isabel Lewando, to work two days a week proofreading and editing correspondence. Twenty years later Isabel would be the *Star*'s most accomplished photographer and most sensitive writer. I have never known anyone who didn't like her, and I wouldn't want to.

Everyone was in place but Jerry's replacement in Kittery-Eliot. I advertised for a managing editor there who would be willing to invest in the future corporation. One of the respondents was the 32-year-old telegraph editor of Maine's second-largest daily, the *Bangor Daily News*. He was Ronald Devine, a Floridian by birth, Mainer by marriage. He agreed to a salary cut to $6,000, so I raised my own and Jerry's salaries to that figure too. I reasoned that Ron's promised $7,000 stock investment would pay for about a year of his salary, and if we couldn't afford that much next year, God help us.

Ron and Lenore Devine settled into Kittery, as agreed. We moved his office to pleasanter quarters and installed a table in it for the new salesman. Ron was a solid newspaperman who worked diligently, filling the *Kittery-Eliot Star* with competent prose. He was a tight, intense man of fixed principles. It developed that he and Lenore were uncommonly devoted members of a fervid, rather humorless Christian denomination. I felt censored in his presence, but we got along pleasantly enough.

With the new personnel in place or in prospect, with the shop full of printing and advertising in July, with incorporation accomplished (but no money yet from Ron Devine), I made the move that was the natural consequence of all the others. The issue of July 29 was the last for the 88-year-old *Kennebunk Star,* for its 5-year-old offspring, the *Wells-Ogunquit Star,* and for their offshoot, the 3-year-old *Kittery-Eliot Star*. While the bodies of all were committed to history that week, their souls would live on. They had not attained Nirvana, nor would their reincarnation the following week as the *York County Coast Star* be without tatters in its mortal dress. Perhaps the soul would sing louder for its tatters, as in the Yeats poem. It had all come sooner than I'd planned — my horoscope had simply turned green, and my *Stars* came together.

The three separate *Stars* had been doomed from the start by the implacable economics of growth and modernity. Next week our readers saw us in our modernity dress, pregnant with possibilities. Either one grows or one shrivels — that is Uncle Sam's Law of Business Evolution. It had become increasingly obvious that to continue to publish three newspapers in one shop for such interdependent communities as ours was wasteful in the business sense and dangerous in the competitive one. What was more, we were running out of challenges, and for a business that relied so heavily on creative enthusiasms, that was insupportable. On August 5 I introduced the new newspaper:

> Eight years ago last March when we came back to Maine for good, having just bought the printing and publishing business called Star Print from the sons of its founder — when the first round of our bout with newspaper work was barely joined — we were already dreaming of the *York County Coast Star*.
>
> Much of our business energy has been spent expanding toward that goal. Ours remained an uneconomical and disjointed operation. The part of the coast between the Piscataqua River and Biddeford Pool could support a weekly large enough to be good, influential and strong.
>
> What you have in your hands is the raw fibre that will need carding, drawing, spinning, weaving, dying, cutting, basting, sewing, trimming, and pressing before it is called a finished cloak, the mantle we want to wear.
>
> We are not apologizing — this is already a fine weekly newspaper, one of the best in America. But we take our newspaper work seriously; being one of the best is not nearly good enough.

In another editorial I introduced the staff to the people who didn't know us yet, the people of the Yorks, where the little *York Weekly* carried on its uneventful life. I had sent out some feelers to its publishers, the Hollingworth brothers, thinking they might be inclined to sell their newspaper and concentrate on the job printing that occupied most of their time, but they hadn't acknowledged my letters. The Yorks represented an unacceptable territorial gap between Kittery and Ogunquit; it was unthinkable to combine the *Stars* without also covering York and its two village corporations, York Beach and York Harbor. So in a third editorial I wrote an explanation of ourselves for the York people that stopped just short of being a challenge, accurately foretasting the years of frustration with official York that lay ahead.

> We are all determined to give you something better than you are used to, whether you are a long-time *Kennebunk Star* reader, a subscriber in Wells-Ogunquit, or in Kittery-Eliot, or you live in the Yorks. It is our conviction that the town without a strong newspaper voice is a town in danger of being doomed to eventual cheapness. You'll find us ready and willing.
>
> Whether we're able or not is, in large measure, in your hands. A newspaper can only be good if it has a good audience. If the newspaper is wringing its brain out every week, warning, extolling,

urging, and cajoling, but its words are directed at a tar-baby, it will never be any good. If it has control of itself, it shrugs and stops trying to get a reaction before it grows rash enough ter hit de tar-baby.

By and large, the people we have interviewed in the Yorks have this idea that a weekly newspaper is a sort of door-slot where they stuff their releases when they want publicity. Or it's something they pat on the head and tell to run along, now, like a good boy, when it asks questions whose answers are unfit for tender public ears.

One story this week led us to interviews with eight people. All but the two who had already had experience with our reporting styles asked us to keep what they had to say off the record, or not to quote them, or just preferred not to divulge anything they knew at all. These six people were intelligent and likable, but they shared this odd conception of newspaper work: that a person who is making a living gathering facts for publication should be told things and then be asked to keep them to himself.

We always try to accommodate people so long as accommodation doesn't mean withholding important news from other people who deserve to know it. This we liken to being accomplices to a deception. . . .

Precious few of our readers in any of our towns would be pleased with the merged *Star*. They had all lost "newspapers of their own." They resented the news of other areas that made them feel their own news was no longer paramount. They grumbled and groused, but circulation never missed a stride. Ever so gradually, as they tested the waters of news stories in other towns and were acclimated to the more varied selection and the larger serial stories, the grumbling subsided. It never quite ceased; the subsiding was more like halving a sum to infinity. Even today I meet people who tell me, "I used to like it better when it was just the *Kennebunk Star*." I don't understand why they feel that way, but I think nostalgia is part of it — memories of earlier days in more exciting youthful times when news of their friends and themselves had a freshness. They were getting more of everything for the same 10 cents, and more newsprint to start their wood stoves with or wrap their fish in, no extra charge.

At first the only ones who preferred the new paper were the advertisers, who were reaching a larger audience at the same old rates. "I suppose this is going to cost me more," they'd say, implying that if so they might curtail their advertising. We assured them that for now the rates would remain unchanged, and for almost a year they did.

The *York County Coast Star* began life with 22 eight-column broadsheet pages. Combined summer circulation grew to nearly 6,500, and for five weeks, when we sampled the Yorks with a thousand free copies, I was able to boast that the *Star* had a larger circulation than "Maine's Greatest Weekly," the *Sanford Tribune,* or any other weekly in Maine.

Instead of four short pressruns each week, we now had three much longer runs of more pages each. Newsprint costs more than doubled. Payroll was higher. The change simply had to produce more advertising, eventually at higher rates. Almost no advertising would come from the Yorks for years. For many months, even years, the new operation looked like a losing proposition riding on the back of a losing operation, a breakthrough only in egocentric terms.

Nonetheless, I was confident I had chosen the right course. To our future advertisers we looked more substantial, half again as bulky and many times newsier than the *Biddeford-Saco Journal.* With a reasonable circulation in the Yorks to add to Ogunquit, Kittery, and Eliot, some day we'd be able to crack the tempting Portsmouth advertising market and go head to head with the *Portsmouth Herald.* Eventually the tide did turn and start running in our direction (upstream), until it became obvious that the new paper really did constitute a financial breakthrough as well: a good gamble, the only way out — and up.

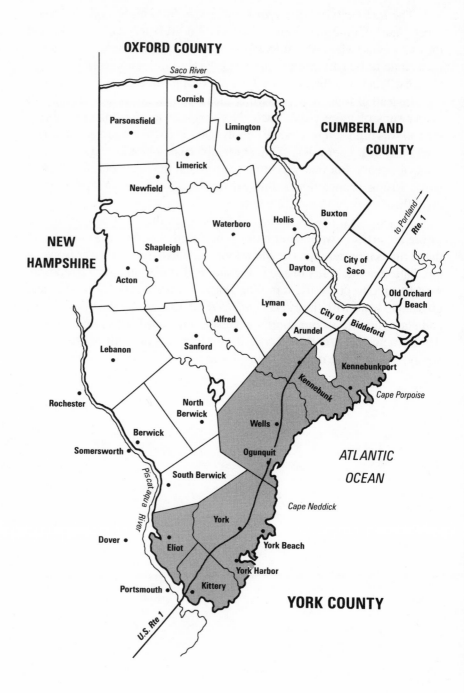

★ 29 ★

"They Did It!"

For us, entering the Yorks wasn't like paddling up the Amazon. York citizens worked in our other communities, acknowledged common ancestors, and claimed common friends. When the York Water District decided to build a 90-foot water storage tower in Cape Neddick, between Ogunquit and York Beach, the unsatisfactory summer water pressure it was designed to improve also affected some of our Wells-Ogunquit readers. Maurice Weare, owner of the four-story Cliff House Hotel at the end of the water main, was among our biggest printing and advertising customers, and his hotel would be the chief beneficiary of the new tower. In August, when Cape Neddick shore cottages were full, and tourism in heat, the drain on the main was plain. Sometimes the shower heads on the Cliff House top floor could only trickle.

The Water District engineer's first-choice tower site had been at the Shore Road entrance to the Cliff House's long driveway. When Maurice Weare objected, his brother, Water District Trustee Charles Weare, helpfully persuaded his fellow trustees to pay Maurice $2,000 for the 100-foot-square, scrub-covered alternative plot Maurice offered them.

This new tower site was well removed from the hotel entrance — even remote. A stone wall, the narrow, winding Shore Road, and a small stone Episcopal church were the only man-made things in view. The church, on its bucolic rise — blunt fieldstone tower against the sky, ocean in middle distance — imbued the spare northern landscape with a rare chthonian ambience. One fancied in the airy, rather Irish-looking stony fields and wind-shaped copse, a temple shared by God and Pan. Much-photographed St. Peter's was used only in July and August, but was popular for its inspiring aesthetics. Young people chose it for weddings, others for last rites. On summer Sundays the genteel faithful flocked there from miles about.

After Labor Day 1966, when summer residents and tourists were gone, and Bishop Ernest Harding had closed the church doors, silenced its bell for the ten-month winter, and returned to his Philadelphia church, steel sections of the water tower's storage bulb and tripod legs were ordered, and work on their concrete foundation was begun. No one but Maurice and Charles Weare, James Lucas, another trustee, and his brother Roger, the Water District Superintendent, knew that the tiny plot Maurice had sold the district was directly behind the church, where the tower's bulbous business end would loom to twice the height of the bell tower. One of its three stilts would be planted in concrete only 23 feet from the church's rear wall.

My first inkling of these plans came over the phone in early November from elderly Mrs. Carl Perkins of Ogunquit. She and her husband, a trustee of St. Peter's, would like to drive up to see me. They hoped I might be able to give them some advice — they were grasping at straws.

The Perkinses arrived, agitated and apologetic, and soon I knew their story. Shortly before leaving for Philadelphia, Bishop Harding had walked over to the church from his rectory. There he found workmen clearing brush on the neighboring Weare property. The men told him they were preparing ground for a water tower, but didn't volunteer dimensions. Assuming that his trustees knew about it, Harding envisioned something much smaller. "Bad plan," he thought to himself, but none of his business.

When the foundation had been completed, a wandering church member came across it and told the trustees. Their immediate response was to request an audience with the Water District trustees. Church Trustee Homer Waterhouse of Kennebunk, senior partner of a Biddeford law firm, spoke for the church.

The three Water District trustees who hadn't seen the plans were "quite upset," Carl Perkins told me, but saw no way of reversing them. District Superintendent James Lucas and Trustees Roger Lucas and Charles Weare defended them — only available lot, right elevation, no complaints received from notified abutters. They expressed surprise and regret at the church people's reaction, but the steel was ready to ship and the foundation was complete. The cost of breaking the $48,000 contract for steel and erection would be "prohibitive."

The Water District's lawyer, Lester Bragdon, suggested that the church people might seek an injunction which, if granted, would require the church to post bond sufficient to cover damages to the district. His bylaws, he said, prohibited unproductive use of district money. Superintendent Lucas estimated damages at between $10,000 and $15,000, either of which Waterhouse considered unmanageable for the church. He suggested splitting the cost with the district, and the meeting adjourned with some outward sympathy for that idea. Lucas would put together more exact figures for a second meeting.

After the meeting, attorney Bragdon privately advised his Water trustees that the Public Utilities Commission wouldn't countenance spending customer money to share costs with the church. When church lawyer Waterhouse called to argue, Bragdon refused to budge without an injunction. The church trustees met again and reluctantly agreed to foot the whole bill themselves, up to $15,000, then requested another meeting with the district. At this meeting they learned to their dismay that work on the tower had proceeded apace, and now relocation costs would be more than $25,000. At this Waterhouse advised his fellow church trustees that their cause was hopeless — the tower would rise.

Here they were, the distraught Perkinses told me, on their own — the other trustees had given up. "That tower will leave our little church looking like a dwarf!" was Mrs. Perkins's understatement. I could picture the green bubble on its tubular legs, against the sky, crouching over the little church and its bell tower.

OK, I told the Perkinses, I was sure I could bring the public up boiling. There were always chinks in the armor, unexpected facts and interpretations to be uncovered by public scrutiny. I'd get right to work, but they had work to do too. First, get another lawyer — Waterhouse hadn't had the heart for the pillow fight so far, and things were going to get heavy. Again I suggested Dave Strater. Next, I said, get a volunteer committee together — not just Episcopalians, and not just churchgoers. Get the artists going, and the summer residents. But get people who'll catch the spirit, who won't mind knocking on doors and raising money. There'd be legal expenses, and maybe a share of tower-removal costs. The church might not be able to afford $25,000, but the collective residents of the Yorks and Ogunquit certainly could.

My job would be to make sure everyone took sides, and I'd do the public name-calling. The volunteers should be reasonable, low key. Let the Water District crowd use up its poison against the newspaper and the lawyer. We didn't want to back them into a hard place. Hell, we'd get the tower off the church's back if we had to raise the whole tower budget. I didn't bluster quite this way to the Perkinses, but they went home in revived spirits to get their end of the campaign train "a-moverin'." I'd get some fire under the boiler.

My first story covered five columns, Page One, with a photo showing the tripod legs rising behind the Church. I buttressed the story with three church-committee-solicited letters denouncing the district trustees, and an editorial call to colors titled, "A Tower of Weakness." All communication with the district, I wrote, should be considered hostile. They appeared to be trying to thwart the church people by hastening construction beyond the church's ability to post bond.

Each week we showed construction progress from the same angle, adding new developments. I conferred regularly with Dave Strater. The volunteer committee was organized and energized. Summer residents were kept informed with *Star* clippings, and their letters were swelling the stream we were publishing. In Augusta, the capital, the Public Utilities Commission was getting letters too, and watching carefully. By November 16 two petitions were circulating. In my editorial that week I wrote:

> A setting of tranquil beauty gives meaning to religious experience denied by a setting of squalor. Obviously, the church would never have been built where it is if the water tower had been there first. To call the setting squalid because a tower of symmetrical, functional design sits nearby is overstating, you may say. If you see a water tower next to an oil refinery you don't say the tower creates a squalor for the refinery. But to place a water tower twenty-three feet behind a rural church where before there was only open land and sky, is to debase the church and to deny many people their accustomed quality of reflection.
>
> It is our hunch that the Water District Trustees would rather be remembered as having made a regrettable, but corrected, mistake, than to be remembered as the creators of a monster. If so, they will willingly halt construction, undo what has been done, and find another site. Before people start playing rough and matters of integrity are brought up, as they are bound to be if bitterness continues, why not bring the Utilities Commissioners together with the District and the Church, and see what can be worked out to correct what all must now recognize as a blasphemy?
>
> If all will cooperate, a way may be found to permit the voters to decide the outcome. We have enough respect for the people of the Yorks to feel confident that they will decide the case, not on the basis of money or convenience, but morality. We can not accept the inevitability of the tower. What men can do, men can undo. What they can spend for the sake of efficiency, they can match for the sake of the spirit.

Next week half the bulb was completed on its stilts, and the full future horror could be imagined from our photos. The district trustees hadn't halted construction, but they were making conciliatory noises. Lawyer Strater thought the PUC might agree not to penalize the district for unwise spending if it used some of its hefty "improvement fund" to relocate the tower, but the commissioners could arbitrate only if invited by the district. The Water District trustees weren't ready for arbitration — they were still insisting that the church would have to foot the whole bill if the tower were moved, and were now estimating the cost at $58,000. Workmen were still busy as we went to press on November 22.

The Water District trustees agreed to talk. A December 7 meeting was arranged between PUC, church, and district. The district trustees accepted a PUC offer to mediate, but otherwise the meeting served mainly to define the lines of battle.

Although the Water District's service lines had often been extended during its lifetime, each year only water users within the original district boundaries elected or reelected one of its five trustees, who usually ran unopposed. No more than a handful of interested people ever bothered to vote. Aside from the Public Utilities Commission, which monitored district financial reports and moderated rate increases, only their own self-amendable bylaws influenced the clubby trustees.

The dialogue with the PUC suggested new strategies to Strater. He arranged an informal "press conference" of three people. I would be the press, interviewing him and accountant Michael Calo, who had studied the district's finances at Strater's request. Strater compiled a list of "suggested" questions for me to ask them.

The questions and answers made a long article on the district's history and modus operandi. Strater and Calo were quoted on the generous proportions of the district's over-sized "improvement fund," which could easily move the tower several times without reducing it to below the regulated minimum. Strater stressed the district's past unwillingness to expand its voting franchise to include new users, in effect creating two classes of customers, and its lobbying against legislation that threatened the status quo. Then the church's supporters started circulating another petition to expand the voting area to include all customers.

Late the following Tuesday, after our advertising deadline had passed, District Superintendent Lucas delivered a large ad to ad manager Kai Suhr. In it the trustees defended themselves against some of the allegations in the prior week's interview. I wasn't happy about receiving their defense in this form, since our news and letters columns were open to all sides equally. I called Lucas with apologies about our deadline. He accepted my offer to turn the ad into a news story at no charge, with the same page position and headline size as the Strater-Calo interview story.

The district's riposte was quite lame. It asserted that "malice" had not been a factor in their choice of tower site, a charge never made. It said the district had tried to cooperate with the church, and blamed the *Star* for being critical of a deed intended to be helpful to others, two patent bits of sophistry followed by another: "After reading the article in the *Star,* one wonders if moving the elevated tank is the primary issue, or is it being used as an excuse by some individuals to harass the Water District?" The district trustees apparently still didn't understand what the fuss was about.

By early January two bills were in the hopper of the State Legislature, placed there by York's representative, a friend of Strater's and Attorney General James Erwin's. As a private York resident, Erwin had called the decision to place the tower behind the church "disgraceful" and doubted the district trustees' pleadings of ignorance (Charles Weare had said that the day he had inspected the site had been so foggy that he hadn't noticed how close it was to the church). One of the legislative bills called for expanding the district to include all users, the other called for relocation of the tower. Hearings on both were delayed till February 7.

To my immense satisfaction, one provision of the bill, as recommended by the PUC, was that the large improvement fund should permit relocation with no effect on water user rates. If we finally succeeded in having the subject put to referendum, the voting would be less influenced by venality. It would still be the voters' money that moved the tower, but it would be money already raised from them, not new money.

On March 8 the governor signed both bills passed by the Legislature, including the provision for an April 1 referendum. Now we had a flock of new voters who had been jilted by the district in the past. I called my editorial "Filet of York Soul."

> On April 1st, voting members of the Water District will slice open their souls and bare the insides to public view. The public is interested in their collective firmness, color, and smell. If the tower is moved there will not be, for all the foreseeable future, this gigantic spider-crablike science-fiction creature crouching over the church, a monument to folly that would otherwise have remained to haunt the District Trustees and their descendants. If they try to influence the voters to leave the tower where she squats, we have misjudged them by giving credit to a bankrupt sensibility.

Part of my March 22 editorial went:

> In York this year April 1st will be no joking matter. That day the voters of the District will either vote to correct an error, or vote not to correct it. If they vote not to correct it, they will be ignoring the humble, heart-sprung request of the people who worship at the little stone church, and all others who love it and the countryside around it.

We have no conviction that the people of York will vote the way we would. Nor, sad to say, has anyone connected with the church. They have hope, but no conviction, and while our wishfulness makes our own thinking positive, our experience tempers it with cynicism.

We assume that all who love beauty will vote the same way as all will who love the church. Together they may not be enough to win, so we must now speak to the people who are guided in all matters principally by attention to the health and welfare of their purses.

I reminded my readers that no rise in rates would be permitted for relocation expenses. Anyway, I suspected the district of grossly exaggerating the expense of moving the tower all along. If they swapped the land for another plot and saved the steel, the expense should be about half what they were saying, a small enough price to pay for preserving a major scenic attraction.

I was worried that the vote might be small. The district trustees and their sympathizers, all out of sight in the long grass, would turn out in force in the privacy of the voting booths to punish the newspaper and the effete group of Ogunquit and Cape Neddick people. If too many church people left the voting to their friends, we could get shellacked. In the usual district elections only a couple dozen voters showed up. In our final issue before the voting, my editorial was "York's Answer."

London has its Tower of London, Paris its Eiffel Tower, New York its Statue of Liberty, York its Water Tower. There must be a name for York's tower, if it remains where it is, because it will become a town symbol, the most memorable of its man-made objects. How about "Weare Tower"? Maybe "Yorking-By-the-Church," or "Lucas What York Built," or "Fifteenth Station of the Cross"?

Maybe St. Peter's will become known as the "Little Miss Muffet Church," the one that was frightened away by a spider that sat down beside her. Certainly, if the tower stays, the church should go, since it would then be useless as a house of God. It could be no more blatantly disgraced if someone came along with an elephant gun and shot a hole near the base of the tower's water storage bulb on the side overhanging the church.

I continued with a long last dissertation on the economics, then a heated rebuke to the Water District trustees, and a few last paragraphs:

The Water Trustees are apparently unmoved by natural surroundings, and must have poor opinions of people who are. If for no other reason, you should vote to move the tower to serve notice on all

Town, State, and Federal agencies that you don't thumb your noses at the people of York. If you know what's good for you, you listen carefully. You're dealing with people whose forebears carved a colony out of the wilderness. . . .

Are the people of York true to their traditions, heirs of the men and women who left the Bay Colony for freedom to worship at peace and as they pleased? Does the tower represent spiritual oppression? "Tower, tower, by my wall, am I the fairest one of all?" So sings a little church on a knoll by the sea. On April 1st the voters of the York Water District will give their answer for all the world to hear.

Heavy, Lopsided Vote, 577–173;
York Water Tower Will Be Moved

It was far and away the largest vote in district history, most certainly larger than all previous votes combined. My editorial — "They Did It!" — expressed my relief:

When we heard the results of the voting in York Saturday our reaction was not to hoot with hilarity or knock the top off a champagne bottle; it was one of sober thankfulness. It was also one of surprise. We had fortified our mind against disappointment, knowing how seldom random collections of individuals, such as townspeople, will put aesthetics before money, or even the certainty of beauty above hope for financial advantage. But we had a little idea in our head that York might be different, and we are in a mood to hug the people of York today, women and children first, please, in that order. . . .

We are encouraged by the enormity of the majority to say to the District Trustees: You have heard the people. You know how they feel, these people who created you Trustees. You know what they want. Do as you deem prudent.

They took it down. But despite an offer by an old friend of mine named George Weare (no relation that he acknowledged) of another piece of nearby high land as a gift, the district never did re-erect the tower. The Cliff House Hotel itself would come down, however, to make room for one-floor motel units that presumably got by with the old water pressure. Life and commerce and Cape Neddick plod onward, towerless, toward the twenty-first century.

★ 30 ★

Raising the Competitive Stakes

Jerry Robinson relieved me in Kennebunkport, adding that town to his Wells-Ogunquit coverage, while I added the Yorks to my Kennebunk beat. The *York Weekly* offered nothing much but releases and social news, not reporting, but for the York people it was the hometown weekly, their "own" paper. Our efforts to improve circulation did have measurable, but not gratifying, success. Those who bought the *Star* bought it as well as, not instead of, the *Weekly*.

Now with nine towns to cover, we kept all three section front pages free of advertising so that each town's major stories could be prominent. Without more advertising I couldn't afford another reporter, and the dilution of our reporting energy was short-changing everyone. Kai Suhr and his assistant, Gene Zaremski, were at capacity, so I asked Peter Agrafiotis, who had been giving us two days a week, to give us two more, spending them on special sales projects.

Peter talked a Portsmouth city bank into an ad — not large, but several times larger than those of our regular local banks, none of which had been willing to rock the budget boat on the upside — and the whole level of bank thought about *Star* advertising advanced one notch.

Our only food advertiser, Red & White, had been giving us half a page a week. There were now two IGA markets in our territory, and when another neared its opening date in Kennebunk, they shared a full-page ad, so Red & White followed suit. A small A & P had also opened in Kennebunk. There was a small A & P in Wells and a full-size one in York. When their managers saw IGA and Red & White with full pages, their resistance collapsed and headquarters began sending us weekly full-page mats. Observing the tactics of the big boys, a Biddeford discount market came in with a quarter page. In two months we went from half a page of food advertising to three and a quarter pages.

With our new Scan-a-Graver we offered free engravings to advertisers. Illustration doubled the size of our realtors' ads, and success increased both numbers and frequency. We talked the local auto dealers into an every-other-week "Automotive Armchair Marketplace," and started a successful restaurant page.

I was elated with the breakthroughs. Before looking for another reporter, however, I had other personnel matters to troubleshoot. Newspaper Production Foreman Bill Dawson left to start a small printing shop of his own. Bezo moved into Bill's shoes, and I hired the first of several semiexperienced printers who came and went at four-month intervals. In July Jerry and Jane Robinson divorced, and Jerry left abruptly for a job with a New Hampshire daily. Shortly afterward, typesetter George Pulkkinen and his wife Fay also were divorced, and Fay, who had been Bunny Sampson's front-office assistant, left town. That same year Peg and Art Hendrick, too, divorced. I pass quickly over these events. I was profoundly shaken by what had happened to six friends, all fellow sufferers of long standing.

One of the applicants for Jerry's reporting beat was a spirited, petite, recent journalism graduate named Kathy Mincher, whom I hired on the spot and was able to introduce to a friendly official atmosphere in Wells. In early August, Gene Zaremski went back to selling automobiles. Two weeks later a former colleague of Kai's at Biddeford's WIDE, Frank DiFrancesco, was a welcome professional replacement. I was particularly relieved to have Frank because Gene's resignation timing had upset me. That very week I had been offered what had until a few weeks before been two weekly newspapers. For $3,000, the good will — meaning mostly an obligation to fulfill subscription commitments — of the merged *South Berwick Chronicle* and *North Berwick Enterprise* could be mine.

North Berwick was a rural but industrial village of 1,800 children and adults nestled inland, proudly insular, on the Boston & Maine Railroad. South Berwick was larger, population about 3,200. South Berwick shared a representative to the Maine Legislature and a school system with Eliot and was a natural reporting addition for us, while North Berwick shared a representative and a superintendent of schools, but not the school system itself, with Wells-Ogunquit.

The *South Berwick Chronicle* was first published in 1920. Five years later Virgil Horr bought the small weekly and printery, carrying on without appreciably expanding circulation. For a year or two the *Chronicle* claimed the distinction of being the last paper in America still set by hand from foundry type, letter by letter. By 1966 Virgil Horr had been dead for six years. I had never met him or his son, Cecil, who had worked all his adult life in the *Chronicle* shop. After his father died, Cecil and his wife Minnie published the newspaper from their home, printing it and the job work in an outbuilding. They labored long hours without other employees. Their *Chronicle* acknowledged North Berwick by including a correspondence column of neighborly trivia written as an unpaid hobby by housewife Hazel Shibles. Though North Berwick had never in its history been reported more seriously than this, its people had a choice of two newspapers. The *Sanford Tribune* also carried a North Berwick correspondence column and was sold in Cressey's Store, only newsstand in town. North Berwickians mostly shopped in neighboring Sanford, and the *Tribune* sold sixty or seventy copies a week in Cressey's, half again as many as the Horrs' *Chronicle*.

Cecil and Minnie Horr's response to being Number 2 in North Berwick had been to encourage Hazel Shibles to write more correspondence and to have Minnie jot down what she learned of local gossip during her advertising sales visits, then to split their paper in two, calling the part with North Berwick news in it the *Enterprise*. They set both news and ad copy on a glorified typewriter, printed on a small offset duplicator, and stapled the unfolded legal-size sheets in an upper corner. The people of North Berwick responded positively to these innovations, but not in a manner that may be called uncontrolled celebration. They had "their own newspaper" at last, an identity on a masthead.

Circulation, however, remained inadequate — the combined total for the two papers was less than 1,000. Worst of all, the advertising incentive the Horrs thought they were providing to North Berwick merchants with "their own" newspaper was virtually ignored. There were so few businesses — one of every essential one but gas stations — that no change in local shopping habits could be foreseen through advertising. The only things that increased measurably were the Horrs' operational headaches and production expenses, so after a while they gave up the *Enterprise* and reverted to one newspaper in the same format, calling it the *Enterprise-Chronicle*. Both towns had lost "their own" newspapers. The unforgiving readers delivered their vocal coup de grace, without the grace.

Discouraged, Cecil and Minnie came to the painful decision to cut their losses and retreat to their garage, where they could carry on the modest job printery alone and at peace. They had observed the *Star* expanding. They knew the *Sanford Tribune* of old. To the southwest, covering Berwick itself and larger Somersworth, New Hampshire, across the river, was that other Alta Group newspaper, the *Somersworth Free Press*.

The Horrs' asking price was beyond neither the resources nor the mounting courage of the Ocean National Bank, which once more remade and extended my notes by $3,000. But if they or I had known what

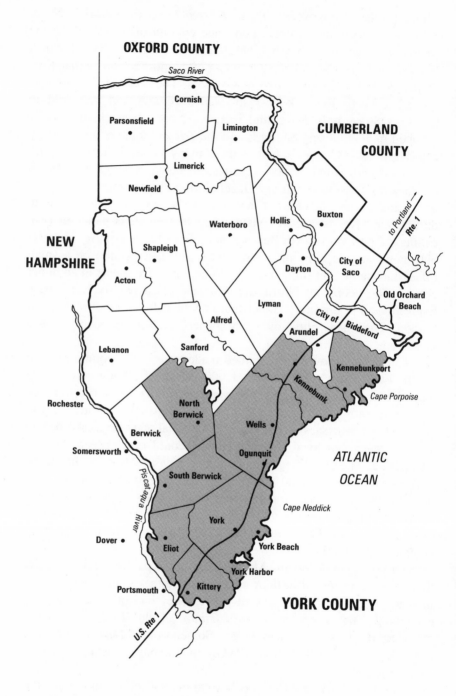

OXFORD COUNTY

Saco River

Cornish

Parsonsfield

Limington

CUMBERLAND

COUNTY

Limerick

Newfield

NEW

HAMPSHIRE

Waterboro

Hollis

Buxton

to Portland —
Rte. 1

Shapleigh

Acton

Dayton

City of
Saco

Old Orchard
Beach

Lyman

Alfred

City of

Arundel

Biddeford

Lebanon

Sanford

Kennebunk

Kennebunkport

Cape Porpoise

Rochester

North
Berwick

Wells

Berwick

ATLANTIC

Somersworth

Ogunquit

OCEAN

Piscataqua River

South Berwick

Cape Neddick

York

Dover

Eliot

York Beach

York Harbor

Portsmouth

Kittery

YORK COUNTY

U.S. Rte 1

would follow, neither of us would have looked on the investment with nearly the same enthusiasm. Whether or not the Horrs had approached the Alta Group, too, with their offer I don't know, and never asked. I assume that by the time I had accepted the Horrs' offer the Alta people had already concocted the plan they carried out immediately afterward, changing their Somersworth paper's name to *Somersworth-Berwicks Free Press* and making it free indeed by mailing it to every household not only in Somersworth and Berwick, but in North and South Berwick as well.

This jolting competitive maneuver was obviously designed to take advantage of the temporary geographic vacuum by flooding it with a familiar, established neighboring newspaper, and without financial outlay, at the same time rendering my investment shaky. Certainly I was now walking into a mine field rather than into one that was stony but at least redeemable. In a September 7 editorial I wrote sympathetically of the Horr plight, in the same breath doing my best to cut off at the pass the subscription cancellations and other manifestations of pique I had learned to expect.

If I could win the battle for the attention of those two rural towns, I reasoned, our southern circulation might be large enough to interest advertisers in Portsmouth, Dover, and Sanford, the point of the wedge I had been sharpening. Once again, expansion had been forced on me before I was in any sense ready for it, but fate was calling the game, and if I wanted to gamble I had to play with the hand I was dealt.

★ 31 ★

Church and Press

A minister I knew as a common, boosterish man with an energetic "get right with God" flock, called me one day for an appointment. The friendlies merely dropped by, so I was prepared for a complaint. He and other ministers, he told me pointedly, were having trouble getting publicity for church affairs. Other weeklies he'd known published his releases unaltered and in time to improve attendance. The *Star* condensed these releases, or even ignored them altogether. Occasionally an affair was mentioned only after the fact — this didn't help attendance. It seemed to him that the *Star* editor preferred the seamy and sensational to the positive, moral news generated by the churches. What was the policy of my newspaper, if I called it a newspaper?

Well, I told him, I was still learning the answer to that question myself. I could only say that policy with respect to church affairs was flexible. When a release had general news value, we used it as a starter for a story we wrote ourselves. If it had more than routine, but not general, interest, it was synopsized for our "Capsulary Comment" sections. Routine items of interest to only one congregation we usually added to the appropriate correspondence column.

For a long moment my visitor stared at me. Would I consider setting aside a spiritual page for church releases? — he was making this request for other ministers beside himself. No, I told him, I preferred not to be bound to anything like that. We never seemed to have enough room for all the stories of more general interest. I'd continue to do my best according to my editorial judgment, but I doubted that my best was going to satisfy him. He didn't challenge me there.

With a few gratifying exceptions, relations between the *Star* area ministers and the editor were formal, if not chilly. The churchmen were accustomed to accommodation. Courteous denial, as I characterized my response on this occasion, confused them. I pictured my visitor before he came, assuring his deacons that he'd take care of this little matter with the editor himself.

Editors and ministers are, in a way, rivals, with parallel though dissimilar missions. In our quiet little Maine towns the ministers each week commanded the attention of a handful of elderly people for a few sabbath hours. There were 40 of them with 40 different messages, and only one of me speaking to an audience several times as large as all theirs together.

My mail was fat with releases, local and national. And the churchmen weren't alone in their frustrations. For most weekly publishers, releases save the price of reporters and earn the gratitude of their senders. The undiscriminating reader, accustomed to soap opera and public relations, is satisfied with releases. While the impersonal agencies that dispatched their national releases everywhere didn't know we ignored them, the local clubs and businesses bristled readily.

I eventually soothed the churchpeople somewhat by starting a page of church notices, allowing each minister about two column inches of small type each week for calendar schedules, with space at the bottom of the page for sponsors. I asked each minister to find one businessman in his congregation who might donate two dollars a week as sponsor, not profit-making for us, but loss-reducing. I can't remember that a single minister did more than send us suggested names, leaving us to try, not very successfully, to sell the idea ourselves.

To solve the other release problem I announced a "Coming Events" page, where readers from all towns could peruse the offerings handily and plan their weekly entertainment. Before then, theatrical bean-ophiles in Wells had been ignorant of the Kennebunk bean supper on the same night as the Ogunquit amateur school play, when they might have wanted to make a night of it. I announced the "Coming Events" innovation in a box on Page One, and explained its glories in an editorial I called "Pins into Plowshares."

This newspaper's sincere attempts to provide free advertising for church and club affairs have probably earned it, in the aggregate, more ill-will and public indignation than anything else it has done. Almost every church or club member has found himself at one time or another mentally sticking pins in a clay image of the editor because a notice of an impending rummage sale has been left out of the paper. Ouch! we say every Thursday as our attention is called to the plain fact that the Red Cross drive wasn't mentioned, or the Bingo party for hospitalized Mrs. X inexcusably has failed to find its way into the chases that hold the newspaper type. Ouch!

"We'll gladly pay for it if you'll just be sure it gets in," so many people have offered. No, we tell them, the item is in our hands in plenty of time. Save the four or six dollars it would cost for a display ad prominent enough to be noticed, we say, smiling magnanimously. And then the darned thing doesn't get in at all. Ouch!

But we have described on Page One what we hope turns out to be our collective salvation. May you all enjoy the new section. May the cake-fanciers of South Berwick learn easily of the cake-sale in York Beach, and swarm there to fill the coffers of the York Beach volunteer fire company. May good will return to York County, and songs of praise rise in the throats of her people! May all our little ouches of the past heal, and the lion lie down with the lamb, and the pipe of peace be lit! . . . May pins be beaten into plowshares, and the mortal clay image of the editor have the mustache removed and be placed in a conspicuous place on the mantlepiece, surrounded by freshly-cut flowers.

Unlike the advertising consolidations mentioned earlier, the church and "Coming Events" pages did nothing to help solve our money problems. They were, however, useful and appreciated services, refined and made handier for our readers and less stressful for us, all stepping-stones to organization.

By 1967, sales volume for Star Press had grown to nine times its 1958 size, and inflation was hardly a factor then. The company had grown despite its crippling debt, its precarious ratios, and its worn-out, inadequate machinery. Long shopping lists under only two headings — Desperately Needed, and Must Buy — were constantly with me, burnished into the back of my mind. Our building mortgage was fresh and new, but stable, while the bank continued to remake the equipment notes in ever-larger denominations.

Early that year I made my largest machinery purchase to date, a new, heavy-duty, offset job press with process color capability. I also bought a tape perforator with electronic keyboard and the device that used the tape to depress the keys on our new, fourthhand Intertype. Ellen Stevens, who had done some typing and allowed as how she might be able to learn to perforate the body copy, joined us. She became eerily accurate and lightning-fast, but she was much more than that — a worker of heroic capacity and rare good spirits. George Pulkkinen monitored the new Intertype while he set heads and ads on the old one beside it. That year George and Assistant Editor Kathy Mincher made us all happy by getting married. There were 23 on the payroll now, as well as others like the correspondents, columnists, piecework women, newspaper-night high-schoolers, and photographer George Stevens, so that Star Press faces kept cropping up hearteningly all over town.

On a Wednesday night while George Stevens was delivering papers to our newsstands, his old Buick had a jarring collision with another car. It at first appeared that no one had been injured, but within a week George, temporarily auto-dependent, strangely listless, announced that he was through delivering papers. We all took turns driving him to photo engagements until Star Press bought him another heap, but he grew increasingly morose and defensive, dropping from public view by moving into the family homestead with his sister Madeleine and brother Carlos.

One morning Madeleine called me with alarming news: after spending several days sneaking around the darkened house hallucinating about fancied tormentors, George had withdrawn into a morbid state of catatonia, recognizing no one, sitting motionless and mute in a corner of the parlor with blinds drawn. I found his condition even worse than described. He was gaunt and remained deathly still, not even reacting to sudden noises or hands passed before his eyes. I reached my doctor, who did a quick inspection and called an ambulance. At state hospital in Augusta a team of specialists exhausted its bag of tricks before recommending electric shock treatment. Unstrung, his family turned anx-

iously to me, and after lengthy consultation with the doctors, I reluctantly agreed — George was by that time unable to swallow food.

The treatment was successful — miraculously, George was eating,
speaking, and moving again. In two months he was pronounced out of
danger and well enough to come home. I had kept his old job open for
him, but urged him to take his time. When I called he'd tell me gruffly
that he wasn't coming back to my lousy job, but he finally came around.
I eased him back a day at a time, first giving him an assignment for quick
money that had always afforded him a gleeful sense of lucrative accomplishment. He would talk — more like bully — the merchants into paying three dollars apiece to have their names on a full-page message of
support for a local high school team.

During George's stay in Augusta my nerves had languished in
unaccustomed tranquility. Now here he was again, bursting into my
office demanding that I take down the eight names he had sold so far and
accept and count the dollar bills and change he had collected — he'd
deliver to no one else. I looked up from what I was doing and told him
that was great. But look, George, things were different now — had to
be. Bunny would take the names and money, and please, save it and give
it to her all at once, not a dribble at a time.

Suddenly George went savage, ranting loudly all over the plant,
returning only to tell me to stick my stinking job, and then driving off.
At the time I was less concerned than I would have been if I had been
seeing this behavior for the first time. I'd give him a ring next day with
another assignment as if nothing had happened. But as the days went by
without response to our calls and knockings, the finality sank in. George
had left us for good, never to acknowledge my greetings again. He
withdrew, not from everything, but from the community for which he
had become, through the newspaper, such a familiar, rambunctious
presence, an irrepressible Saroyan-esque character, heroic, unforget-
table, larger than life.

★ 32 ★

The College Caper Exposé

York and its two village corporations, York Beach and York Harbor, exerted essentially the same strain as the Berwicks on our elastic editorial department. Sports events were intertown, so our reporting had a built-in duality. We began to look for stories of regional interest, like a series on Camp Waban for the retarded, whose volunteer helpers and wards were recruited from all our communities. I took on the county's wastrel Community Action Program. These and eight or nine other campaigns that year, among them a study I initiated on starting a college of oceanography in the Kennebunks, were to win us an unprecedented special New England Press Association prize in 1967 for Community Service, continuing a string that went to eight straight — that special one, six firsts, and one third — before we stopped competing.

York officials were particularly hostile toward publicity, their attitudes a curious mixture of hubris and paranoia. Our journalistic purpose was to divulge, their paternalistic one to conceal. The script of our relationship came to resemble that of a soap opera, full of confrontations, with an ever-receding denouement. However, we did manage to establish our competitive imprimatur in the Yorks with the water tower campaign and another quirky one that dropped into our lap. Like Huck Finn seated in the parlor disguised as a girl in a skirt when the farmer's wife tossed him a spool of thread, we gave away our gender when we caught the two subjects by clapping our knees together.

The story of York Harbor Institute rode a swift current that took it in and out of Maine in just two months. The service the newspaper performed for the mostly oblivious villagers was accomplished with subjective news stories carefully dressed, like Huck, to make themselves look harmless. I think I just heard Adolph Ochs groan in his crypt — there it goes again.

Our first correspondent in York called me one late-June day to say she had a story too big for her column. A man named Granville Rideout was planning a college of oceanography in the old Emerson House, a refined, idle, summer hotel in York Harbor.

I sent Kathy Pulkkinen down that afternoon. When she returned with her notes she said, yes, it was a front-page story. Rideout himself was a positive man in his early fifties with an impressive background in business and education. The college could be the down-season flywheel for York Harbor's one-cylinder summer economy. When I read Kathy's long story I, too, was impressed with Rideout's credentials, and I admired his goals. I gave the story second lead, Page One.

But after the paper went to bed I had time to read it again. I wondered: Rideout was planning a mid-September opening, two and a half months away. I asked Kathy to tell me more of her impressions. What kind of shape were things in, down there? Was the timetable realistic? How did the interview go, exactly? Only seven months earlier, when I and the others had studied starting a college of oceanography we had learned how difficult it would be, and after many meetings and consultations with educators and scientists, we had decided that it was pointless to persevere. During the decade following World War II the science of oceanography had become the hottest game around. Every existing college with so much as a single teat of an oceanographic program was milking it hard, and every coastal college without one was trying to grow one. Even if every graduate of every one of them went on to teach, for many years to come there still wouldn't be enough knowledgeable teachers to go around. Even within an existing university, a bare-bones start-up budget would exceed three million dollars. Kathy nodded; she too was having her misgivings.

Once-elegant Emerson House on its two crowded acres had suffered from unprofitable, intermittent use. Restoration alone would be formidable. Rideout had airily spoken of concurrently — that very autumn — opening a sister college of classical studies in Greece under the deanship of his York Harbor Institute associate, Donald Terwilliger, and three other sister colleges during the next few years.

In odd moments during the next week and a half I used the phone to check out the credentials Rideout had volunteered during Kathy's interview. Two weeks later I used the same front-page layout and space for my follow-up story. The first story, I announced, "appears to have seriously misrepresented Mr. Rideout's educational background, and may have been misleading in other respects as well."

My format was to juxtapose, one by one, paragraphs in Kathy's first story, reprinted in boldface, with paragraphs of retraction in the regular typeface. Rideout had claimed a civil engineering degree from Northeastern. In the correction paragraph I reported that he had attended Northeastern, but for "academic reasons" had received no degree. Rideout next claimed an electrical engineering degree from Worcester

Polytechnic. He had attended only in 1937; he received no degree. He said he had then attended Yale to study electronics, too vague a claim to investigate.

I had called Belleville Area College in Illinois, where Rideout had said he earned a master's degree in education shortly before World War II. The dean of admissions told me that Belleville was a two-year junior college that awarded no degrees, certainly not master's degrees. I asked if Rideout had stayed on at Belleville as a professor of radio engineering, training men at nearby Scott Air Force base, the "war replacement" for Belleville. The dean said there were no records that Rideout had ever been to Belleville, as student or teacher. Anyway, the college hadn't even been established till 1946, after the war.

Rideout had told Kathy that after Belleville he had entered the business world as an engineering consultant, and as president of three firms he'd originated — a water company, a land-development company, and a commemorative-cannon manufacturer — and had built eight lakes in three states, one a multimillion-dollar project in Ashburnham, Massachusetts: three hundred acres of water surrounded by a thousand-acre housing development.

The chairman of the Ashburnham Board of Selectmen was warily noncommittal, referring me to a lawyer, but the secretary at Town Hall told me a dam had burst in 1936 and that Rideout had bought the property around the hole and built another dam. The whole property, otherwise undeveloped, had changed corporate names three times since. When I called the lawyer, he said, "You'll get nothing from me!" Another Ashburnham man said, yes, Rideout assembled nonfunctional cannons in his backyard with castings from a local foundry. The man sent me a snapshot of the backyard of a rather messy lot surrounding a modest dwelling. Three castings were visible scattered about the yard, one sitting on a homemade carriage.

After forming his companies, Rideout had said, he had felt the old education drive return. He had jotted down his concept of the ingredients of a good college, and then in 1962 had acted as chief coordinator in the founding of Nathaniel Hawthorne College. After the start-up he had served the college as trustee, meanwhile going on to teach new engineering concepts at Franklin Pierce College in 1963 before returning once more to Ashburnham.

The dean at Nathaniel Hawthorne reacted drily. The college had been founded in 1962, as Rideout had said, the year before the dean himself had been hired. He was quite sure that Rideout had never been there, certainly at no time as trustee. The dean at Franklin Pierce was more voluble: he knew the man well. Granville Rideout had been hired as a fill-in teacher of U.S. history, not "new engineering concepts," when a faculty member had died in midterm. He had taught one semester, "then we let him go," the dean said, because, among other things, "Rideout's claims to degrees were quite questionable." All this hadn't been in 1963, the year the college had opened, but rather in January 1966, only a year and a half ago, and Rideout had been let go in April, three months later.

When he returned to Ashburnham, Rideout had said, he had incorporated the Ashburnham Committee for Higher Education, serving as its chairman. The committee had successfully solicited funds for a four-year Ashburnham college called "Converse Grant," scheduled to open next year. Converse Grant was off the ground, but "still clung to [him] for guidance and support." He had gone on to teach at Canaan College, where he had been until very recently, leaving to pursue his plans for an oceanographic college.

The Ashburnham Town Secretary said she had heard about Rideout's Converse Grant plans, but nothing had ever gone beyond the talking stage. She assumed the idea had been dropped. Canaan's Dean Conrad, whom I called next, gave me an earful. Yes, he certainly did know Rideout, and his sidekick Terwilliger too. Both had been faculty members from September 1966, through May 1967, only a month before Rideout had appeared in York Harbor. "Rideout claimed to have certain degrees." He was dropped from Canaan; Terwilliger had chosen to go with him. For motives Dean Conrad said he couldn't fathom, Rideout had tried to stir up faculty dissent — "he seemed to want to take over the college." Rideout had formed an unspecified relationship with Dean Conrad's secretary, who had chosen to leave Canaan with him, the same Ramona Roche posed in a secretarial role in our photo of Rideout at Emerson House. Dean Conrad said both Rideout's and Terwilliger's records had vanished from his files when they left.

I was popping. I called Sanford attorney George Willard, Rideout's lawyer for incorporating York Harbor Institute. I told him that I'd been checking the credentials of a man named Granville Rideout, and had come to some disturbing conclusions. Willard said he had read the first glowing account of Rideout's plans and background in the *Star,* and was having his own qualms, particularly about the part that listed him as a trustee, along with Terwilliger and some others of remoter address. Following a few minutes of reticence at both ends of the wire, Willard loosened up and told me his story.

Rideout and Terwilliger had appeared at his law office one recent afternoon, introducing themselves as staff members at Canaan College. A real estate man whom Rideout had picked out of the phone book and visited in search of college sites had suggested Willard as someone to see about incorporation. In Willard's office they had "wanted much data in a short time." Willard said Terwilliger seemed to have a "binge on" about education, saying "all they taught nowadays in college was a bunch of slop." Willard said his two visitors were in such a hurry that "there wasn't much information for me." When they left, "I looked out the window for their automobile. They'd said they were in such a hurry, but I saw them walk across the street to a restaurant. I looked into their car; it was filled with papers and magazines. It looked like a trip to the dump." Willard's name was on some papers, he said, because "you need some names to incorporate." He was a straw corporator who would bow out later.

All these discoveries, contraposed paragraph by paragraph against the claims in Kathy's first story, were revealed in the second.

From others in Ashburnham I had heard plenty more, mostly opinion and assessment of Rideout's personal dealings and qualities, inappropriate for a news story. I now confronted the unavoidable questions: How much objectivity was either possible or desirable in future York Harbor Institute stories? What was Rideout's likely response to the second story when this issue hit our fans? Rideout had broken no law I knew of. He wasn't a public servant whose actions and motives could be discussed as having a bearing on his fitness to hold office. Rideout was a private businessman who had so far done nothing but misrepresent his background. If I wrote things that could be construed as pejorative to his success, I deserved to be sued, and deserved to lose.

What I chose to do was to balance carefully along the edges of libel, to masquerade as a reporter agog, shaking his head in wonder and admiration at Rideout's optimism in confronting the obstacles I would repeatedly call formidable. I must warn, but guard against all appearance of malice. There must be no discernable pattern of criticism that could be called into account in court.

In 1967, when the postwar babies were in their late teens, the old colleges were full, turning away so many students that new colleges were sprouting all over the place. I reasoned that Rideout should easily be able to find 200 desperate students. Colleges customarily asked for a semester's tuition and expenses in advance, perhaps three or four thousand dollars per student. Rideout and Terwilliger, the only voting members of the Board of Trustees, could vote themselves all the advance money as salaries, pay none of the bills, then declare the corporation bankrupt and head south. The parents would lose their advances, the students a year of opportunity, the teachers other job prospects. I could picture the crowds of joyous young optimists carrying their luggage, descending on Emerson House in September to closed gates and locked doors, the two deans flown and beyond reach of the law. Even so, what laws would have been broken?

My York Harbor Institute scenario was complicated by other unsettling factors. I wasn't surprised to learn that not even earnest money for Emerson House had changed hands, or that the hotel's owner was two years late with property taxes, or that York had a lien on the property that matured in November. What really shook me was the identity of the owner. He was George Kattar, not long afterward tried, convicted, and jailed on serious charges. Kattar was generally assumed to be an associate of New England Mafia boss Raymond Patriarcha. It was theorized that Kattar was laundering Patriarcha money in New England real estate.

I had already written more than once about these Kattar operations in connection with his ownership of another old summer hotel in York Beach, White's Hotel, which later burned flat in minutes during a fire of uncertain origin. A Kattar associate, Leo (Buddy) Dowd, was known to have bought Candlewood Lodge upstate in 1962, insured for triple its value with three separate insurance companies. Candlewood had also burned to the ground. Dowd's wife, listed as owner of Candlewood, was a director of North American Enterprises of Boston. Kattar was president. Another resort hotel owned by Kattar in Cape Neddick had burned in 1964. Kattar had connections with loan companies, trucking firms, and at least one insurance company. I phoned Kattar, who had no idea when Emerson House papers would pass, but would say nothing more. I called his Methuen, Massachusetts loan company too, with no useful results.

The morning my "retraction" story was on the stands, Rideout called. Could he come up to see me? We talked alone in my office. Rideout was a rather tall, well-constructed man with dark hair and courtly mannerisms. First he delivered a letter to the editor, which I published the following week, a low-key, reasoned exercise that said the newspaper's informants were entitled to their own opinions and values, both questionable — he had enemies who would like to see him fail. "Truth is a blend of black and white." He refuted nothing specific. He was slick enough. We both smiled earnestly as we dueled. Until that morning, he apologized, he'd read only a few paragraphs of Kathy's first story (he assumed that she had also written the second), so he hadn't noticed the many reporting errors. Her second story contained even more errors. He knew the problems of an editor — obviously, I couldn't check everything.

I was more than anxious to correct whatever was wrong with either story and besought him to use all the *Star* space he needed to set things straight. No, he said, he preferred not to bother with that — nothing constructive would come of it. He wanted the next part of our discussion off the record, and we had a long talk about how things had gotten so twisted. I listened from my vantage point of having conducted the first-hand interviews, and spotted more discrepancies. I gave him the understanding that I was still unconvinced, defending my reporter. No voice was raised. Rideout hoped that in the future he could count on us to give his college the publicity it deserved, and I was quick to assure him that this was not only my desire, but my duty.

On the record Rideout told me that 28 students had enrolled, several teachers had been engaged, and that he was considering more applications for both. I expressed surprise — coincidentally enough, I told him, I myself had been heavily involved in a study of the prospects for starting a college of oceanography, and one of the things that had discouraged us was the almost total unavailability of teachers. It was then that Rideout glanced at his watch and wondered where the time had flown. He was late for another appointment, and left hurriedly. In my next story I capitalized on my opportunity to expatiate:

> Because Mr. Rideout's time was limited, this conversation was not pursued. But for the record, and to put Mr. Rideout's plans in perspective. . . .

I went on to discuss the many obstacles confronting him, the time, money, and planning required before a college of any sort could be started, let alone a college of oceanography.

> But miraculously, since he plans to open two other colleges as well this fall, Mr. Rideout has apparently surmounted all these obstacles and feels he is in a fair way of gathering a faculty, completing incorporation, hiring staff, and providing classrooms and campus, all from scratch in unfamiliar areas during the next two months.

I drove down to York Harbor next day and snooped around Emerson House, now "Emerson Hall," seeing no evidence of renovation, then went over to lawyer Dave Strater's office, where I unburdened myself of my fears. Dave advised me to be careful, that in a legal sense nothing could yet be done. I called Attorney General James Erwin, Dave's former law partner, who reacted gratifyingly, but agreed with Dave.

Next I called the State Department of Education and talked with a man named Anderson. He told me his department had no authority to investigate private schools or colleges — the state's leverage was very restricted. What leverage? Well, Anderson reflected, about all the state had control over was which institutions called themselves colleges and conferred degrees. Before degrees could be conferred, meaning some time between the opening of the college and four years later, when the first class graduated, the Legislature had to approve the college. But approval was fairly routine.

Supposing Rideout were advertising YHI as a college that conferred degrees, without noting the technicality of pending state approval — could Anderson's department step in and investigate? Anderson thought maybe — he'd get back to me on that. But he'd have to have something concrete. I told him I'd see what I could find.

Next day I asked a friend of mine to visit Emerson Hall to inquire about enrollment for his son. He was greeted by a Mrs. Helen Carrignan, alone in the building. He asked for Ramona Roche, but was told that Mrs. Roche had left YHI employ. He came away with a copy of the Institute's student handbook, and its only brochure. The brochure was illustrated with photographs of laboratory, typical classroom, student quarters, and other bogus facilities. Eighty-five courses were offered. The college would employ teachers from the finest graduate schools in the country. Academic scholarships were available. Summer sessions would be conducted for accelerating students. Quarters were gracious. A full athletic program was promised. Specific degrees would be awarded. I underlined the words *college* and *degree* wherever they appeared, and sent the brochure to Anderson.

Nowhere in either document did I find Rideout's name, but I found attorney George Willard listed as trustee. I called Willard and learned that he had told Rideout he was too busy to pursue incorporation, and to hire another lawyer. He was finding the *Star* fascinating these days.

I knew the name Helen Carrignan. It belonged to a York woman who had been writing long, rambling letters to the editor that made me suspect her rationality. I called her at YHI and introduced myself. She was pleased with her new job — Rideout had promised that she'd be head of a department when college opened. No, Mr. Rideout wasn't in just then. I learned the names and phone numbers of the six students she knew of, and the only three teachers signed up so far.

I called the teachers. One, a substitute teacher at Portsmouth High School, had been referred to YHI by a local teachers' agency. She confessed surprise that Rideout had demanded so few credentials, but was satisfied with his explanation that the college was so new that it wouldn't be able to attract more experienced teachers. A Mrs. Carrignan was to be her department head. The two others were also high school teachers. As candidly as I dared, I urged them to do more investigating. When they had convinced me that they were legitimate, I hinted that I didn't expect the college to open next month, or ever. They promised to inquire further.

About this time the dailies began running their own stories about YHI. Rideout had turned to modest understatement of his own credentials, but not of YHI's. The stories complicated my job by being rather promotional — the *Press-Herald* spoke copiously about the fall athletic schedule, not yet quite firmed up.

On August 16 I brought the whole YHI story up to date in the *Star,* emphasizing incongruities, doing my best to warn off local contractors. I needn't have — no work at all was going forward. I called the three teachers again — all had resigned. I called the homes of the six students and alerted their parents, who took steps to retrieve their substantial deposits. I learned that at about the time the two deans had visited Willard's office, Terwilliger had applied unsuccessfully to an eastern college, then had accepted a western college job. Two of the potential students had enrolled in Terwilliger's college-to-be in Greece.

Next time I called Emerson Hall a young "temporary secretary" told me Rideout was in New York interviewing student prospects. Fifteen or 18 had now enrolled, but she couldn't give me their names. She did know of four teachers, and named Helen Carrignan and the three I knew had resigned. I asked about the athletic facilities, and the laboratories and classrooms. She was new there, she said — I'd have to talk to Dean Rideout. No, there were no teachers there at the moment, she was alone except for the maintenance man. She'd seen one classroom. Yes, there were desks in it. Enough? That depended on what I meant by enough. No, she couldn't tell me anything about the sale of Emerson House. September 18 was opening day.

With the literature I had supplied, State Department of Education man Anderson had visited Attorney General Erwin, who had gone to the state Supreme Court. Justice Talpey lost no time in ordering Rideout to appear before him. A lawyer in Erwin's offices told me the contents of Talpey's injunction. There were no surprises. Rideout asked York attorney George Hutchins, who was presumably also now working on incorporation, to represent him, but by now Hutchins, too, had been reading the *Star* and suggested that Rideout go up alone — he couldn't contest the charges.

When he faced Justice Talpey, Rideout did a little halfhearted double-talking, saw it was useless, and admitted everything charged. Justice Talpey was unprofessionally outraged. He excoriated Rideout, ordering him to recall all his brochures and enjoining him to acquaint his enrolled students with the truth by certified mail. He then issued

Rideout a permanent injunction to cease calling his enterprise a college and advertising degrees, and to stop recruitment.

Finally, I dared an editorial, but not a full accounting — Rideout had been enjoined, not sentenced. I alluded to what had happened, to make a case for improved protective legislation. The laws governing private colleges were weak, I wrote, but at least this time, with a little luck, they had served.

That was the end of the story. Few enough people in the Yorks even read the *Star* in those starting days, and even among them, I doubt that there was anything resembling a full understanding of the part their new newspaper was playing, or an appreciation of the race against time being run right under their noses.

A couple of months after Rideout vanished I took a phone call from Baltimore. My caller said he was a vice president of George's Transfer, a trucking firm in that city. My name had been supplied as someone who might be able to tell him something about a man named Granville Rideout, who had applied for a job. Could I give him the benefit of my impressions of Rideout?

(George's Transfer — George Kattar? I could sense a bug on the line.) Well, I demurred, I didn't know much except that he had been involved in an unsuccessful attempt to start a college locally. Things hadn't worked out for him. *Star* reporters had done a few stories on York Harbor Institute — I could send him those. My caller didn't think those were likely to help much but thanked me for my time.

The old Star Print Company building on Garden Street, Kennebunk, in 1958.

In the Garden Street shop at the two-page newspaper press: left to right, George Ange, Peter Cox, Paul Bannon, printer's devil Bill Perkins, Vic Sampson (partially hidden), Bob (Bezo) Bissonnette, former co-owner Perley Watson, John Cole, and Sandy Brook.

Eben (center), Lisbet (left), and Megan (right) in 1958.

Anneke in 1974.

The Brooks' Cape Porpoise home in 1962.

New quarters on High Street, 1965: two old houses with shop built between them.

Bob (Bezo) Bissonnette (standing) and George Pulkkinen (seated) at his Intertype machine in the High Street shop, 1965.

Some of the 1976 Star crew at a party for a co-worker. S.B. is in the center of the next to last row.

Eben and S.B. in 1965.

John and Pamela Wood in 1969, shortly before he bought shares in Star Press.

Megan at nineteen (1971).

Lisbet at seventeen (1971).

*Second wedding day,
Bass Island, 1976.*

S.B. at the helm of Crazy Horse.

Peg Hendrick (left), collator Hazel O'Dell, reporter Tom Heslin, and pressman Jerry McBride harmonize at the 1977 Christmas Party.

One of the Community newspaper presses at Water Street, 1976.

Anneke and S.B. on the porch of the Cape Porpoise home, 1981.

Partner Robert L. Brigham (right) talks with Joe L. Allbritton, whose Washington Star Communications bought the York County Coast Star in 1977.

★ VI ★

IV

★ 33 ★

A New Partner

My assistant editor and prospective partner, Ron Devine, was reporting Kittery and Eliot; Kathy Pulkkinen was in Wells, Ogunquit, South Berwick, and sharing the Yorks with me, while I had also the Kennebunks and North Berwick; Al Dalton covered sports for the whole territory. We needed help. I hired a young journalism graduate named Jack Casey for the Berwicks. Reserved and inexperienced, Jack had trouble finding stories and by default concentrated on a pointless hassle between South Berwick's two policemen and their tire-squealing young-blood tormentors, an unworthy story line that suggested itself to him by its coffee-counter decibels. Instead of coming to town like a breath of fresh air, we came in like flatulence. Dispirited by his reporting experience, Jack left a few months later, replaced by a former daily feature writer, Maryline White.

Early that year, 1967, when I had all but despaired of getting the $7,000 Ron Devine had said he would invest in Star Press, Ron announced that he could spare only $2,500, but he was now ready to invest it. I hid both my disappointment with the sum and my doubts about accepting it. My relationship with Ron had been symbiotic at best. We reached agreement about the number of shares his money would buy and issued documents. Three months later Ron, his face alert, announced that he had decided to leave us for the *Portland Press-Herald*. I wished him well and told him I'd arrange to return his money with interest. His next communication was in writing. He had spent a year and eight months with Star Press, so he'd expect to get back at least double his investment. Strater's new law partner suggested a meeting in his office. There he argued that for Ron's three-month investment, a 10 percent profit would be more than generous. Ron, scowling blackly, protested with disconcerting conviction, but he finally accepted the check. There he went, my first business partner, stomping out of my sight forever.

With 11 communities to report, we were spread perilously thin, but

I couldn't do any more hiring. We were losing money again, and debts were piling up. I advertised for a partner who could make a substantial investment.

Bankers and accountants judge business values by looking at financial statements. The established Main Street shoe store is worth the wholesale value of its inventory and fixtures, plus a miniscule amount for good will, meaning that people know the store and its pleasant owner. But a cut-rate chain store in a new shopping center, or a young price-cutter next door, will place the old store in immediate peril. The widget manufacturer survives only until he is outsold, or someone introduces the whatgit. Those businesses are not like the newspaper business.

Newspaper readers get hooked. They get comfortable with a paper. They form habits of buying it. They have proprietary feelings about it. All the paper has to do is survive and publish, one issue after another. It may have acne, it may have rickets, but it is no widget. When the publisher is ready to quit there will be buyers out there, even as I was out there in 1958, ready to pay handsomely for the opportunity to own an opinion-setter, the only one like it anywhere.

I must have had a dozen replies to my trade magazine ad for a partner, and five serious interviews. I was about to call one of the candidates back and firm up our deal when Bill Bishop called me. We met on a sunny, late-spring morning. Bill arrived promptly with his wife, Linda, who excused herself to drive around town while we talked. Bill was 48, four years older than I, casually well dressed, putting on some weight, light brown hair graying at the temples of a good forehead, jowly, blunt-featured, with a wide-eyed, direct smile and a decided twinkle. He moved deliberately and spoke with a hesitant drawl, relishing the words but releasing them economically. We toured the empty plant before settling down again in my office.

Bill began with characteristic directness: "What is there to say? You know me."

I had learned quite a lot during our first meeting at Bill's *Reading Chronicle* plant when he had sold me his old Premier newspaper press four years before. Linda had inherited the *Chronicle,* and Bill had run the business. He had discovered that he had a talent for journalism and had become happily involved in his community. At New England Press Association conventions I had known both Bishops as jovial company, sensitive sophisticates, neither too light-hearted nor too serious. I had heard about their sale of the *Chronicle*. Reading, ringed with large weeklies and strong community dailies, was urbanizing unattractively. The Bishops had sold their home, too, when they sold the *Chronicle,* and so had the cash to buy a Maine home and invest in Star Press, if I liked the idea. Bill had followed the *Star*'s progress and thought his experience in Reading would be useful. He'd be satisfied with a minority share of something he could enjoy, work at, and profit from. Neither of us had ever known the comfort of a partnership, but he saw it as much less stressful than plugging away alone.

I showed Bill the books, the equipment, and the buildings. I recited our recent history, withholding nothing. Yes, Bill said, it all sounded familiar enough, but now, at least, it seemed by way of getting pretty solid. There was plenty of room on the up side for ad rates and printing prices. The arrangement I outlined seemed fair — he had just been through it from the seller's angle. I suggested that we pay ourselves $10,000 each, a big raise for me, but a substantial cut for him. That was all right too, Bill thought — the business should soon be able to afford some improvement there. He was prepared to invest $80,000.

We arrived at his ownership share by following accepted weekly newspaper trade logic. For home-printed papers in their own quarters, you start with annual gross sales volume — in our case, by then $220,000. Then you subtract debt, long-term and short. You then add receivables, less 10 percent for bad debts. That brought us to a net base value of about $135,000. If other pluses and minuses balanced, as we agreed they did, my current $135,000 interest would give me 60 percent to his 40. He would have something of a bargain in return for something of a gamble, and I would have salvation. Each of us would gain an experienced consultant and a hedge against personal illness. With its fresh money, Star Press could handle its recent expansions more comfortably. We came easily to terms, and I called off the other aspirants.

Starting from zero nine years before, the Brooks were now worth $135,000. Even Anneke had never been able to swallow my lonely speculations — wishful thinking, they'd had to be, to lift her spirits. Now I would have my raise, and the worst of the economic heat was off.

Bill and I decided together what to do with his money: $25,000 of it would knock current payables down to a less awkward balance with receivables; $15,000 more would retire the Cochrane notes and some others to finance companies. The remainder, $40,000, would be used to retire that much of our bank loans. Bill brought it with him in a single check when I took him out on our first day to introduce him to Bob Stinson at Ocean National Bank.

Each time I had renegotiated my debt with Stinson I had made the same case I had made to Anneke, and he, too, had never for a moment believed it. I had argued that we were worth far more than our puling little book value — that his directors were at less risk than they thought.

If I defaulted, they could sell the business for twice what they had in it. Bob would shake his head and say, "Sure, sure."

Now, side by side, Bill and I faced Bob across his desk, making introductory small talk. When Bill laid his check down and pushed it across the desk, Stinson acted like a proper banker: his eyes did not blink; his expression did not change. He retained his composure even when he heard that the Cochrane notes had been retired, and some finance company notes, and half the current payables, even when I suggested that the remaining bank debt might be renegotiated over an extended term at lesser rate. But when he turned casually to look at me, I crossed my eyes.

Bill and Linda Bishop found a gracious old home in Cape Neddick and moved in. Before Bill came to work we had only sketchily discussed our respective responsibilities, other than that they should overlap to make us interchangeable. I assumed that Bill would report the Yorks, where he'd live, and perhaps free Kai for early-week selling by handling the walk-in trade. I expected him to share the larger printing customers with me, and to do some of the estimating.

Casually Bill confided that advertising wasn't his field — we had a senior man in Kai, anyway, so he'd rather not meddle except for the occasional policy discussions. I broached the subject of editorial responsibilities. Oh, he protested, I was the editor — he wouldn't want to interfere. Well, I said, what sort of writing did he want to do? "I write a column," Bill replied. I gulped mentally and went on to other subjects. Printing? Yes, he thought he could keep a general eye on that — efficiency, budgets and things. He could also troubleshoot the front office, billing, and bookkeeping, and deal with the bank and the accountant. We'd see how things went.

I was growing alarmed — Bill must have operated the *Chronicle* the way Bud Wright did his *Sanford Tribune,* as an administrator who studied reports from department heads, offering advice to the people who worked the nuts and bolts. We were in no sense so advanced in our corporate order. Supervision, yes, of course — that was how we protected our investments — but that was the spare-time job.

Bill did agree to do some reporting on York Village, but it would be impossible, come summer, for Kathy, Maryline White, Al Dalton, and me to cover the other ten communities. I picked the outstanding choice among many reporter candidates, an agreeable blond bear in his middle twenties named Bryan Chernak. Bryan had an infectious laugh, mature judgment, general savvy, and a clear, effortless writing style. He settled in York Harbor with his wife and took on Ron Devine's territory.

My new partner spent what would be considered in better-established businesses a normal amount of time getting the feel of Star Press and settling into his community. One of Bill's early operational jobs was to lay out the front page each Wednesday, something I had been doing in five minutes after dashing off my final stories and spiking them onto Ellen's copy hook an hour after deadline, then manning the Ludlow to set front-page headlines. Bill enjoyed page layout and was good at it. The task became his nearly total Wednesday morning concern. He wrote his column, well-crafted spoofery and comment on subjects of current national interest, the sort of thing I had determinedly excised from the editorial page in favor of comment on the local scene.

At the end of each month the front office bubbled with the billing ritual, the hectic gathering of figures for the accountant. My own involvement in this arcanum had always been first to question Bunny Sampson on the state of her progress, next to acknowledge the validity of her argument that if she could just be relieved of her phone answering and receptionist duties things would go a lot faster, then to make room at a remoter desk for her concentrated assault on the books while I shared her front-office duties with other recruits. Finally, I'd wave "so long" several days later as she triumphantly drove off to deliver her documents to the accountant. When the accountant had finished, Bunny would pick up the monthly statement and her own accounts, bring them back, and deposit the statement on my desk. I'd glance at the bottom line, shrug, and file it away till next month.

More professional, Bill made a proper production of all this, fidgeting a lot beforehand, delivering Bunny's stack of papers himself for lengthy discussions with the accountant, later discussing the results with him in greater detail, and finally bringing them back for discussions with me. I'm sure Bill was shocked to see me in such a lather of work-clothes motion, setting a sweaty example for a crew that had to work hard to keep us all afloat.

I had closed the Kittery office when Ron Devine left; now it made sense to rent a desk in York. There Bill could maintain a *Star* presence and save himself the commute to Kennebunk three days a week. Away from the hyperactivity at headquarters, he could keep civilized hours and go home for lunch. Wednesdays he spent on the layout and the communal paper-night collating. Thursdays he was in York again, and Fridays back in Kennebunk for payroll and management discussions. I was too busy for much in the way of discussions, and Bill wasn't anxious to assume the operational duties he'd left behind him years before. I reminded myself that his money was making a world of difference, and enjoyed his company whenever I stopped for a few minutes to keep it.

★ 34 ★

Reflections on the Weekly Reporter

The primary, often the only, concern of most people in business is making money. I think of these people as being as varied as horses. Among them you find the Percherons, Shetlands, Mustangs, and Arabians. But I think of owner-editors as being as varied as dogs, among which are Chihuahuas, mastiffs, collies, Pekingese, whippets, bulldogs, dachshunds, St. Bernards, Scotties, bloodhounds, and scavenging strays. The wider genetic spectrum among newspeople has something to do with marching to many drummers besides the ones who are drumming up money. Like masters, independent weeklies often look and act like their dogs. I myself am rather forensic, socially insecure, resentful of authority. I tend to identify myself with underdogs — perhaps that is the kind of dog I am.

Before I bought the *Star* I had lived for only three brief periods in communities served by weeklies, and had taken no interest in any of them. In the beginning my figurative pages were blank; the germs of journalism that spread and made them a newspaper grew from their own culture, isolated, Darwinian. I had never, in any sense, been interested in advertising — I responded to it almost negatively. Money occupied my thoughts only in the abstract. I don't shop around and am not a bargainer, a preference that has often made me brag that I've never gotten the better of a deal. I kept Star Press ad rates and printing prices low partly because of this unbusinesslike attitude, partly because my manufacturing experience taught me that volume was healthy for unit cost, and partly to discourage competition. Of these three reasons, a determination to give better than I got — the underdog attitude — was strongest. The field of business was not my field of honor.

What my neighbors, or even criminals or glamorous people, are up to, interests me less than it should. My friends are repeatedly shocked by the gaps in my gossip repertoire. The usual weekly news fodder of social events, announcements and reminders, local decisions, elections, and changes, interested me only when I could influence them. I assumed that others as incurious as I could only be interested if what was written was at least as exciting and entertaining as the subjects. The challenge of making it so brought my interest in local news to a simmer. It boiled when I found reasons to support decisions or argue for different ones, developing convictions in myself and my readers, thereby influencing the course of affairs. A head of steam was reserved for the times when minds were won and the newspaper triumphed.

I was miscast as both journalist and entrepreneur. With normal journalistic instincts I never would have wanted the Watsons' *Star*. With normal business instincts I never would have bought it. Any good businessman or trained journalist soon would have quit, bankrupt. Later on, when the business was reasonably sound, I would have made more money with normal instincts, but I suspect that running the newspaper as a business could only have been done at the expense of its spirit, and in the end it was spirit that made it valuable. I didn't change my habits; I merely did my best with the ones I had. I'm reminded of the story of Evelyn Waugh in uniform. When his commanding officer found him drunk and said sternly, "Waugh, you're making a spectacle of yourself. I must ask you to stop," Waugh is said to have replied, "Surely, sir, you can't expect me to change the habits of a lifetime to accommodate your whim."

I admire journalists who sustain their interest in imparting facts to inform and entertain — the who, what, where, and when — but I am not one of them. I am much more interested in the how and why. I look on journalism as one of the most admirable of professions, and on journalists as being working aristocrats, artists of the rough-and-tumble. The most successful of them lead exciting lives digging up pieces of information that redress wrongs, avert disasters, advance discovery, sway governments, and promote order. They are the least specialized of artists, the most dashing of professionals. They are not all good at what they do, God knows, any more than other professionals are. The bad ones can make a great deal of mischief before their inadequacies are discovered and they are encouraged to find other work. But the good ones belong to a fraternity of inquiring skeptics, humanized by their calling, with more than the usual humility, tolerance, and good humor.

While he was my partner, Bill Bishop reported York with lucidity and insight. His copy, like himself, was easygoing. The notes he took were spare — single words, phrases, names. He got the better quotes and salient figures down on paper, but mostly listened and observed for the short summaries he would concoct at his typewriter. His occasional editorials were short, literate, thoughtful pieces of work, rational comment on selected detail by a sound student of community affairs. When he had written one, he was done with that subject, had made his statement, if anyone were interested. If not — aeingh! In this fashion the *Star* maintained a subdued, courtly presence in York, and circulation remained about where it was when he started.

At 48 Bill approached reporting in the usual way, as though it were a rather simple matter of understanding what went on and getting it into plain language so that everyone had access to the information. His stories were abbreviated versions of the stories I demanded from other reporters. They were good because he was experienced and observant, but small-town reporting was a job Bill had outgrown.

The house fire that leaves a family homeless, the weekly's story, offers its reporter a chance to rally his community to the aid of known individuals. The daily's story of the hotel fire that claims many lives and renders corporate losses in seven figures satisfies other curiosities. The daily reporter tries to be first and cleverest in learning what he can repeat to readers he doesn't know. The weekly man writes of a personal tragedy. What the weekly reporter misses of the sensational, he finds in the personal.

But reporting, daily or weekly, is a young person's game. To do it well the mind must be fresh and eager. After writing a dozen fire stories, the reporter has exhausted his imagery. He dips in vain for fresh words to describe what happened. After 15 years of wringing his talent dry, his writing becomes mechanical and he loses interest.

For the middle-aged weekly reporter there is, moreover, an indignity in much of what he does. He has a sense of the ridiculous when he sets forth to interview the elderly husband and wife who have for 40 years been gathering together an extensive collection of hotel ashtrays. He helps them arrange a sampling of their more Byzantine treasures and poses the couple behind it for a photo. He tries to squeeze from inexpressive minds their most vivid memories of ashtray collecting and their observations during pursuit. Disappointed there, he urges them to recite the humdrum events of their lives that led to the first stirrings of interest in hotel ashtrays. When he sits down at his typewriter, all the middle-aged reporter can do is get a tintype, not an essence, because he found no essence. He has lost the exhilaration of contrived fun and hyperbole. The story he completes is obviously not worth the indignity he has suffered to get it, or the space waiting for it in the newspaper.

His sense of his own inconsequentiality doesn't end there. Most newsmakers he interviews are young doers, athletes, adventurers, politicians, bureaucrats, or professional people. For them the interview is a form of flattery: the reporter is moth to their flame. The experienced reporter, often more substantial than his subject, finds himself growing resentful, and the interview flops.

The reporter who fails to move on to special assignments at larger publications, or into comment writing or editing, enters middle age as the familiar caricature, the cynical wiseacre who plays poker with cronies, knocks out his stories offhandedly on two fingers, his fedora pushed back from his forehead and a cigarette stub drooping from the corner of his mouth. The caricature is an armor that protects his self-esteem from the abrasive world of action filled with movers and shakers who notice him not. At least to his colleagues the veteran on the major newspaper is an elder statesman of journalism. The wealth of his employer, and his own longevity, assure him a comfortable salary. But the aging reporter on the weekly paper has no such consolations, which is why there are few middle-aged weekly reporters.

Bill Bishop had lost most of his reporting enthusiasms, as I was to lose mine later, because he had written himself out of metaphor. Had I not been there directing *Star* destiny, he might have taken hold and directed it better. He didn't need any more of my relentless 80-hour weeks. He didn't burn for his share of the action. For most of Bill's year and two months with Star Press I failed to appreciate his difficult position, how I was sapping his vitality by carrying on with his investment almost as if he were a silent partner. I don't think he resented me for it, or even that he blamed anyone but himself, because he was that kind of man.

One day in June 1968, Bill slipped a letter under my hand on my desk and asked me to read it when I had a minute. In it he had written that he had reluctantly concluded that when he left Reading he hadn't been trying to escape urbanization or the encircling competition, as he had thought, but had been running away from weekly journalism. He was no longer suited to it, and so wasn't the right partner for me. He was leaving, and hoped I'd help him find a buyer for his shares — he knew Star Press was in no shape to buy them back.

I wrote him back — it was easier for both of us to write. I keenly regretted his decision, but thought I understood it. I promised to help him find a buyer, agreeing privately with his financial conclusions by studying our monthly statements. For a year we had hardly grown. Payables were on the rise again. We were losing money. According to the formula we had used for share value when he came, we were worth less when he left.

★ 35 ★

Backing an Underdog

Something else checked our growth momentum in 1968. It had to do
with a series of connected incidents that were to preoccupy my editorial
life in a nightmarish way for more than three years, and in diminishing
degree, like remnants of a recurring dream, for the rest of my time with
the *Star*.

One November evening I was covering a Kennebunk School Board
meeting, during which the board heard a taxpayer's request. This taxpayer lived in the only habitation at the end of a half-mile-long gravel
road in the sparsely settled farming section of town known as Alewive.
He wanted the school bus to turn up Kimball Lane morning and evening
to pick up and deliver his two young granddaughters, relieving the
petitioner and his wife from the chores of delivering the two little girls to
the main road to wait for the bus, and driving out again to wait in the
afternoon.

The School Board routinely considered such requests for extended
bus service. Like this one, they were usually denied. Pressed by the
angry taxpayer, the superintendent agreed that Kimball Lane qualified
for bus service as a public way, but argued that the extra time and
mileage would inconvenience other passengers, and that the pitted,
dead-end road, otherwise uninhabited, would be rough on the bus.
Listening to the debate, I agreed with the School Board — the other
children and their parents would spend perhaps 40 additional minutes a
day on the bus, causing them all to rise earlier on the dark winter
mornings and wait longer for homecomings in the evenings.

But the petitioner this time was not an ordinary mortal. Herman
Cohen and his wife, Sallie, in their middle fifties, were caring for their
granddaughters while their son and daughter-in-law were overseas on an
engineering assignment. Cohen took the School Board's denial as a personal insult, assuming that if he had been a native Christian Yankee member of Kennebunk's establishment the decision would have been different.

It was "COHEN" that had been scrawled on a board tacked beneath the stuffed black leotards hanging in effigy on the signpost at the

entrance to Kimball Lane that Halloween night seven years before. Photographer George Stevens and I had driven out to Alewive to meet Cohen for a photo and my front-page editorial. Later, Cohen had called me for a bit of publicity when the Army chief of staff, accompanied by other generals and Pentagon officials, had visited the enormous barn he had converted into a workshop-laboratory for a demonstration of a device Cohen had invented to remove carbon monoxide from internal combustion engines, notably those in tanks.

We had met again when Cohen had wanted to show me his plans for a grandiose scientific research center on his Alewive land. He seemed to be trying to arouse my indignation against the bygone Chamber of Commerce directors who had rebuffed what one described to me as an impertinent demand. I agreed: Cohen wanted the directors to pressure a local oil dealer of ancient Kennebunk pedigree to sell his ancestral homestead land across Kimball Lane from Cohen's extensive acreage; he warned them that unless he could buy it he wouldn't build his research center. Cohen interpreted that rebuff as a combination of timidity, stupidity, turgidity, rigidity, insult to his own credibility, and anti-Semitism, just as he had interpreted Police Chief Stevens's inability to bring someone to justice for hanging the effigy.

Cohen was to invite me out to Alewive on other occasions and to drop in for conversation in my office, an outwardly self-sufficient, apparently lonely man. I learned much more about him than he did about me, because he was a marathon talker in unhurried, gravelly tones, a man of huge and varied experience. He was of shorter than average height, with heavy, sallow features, meaty hands, and a compact body with the hard, protruding stomach of an aging laborer; he was a smoker, a chuckler, dressed always in his raffish uniform of soiled khakis, cheap black shoes, white cotton socks, and peaked twill cap. On the rare occasions when he kept city appointments he wore an expensively cut herringbone suit, an off-white wide-brimmed Texas hat, a white shirt with large monogrammed cuff links, and a string tie with diamond stickpin. The bug-eyed reaction he got from his local acquaintances to this rare sartorial solecism never failed to delight him.

Given Cohen's barely perfunctory attention to conversation not initiated by himself, it was impossible to avoid the conclusion that his ego was as big as his talk and experience put together. Withal, there was something childlike about Herman Cohen that I decided had to do with his yearning for companionship and recognition, and once I had satisfied myself that he was genuine, I was happy to provide both.

Cohen was an enigma to Kennebunkers. They wondered about his life before Maine, the source of his money and how much there was of it, why he had chosen Alewive, or Maine at all, and what he was up to at the isolated end of Kimball Lane. Who were the out-of-state visitors? What was being delivered to him by common carrier? Why was he so rabid about the trespasses of local deer hunters?

Herman's brain was agile, complex, and extraordinarily retentive, but there was a segment of it that seemed to be missing, a peculiar deficiency. He was shockingly oblivious to the niceties of social behavior. He could irritate his enemies, but he didn't seem to know how *not* to irritate his friends. He was quick to react to slight or injury, but his own tactlessness was legendary, his vainglory undisguised. He viewed the world through an unmatched pair of spectacles, one lens paranoidal, the other megalomaniacal. Through the first, the motives of his antagonists appeared as tendentious as his own, and through the other the admiration of his supporters shone boundless and unflawed. He was the implacable foe of advantage, who consistently sought advantage for himself. He was politically intolerant, but was the self-appointed champion of what he called the "little people." He was a reactionary who was warmly generous of himself; a man of subtle reasoning who was oblivious to the fragility of nature. The world had never fully turned on to his talents, perhaps because his social habits turned it off. A starker contradiction of worldliness and immaturity I have never known.

The sum of these observations doesn't describe Herman Cohen adequately, even for my purposes here, even when it is qualified by his rather ordinary origins or the professional disappointments he attributed partly to his being Jewish, and partly to the natural jealousies of lesser intellects. Certainly none of it explains the attractive qualities of the man. For these one must turn to his physical and intellectual bravery, his trueness to stated purpose, and to the assistance he was forever offering to his few friends and nonestablishment citizens. It was the curse of my own underdog syndrome that forced me to risk the fortunes of my newspaper in following where Cohen was to lead. Even when he violated his repeatedly proclaimed standards, as he did effortlessly, I had to support his condemnation of Kennebunk officialdom for violating the same standards. In this way I was seduced into a lurid adventure with a tainted but oddly appealing collaborator.

The day after the School Board meeting, Cohen drove purposefully down to Town Hall in his recycled Oldsmobile. One of the School Board's reasons, albeit a minor one, for denying his request for bus service was the roughness of Kimball Lane. Past selectmen had promised to schedule Kimball Lane for rebuilding and tarring, so, Cohen put it to Town Manager Earl Hardy, how about some gravel and grading now? Hardy was a smugly simpering, flabby little man of bland demeanor and faint, enigmatic smile. The budget couldn't stand more gravel, he told his grim visitor.

"I see," said Cohen, who then exited and drove down to Seabreeze Acres, a large housing project behind the beach recently prepared for construction on sand, peat, and marsh with free muck from the Kennebunk River dredging. The developers, a consortium of local men led by George Timson, had bought the marshland for a song and then arranged privately with the Army Corps of Engineers to use the property as a spoil area. Cohen would often refer to the development as "Sinking Acres," and once Timson threatened suit.

Down at Seabreeze Acres Cohen watched the trucks of a Seabreeze Acres partner, a native-son earth-mover, hauling load after load of gravel to build Seabreeze Acres roads. He trailed an empty truck back to the municipal dump where it was reloaded with gravel from the pit. Back to Town Hall went Cohen. Town Manager Hardy was out, so he talked with one of the office women. He asked to see the town's records of dump gravel sales. There were none — the town received no money for the gravel. Who had authorized the taking of the gravel? Cohen was told he'd have to get his answer from Hardy.

On his way home Cohen stopped in to see me. He said he had a very interesting follow-up to my report of his School Board denial. What came out of our conversation I published under a headline whose kicker was: "Time to Lift the Lid, the Man Says." Cohen was promising to take the cover off Town Hall to see if the insides were as rotten as they smelled to him.

That week Cohen wrote the first of his letters to the editor. From then on, and for years, he'd write a long letter each week, his personal newspaper column. If he planned a trip, he'd leave me installments to publish on specific dates. In the war he waged with the local establishment, these letters were as feared as anything else in his arsenal. The first scathingly denounced Town Manager Hardy and the School Board, and called upon all taxpayers to arise and support "Herman Cohen, a citizen of Kennebunk," in what he billed as a second-class citizen's fight against bossism, arrogance, and privilege. He promised a full investigation of town records, addressing rhetorically the questions he'd try to answer and repeating eight specific ones he had posed that week in a formal letter to the selectmen, with the demand that agenda time be provided for the answers at their next meeting. Just prior to that meeting Town Manager Earle Hardy surprised everyone by submitting his resignation, citing the town's "deterioration."

Cohen threw himself into his parlous tourney with an élan that was startling. He ceased speaking of all else, but spoke constantly to anyone who'd listen. He commenced a regimen of attending every meeting of every town board and committee, interrupting with rude and pointed questions, ignoring all protocol, being gaveled out of order, making audible comments to the audience, engaging committee members in heated cavil. Many hours were added to meeting times, and much business neglected. I quoted copiously from Cohen's inflammatory speeches and the angry responses.

The selectmen particularly were infuriated by his insubordinate insistence on answers to his questions and demands for action on Kimball Lane maintenance. They had been shamed into stopping the dump gravel giveaway, but Cohen wouldn't shut up about it, lecturing them on the loss of future dump cover and hinting broadly at hanky-panky. The selectmen retaliated by refusing to answer his insinuating written questions, announcing, with some reason, that the research would take too much time. Cohen would let nothing drop. Like the patient wolf stalking the guarded moose calf, he prowled and snapped just out of reach of the defending hooves and antlers, sniping, sneering, demanding, interrupting, suggesting other reasons for every official statement as well as for the selectmen's refusal to answer him.

After a few weeks of this treatment the selectmen asked Town Counsel Chester Cram to attend their meetings, to keep Cohen in line. Cram was a man of wry wit and prickly disposition in his midforties, diminutive in stature but quick to strike. As the selectmen's protector, Cram was a worthy adversary with a sensitive behind for Cohen's brand of sting. Cram would be kept hopping mean for years.

It may even have been Cram who first suggested the plan to rap Cohen's knuckles — certainly he was consulted about it and became its chief proponent. The Maine Legislature had recently enacted a "limited-user" law having to do with little-used roads that towns no longer wanted to maintain. Formerly, "abandoning" such roads — lovers' lanes, logging roads, roads used only by fishermen or hunters — had required town-wide voting and was often successfully resisted. The limited-user law permitted selectmen merely to hold public hearings before they could unilaterally declare roads to be of limited use, relieving the town of the obligation of further maintenance. What the selectmen now proposed was to hold their hearing and then declare half-mile-long Kimball Lane a limited-user road. Thereafter Cohen would not own Kimball Lane, but to reach his home at the end of it he would have to plow it himself in winter and grade it in spring.

I had been slow to editorialize on the subject of Cohen's aggravations — he had been overresponding to personal matters in an unattractive public way, and the dump gravel authorization remained a mystery. But this rash bit of official retaliation left me in an unavoidable position. On December 13 I wrote the first of nearly two hundred editorials on matters in the Cohen shadow. I called it, "Oh, He Was Herman, and They Done Him Wrong (Because He Done Them Wrong, Because They Done Him Wrong)."

Three wrongs don't make a right, any more than three lefts do. The question is: Are they all wrong?

There is a fascination in the story of Herman Cohen and his boresight on Kennebunk officials. "There are nine and fifty ways of constructing tribal lays," Kipling observed, "and every single one of them is right." There are as many ways of entrapping selectmen. If you look deep enough into any public official's work you'll find things done for the sake of expedience, or done the easy way, or the pleasant way, or the political way, that should more properly have been done another way.

The fact is that in Herman Cohen the town officials are up against something they couldn't have bargained for. And bargaining will do them no good — there is no price. For one thing, Mr. Cohen has nothing to gain or lose. He starts with a quarrel with what he calls the "Good People" of Kennebunk, the "Four Hundred," the ones with the privilege, social, economic, political. He lines himself up against them as a matter of course.

He thinks the taxpayer is subsidizing the money-making schemes of the developers. He thinks the Selectmen have perpetuated a gravel give-away program which leaves the dump short of covering and grading material. He thinks developers should complete their roads before the Town accepts them. He is probably right.

He is asking questions that are designed to elicit embarrassing answers. He has confronted the Selectmen with hostility, and they have reacted with hostility. After asking him to put his questions in writing, then seeing the unexpectedly long list, demanding considerable research, they have decided to let him answer the questions himself. Cohen calls this arrogance and secrecy, and assumes the officials have something to hide.

This infuriates them further. In a fit of pique with his earlier insistence that they were trying to avoid rebuilding Kimball Lane, they try to turn the tables on him by demoting his access road to "limited-user" status. The Selectmen don't like to be pushed. This time they pushed back recklessly, and their action has provided Mr. Cohen with an obvious fowling-piece. He has been quick to use it:

if the Selectmen defend their action now, they will only be lining themselves up in a row.

"I am completely impersonal about this," Mr. Cohen says. When his comparison of the Selectmen's attitudes with those of Hitler and Stalin is doubted, Mr. Cohen says: "It starts right here." Ignoring bossist attitudes, or the official favoritism he thinks he's uncovered, is the way things start, he says. He sees his role as that of Defender of Kennebunk Democracy, and he's enjoying it. He has found some support from "second-class" taxpayers, for whom he is the self-appointed champion.

We don't see things as clearly on the one hand as Mr. Cohen does, or on the other as the Selectmen do. However, despite Mr. Cohen's provocative behavior, we are more in sympathy with his position than the Selectmen's who, as public officials, must avoid all bias, no matter what their personal feelings may be.

The *Star* publicity packed Town Hall for the limited-user hearing. Cohen loved to hear what came orotundly from his throat. He talked and talked. The developers had their hands in the taxpayers' pockets, he said. He was paying first-class taxes as a second-class citizen. He smiled slyly to his audience as Counsel Cram and the selectmen fumed and retorted intemperately. They stood it as long as they thought decorum required, then retreated in orderly haste by declaring the hearing closed, leaving the field to their still-speaking tormentor and going downstairs to their own quarters where they voted to give four roads limited-user status, three of them uninhabited, the other Kimball Lane.

A few days after the hearing, influenced by their deepening hatreds, the selectmen made their choice of town manager to succeed Hardy. He was a seven-year Augusta city councilman from a tainted regime, who had since turned to town management, holding three jobs, each very briefly. He was Donald Dulac, a 40-year-old, bullet-headed, knot-bodied former merchant seaman of French Canadian extraction who spoke rapidly in gutteral tones; a tough, expedient man of mill-town cunning. He had been told about Cohen and me, and would put the quietus on both of us.

Thoughtful Establishment emissaries kept coming over to talk sense into me. I was responsible for the Cohen uproar that was tearing Kennebunk apart, they told me. Cohen was setting neighbor against neighbor, wrecking a nice little Maine town. People were hating; the game was getting dirty; business was suffering, and the town's image. I was encouraging a rabble-rouser by giving him undeserved space in my reports and permitting him a weekly soapbox in the letters column, from which he was shouting intemperate bombast. All I had to do was ignore Cohen and deny him free space, and he'd dry up and blow away. Now that I saw the evil genie I had unstoppered, it was my duty to stopper him up again. Please, for the good of the town!

They were decent people, and they had a point. But, I asked, didn't they see the other, worse dangers in hushing things up, muffling the voices of the aggrieved? If they were in my shoes, what would they do? Not what I was doing, they assured me; I was a traitor to stability. They were accusing me of causing what amounted to a localized civil war merely by meticulously reporting the words and actions of a hitherto obscure citizen and awarding him space in the letters column. Then they were saying I had the means to stop the war or let it run.

There were others, rude worthies and independents of all ranks and stations, who saw things Cohen's way, and others too, suppressed or free of who knows what forces move society to pull its wagons into a circle, who were coming to me clandestinely with a common message: "Sic 'em!" The Establishment saw only the tip of this iceberg.

★ 36 ★

Herman Cohen Center Stage

Audiences at all board meetings were swelling, first with Herman Cohen's supporters, the "little people" come for the show and to see the mighty slam-dunked, then with Establishment types, recruited for balance. Cohen himself was at every one, like the polecat at the lawn party, comporting himself with a disdain for the evident opprobrium that was at least admirable. He had studied law and appreciated the restraints on slander, libel, and public nuisance. He paid me long, unannounced, quasi-social visits at least once a week, using those occasions to deliver his letters. He would sit quietly watching my face as I copyedited, probed allegations, weighed adjectives, suggested word changes, and deleted what was libelous or untrue or counterproductive or simply eggregious exaggeration.

I could report all words spoken at public meetings — being careful to get them right and in the proper context — and in my editorials I knew how to minimize my risks. Cohen's letters were more dangerous. No one could sue him for what he wrote to me — the accountability was mine for making it public, and there were plenty of dyspeptic people waiting for me to slip. For three years I would be repeatedly threatened with libel suits, twice by embittered lawyers. Most Kennebunk business people stopped bringing us printing and many stopped advertising.

Would-be leaders and climbers were outdoing each other in pronouncing anathema on Cohen and the *Star*. One of my tenth-anniversary "April Fool Wire Service" stories had Cohen deciding to join the Establishment and all the other members scurrying to resign.

Cohen's letters were replete with blustery rodomontade and polemic hyperbole. Almost every sentence ended with an exclamation point, often two or three in a row: "The need to eliminate the virus of utter contempt for the taxpayers that affects our Selectmen and appointed officials is as great as ever!"; "To Mr. Dulac I answered that we would meet on the field of battle, with no quarter asked, and the conversation came to an end!"; "saddle the backs of the Kennebunk taxpayers with this burden of privilege of these parasites!!"; "proof that the Board considers their actions to be NONE OF THE TAXPAYERS' DAMN BUSINESS!"; "cesspool of moral bankruptcy in the Manager's office!!!" Cohen's fear-filled targets hadn't the sophistication to parody this sort of language into comic obscurity; they were strangling on their own spittle.

Annual Meeting that year would be held March 18, a day-long affair that would begin with the election of a moderator who would first supervise the daytime balloting, then climb to the main hall to preside over the evening session on budget and policy warrant articles. By this time "Herman" and "Cohen" were the two most-repeated words in York County. His adopted second-class confederates were visiting him covertly with their legitimate gripes and mischievous anti-Establishment scuttlebutt. Cohen the strategist strode the front lines in khaki fatigues and rumpled, peaked combat cap, the GI's general, ignoring enemy fire. "Let's see who's boss!"

Six days before Annual Town Meeting and elections, Cohen rented Town Hall for an evening meeting of his own that would be known as "the First Cohen Town Meeting" or, for short, "The First Coming." All six candidates for the three open seats on the Board of Selectmen had been formally invited, and none dared decline. Ralph Curtis, a defensive, small-eyed plumber, had decided not to seek reelection. For his seat, one of the early Cohen admirers, Heber Smith, an anti-authoritarian local activist, was opposed by young Cohen-hater Richard

Bibber, son and business heir to undertaker and former State Representative Earle Bibber. Incumbent Eben Cook, a jovial, outspoken fellow of short but impressive construction, was being challenged by large, heavy-set Hugh Googins, owner of a local garage. Norman Stevens, father of the police chief, was opposed for the empty one-year seat by Richard Brown, an antiques dealer, brother to the Cohen-hating earth-moving contractor for Seabreeze Acres.

The incumbent board chairman, with a year left of his three-year term, was Ed Winston, an even-tempered man in his early fifties who moonlighted as the *Press-Herald*'s Kennebunk stringer but whose main job was as assistant to Postmaster Lewie Burr. He was courtly, a sometime town moderator and a strict *Roberts Rules of Order* man, conscious of his duty to be civil even to so chiggerish a taxpayer as the one confronting his board. The other incumbent selectman, Warren Bowdoin, had two years still to serve. Bowdoin, in his early forties, had inherited his father's drugstore and was known as a shrewd businessman and workaholic — a saturnine, chunky man with an expressionless face noticeable for the thick glasses he wore and his short, broad, upturned nose, with prominent nostrils.

In my March 13 editorial I stated my preferences — Smith, Stevens, and Cook — then turned to the subjects that overshadowed both elections and budgets, the "Cohen Issues." I reminded readers that so far I had supported Cohen in only two, the limited-user affair and his contention that —

> . . . there were some people blessed with greater official favor than others, and that this was being manifested, among other ways, by the drain on the dump gravel, a potentially expensive loss for the taxpayers. We too thought the gravel give-away should stop. So did the Selectmen; the present Board hadn't started it. They stopped it.
>
> We have approved of Mr. Cohen's stubborn purpose to inspect the dark areas under the official bed and run a finger over the tops of the door lintels. Privately, we have enjoyed knowing Mr. Cohen and observing his relish of the spotlights — both as he turned the harsh white one this way and that under the beds and through the cupboards, and as the other multi-colored one followed him about on-stage. Indeed, the whole episode has this quality of a social satire acted according to a script and leading to a pre-ordained ending. Cohen is the improbable blithe spirit, exasperatingly invulnerable to attack, and the others are the often well-meaning heavies who plod along clumsily, prey to his mockery and practical jokes. In this way Mr. Cohen has been of service: he has pinched us

awake. He has lured the heavies into the parlor on-stage in their skivvies and snapped on the light. He has lifted the lids of the pots on the public stove and invited the citizens to apply their nostrils to the fumes.

To Mr. Cohen the pots are all chamber-pots, and the fumes smell to him pretty much as you'd expect. His stock remedy is drastic: throw pots, pans, lids, implements, and stove out the window and start over. Here we part company with him. To us, the smells from the pots can all stand some improvement, but all are generally wholesome.

We think Mr. Cohen is rocketing around too impetuously in the fragile framework of Kennebunk democracy. Much of his thinking is sound and many of his ideas are good. But there is some question in our mind that his first thoughts are for the welfare of Mother Kennebunk, as he insists they be for other public figures. It seems to us that he is looking on Kennebunk more as if it were a Goliath armed with the slings and arrows of outrageous fortune, and himself as David armed only with two spotlights, one on him, the other in his hand.

The restive Establishment pointedly ignored the Cohen meeting, but Town Hall was crammed with people in work clothes, undeterred by the blizzard piling up outside. For three hours khaki-clad, vitriolic Cohen lounged against the stage podium, expatiating on everything he had learned while probing the Town Hall labyrinth. In closing he announced puckishly that he would be a candidate for moderator of the Annual Meeting six days thence.

When the card-carrying Establishment members heard this they went off like Roman candles. The moderator not only supervises the balloting but also wields subtle power during the evening floor meeting. He can cut off debate he doesn't like. He can recognize some speakers and ignore others. He settles points of order and calls for voting at moments of his choosing. Usually a single experienced moderator agreed to accept nomination for the paid job in advance, was then nominated unopposed, and was elected by a few chosen people assembled for the formality. This time the election would be a symbolic test of strength. Kennebunk buzzed with partisan activity for the rest of the week.

In retrospect it seems incredible how much fear and loathing on the one hand, and votary support on the other, Herman Cohen aroused. Telephones jangled all over town, the organized callers in both camps urging their troops to vote for moderator at 9 A.M. By the appointed hour, the corridors and surrounding rooms were a-jostle with purposeful Establishmentarians and common folk in carnival spirits.

Earle Bibber, the undertaker whose son was a selectman candidate, was the Establishment nominee for moderator; Cohen was his opponent. Never in Kennebunk history had there been a moderator election remotely like this one. Seven hundred sixty-four ballots were cast by people inching forward in the long line that stretched from the polling room, down the corridors, out the street door, and halfway around Town Hall in the rain. It was 11 before the ballots were counted and the results announced. Bibber was the winner, 422 to 342.

Two hours behind schedule, with only eight hours left for the election balloting, voting began. A total of 1,207 ballots were cast, 67 more than ever before. The evening meeting was six hours long, every seat filled, balcony and orchestra, and all floor space was packed with standees. Others jammed the vestibule, and others sat, as I did, on stage on folding chairs behind the moderator. Cohen spoke on every one of 50 articles.

Cohen's own petitioned article, calling for a rescinding of the selectmen's limited-user designation for Kimball Lane and for $3,900 to repair it, occasioned the lengthiest debate. The Budget Board had voted eight to one for a negative recommendation. Town Manager Donald Dulac, making his first public appearance, oozed self-confidence as he double-talked against the article. An Establishment leader, moving confidently for indefinite postponement of Cohen's article, was as shocked as the rest of us when his motion lost to a standing vote. Moderator Bibber permitted debate to rage on until forced to "move the question" of Cohen's motion. He called for a show of hands: yes, and then no. From behind him, facing the hall, I thought the two forests of hands looked pretty even, but with conviction in his voice Bibber ruled against the motion. The Cohen people wouldn't let him get away with it, shouting him into a standing vote. While some three hundred timidly abstained, Cohen won it, 204 to 194. The limited-user status was nullified; Kimball Lane was again a municipal responsibility, and $3,900 had been raised to improve it.

Between adjournment at half past midnight and 8 A.M. I wrote a 25-page meeting story and three "Post Mortem" editorials for that day's paper. The first described how I saw things turning mean:

Sift the true motive from the false as you read a detective story, and you've found the murderer. Try it — it doesn't work. All the major characters have motives. You are playing against the author, who wants to surprise you. Better to find the person without an obvious motive; concentrate on him.

That is the way fiction is played; fact is usually played otherwise. But Kennebunk officials, no less than the supporters of Herman Cohen, have been playing like fictional characters. Cohen himself has looked for obvious motives. People are taking gravel from the dump — what could be the motive? Cohen says the motive is that they want the gravel. Without taxpayer authorization the Town acquires an ambulance. Cohen says the deal was made because they want a new ambulance. He ascribes no ulterior motives to these actions, or to many of the others. But he objects to how they are done. Some of his charges are overplayed, some not. From the official point of view, of course, all are.

But official Kennebunk, and the members of what Cohen calls the Establishment, are doing something else. They are looking for Cohen motives and are infuriated that the ones he claims (better government, democratic process, secret ballots, open discussions, citizens' rights) are too pure to fight. The ones he doesn't admit, but are ascribed to him (being a sorehead, or an egoist, or a mischief-maker) are human failings that don't constitute crime, and so don't lead to a sentence, only a reprimand. Official Kennebunk refuses to settle for a reprimand, apparently.

So other motives are sought, and crime is hinted. The people who guard the institutions he has criticized attack him personally. They attack his sense of the truth. They attack his character. They do more: they try to paint him as a dangerous, deranged, subversive criminal against society. He is criticized for keeping to himself, for being different, or unneighborly. People are infuriated that he doesn't seek out and enjoy the approval and fellowship of his townsmen. These social stigmata are applied to all independent souls. Eccentricity is a crime in Kennebunk. It is hinted that there is reason to think Mr. Cohen is a Communist! His citizenship is questioned, and in fact has been investigated at official request. Not satisfied with learning that he is, in fact, a citizen, others are launching an investigation to learn if he has ever been temporarily not a U.S. citizen. It is hoped that this crime of temporary non-citizenship can be pinned on him.

Mr. Cohen's business affairs are also scrutinized. Has he ever avoided payment of Maine sales tax? What is the source of his income, and is any of it not declared? A dozen Kennebunkers have hinted darkly to us.

Finally, we were told by an intemperate town official Monday morning, when the Town Meeting is over a "thorough check" will be made on at least seven local people, and we can assume that the writer of this editorial will be one of them. It is not known by us whether or not this investigation finds favor with all officials or was simply a veiled personal threat by the one who made it.

To all this Cohen replies (and so do we): "Fine, I welcome it!" Let those who live in glass houses cast the first stones.

In another editorial I analyzed the voting, calling it almost unbelievable that after having criticized every board in town, teachers, developers, firemen, police, merchants, deer hunters, candidates he opposed — all the sure voters and their families — and after frightening all others with the promise of a three-day Town Meeting if he were elected moderator, Cohen lost by only 80 votes. There was fear in the vote against him — one smelled it in the air, like ozone. With it came hatred, for Cohen and for me. The fear manifested itself in frenetic activity against a man who ambled about town talking to everyone, always talking, never raising his voice or changing his theme. The fear welded together a brotherhood of strange bedfellows that gained a temporary triumph.

Directly following the meeting the three new selectmen, Googins, Brown, and Bibber, all hard-liners, voted to bestow the chairmanship on angry druggist Bowdoin rather than on incumbent Chairman Ed Winston, who was too soft on Cohen.

Cohen was difficult to support. His tactics embarrassed me — repelled is too harsh a word. He was uncompromisingly rude and unmannerly, indiscriminatingly insulting to all members — worthy or unworthy — of every board and committee. He was wantonly adding time and turmoil to their volunteer work by coarsely exaggerating, doubting honesty, challenging ethics, interrupting, calling things by nasty names, preempting energies from other business. It was easier to be philosophical about a mosquito.

Supercharged Town Manager Donald Dulac was beginning to chafe his departmental employees, who were resigning and going to Cohen with their gripes. Dulac made the mistake of telling one of the few non-Establishment businessmen, Mike Tranci, that it was "none of his damn business" why the dump-keeper had resigned. Tranci took his outrage to the new chairman, Bowdoin, who brushed him off, and then to the public in a letter to the *Star*. Predictably, Cohen jumped on the issue too.

Establishment leaders had formed a Citizens Committee for Responsible Government, a euphemism for "get Cohen and Brook." Overnight half the town's influential citizens hurled themselves into membership. Free rein was given to discussions of returning stability by starting an alternative newspaper funded by Establishment shareholders and backed with their advertising. The better news would be prominent, and Cohen would be blanked out. ("They would publish a spayed newspaper," I commented, "but they wouldn't call it a spayed.")

It was hard in 1968 to avoid comparing what was happening in Kennebunk with what was happening all over America. Of all the 192 years of the Republic to that date — and since — 1968 may have been the most demoralizing. It was the year of the Tet offensive and the growing perception that we were not only losing the war but also that we deserved to lose it, that our government was unprincipled, our leaders corrupt, our American boys at My Lai and Song My, brutes. Martin Luther King, Jr., and Bobby Kennedy were assassinated. President Johnson stepped down after saying he couldn't unify America. It was the year that gave the Republican nomination to Richard Nixon, who then chose Spiro Agnew as his running mate. It was the year of the worst of the student riots, of college deans at gunpoint, of the abandonment by our youth of all former standards of behavior, of indiscriminate rebellion against authority and old values, rejection even of soap and water, a year of marches, police brutality, sexual promiscuity, obscenity, nudity on stage, bizarre dress and life-style, hippie and yippie cultures, jeers and confrontations, irreverence in the church, demonstrations, arson, communications gaps and generation gaps, no laughter anywhere.

Inflation was smashing the hopes of the elderly. Prices bore no relation to values. Workmanship had turned shoddy. American productivity and leadership were on the skids, the dollar weak, pollution rampant, the drug culture out of hand. While world hatreds deepened, nuclear bombs proliferated. In York County the already frightened local people of property who had worked and planned and made lifelong sacrifices for their families' security — people for whom Kennebunk, with its reassuring continuity of native families and trusted values, was a rock of ages — saw the fabric of their birthplace coming apart, and were afraid. Cohen was a highly visible symbol of all that was threatening their way of life, the personification of the evil spirit of '68.

I too saw Cohen as a product of the times, but differently. I hated the current wild excesses, but I hated what was rebelled against, too. In a way I had been hooked by Herman Cohen against my will and better judgment. I and my paper were old-fashioned for the times, calling for restraint, and respect for experience and time-tested standards. At the same time, with my underdog sense of outrage, I too was a creature of the sixties.

I was generally sympathetic to Cohen, but felt tainted by his tactics. I was a collaborator in principle, not spirit. I looked on his letters as bad literature, full of fractious cavil and ludicrous overstatement. The endless gushing forth, week after week, of patent, ad hominem diatribe mesmerized his audience. I was being shown forcefully what I had been learning on my own — that if you hammer away long enough with the same point, you can penetrate anything. Repeat something, truth or lie, with enough assurance often enough, and pretty soon you'll start hearing your own words coming back. The lesson can chill you.

★ 37 ★

Town Hall Revolution

Even today I hear people explaining disagreement as a "communications problem." In 1968 the phrase was at its most oppressive. What people meant by communications problem was that their stubborn opponents couldn't be made to listen to reason. The Establishment was in agreement that what was keeping me from seeing reality — that Cohen was trying to destroy Kennebunk and that I should be gagging him — was a communications problem they were having with me.

Four of the selectmen were having another communications problem with the former chairman, Ed Winston, the controlled moderate on the board. Winston couldn't seem to grasp the idea that they should be dropping napalm on Cohen's fire. Town Manager Donald Dulac understood; Town Counsel Chester Cram understood; most town employees had the same idea; the other four selectmen got along fine on this subject. Winston, they felt, was deficient in at least two parts of his anatomy, and this deficiency was causing a communications problem with him. To solve it they stopped communicating with him.

So it came as a surprise only to Winston when, a month and a half after Annual Meeting, the new chairman, druggist Warren Bowdoin, his sullen expression unchanging behind his thick lenses, formally moved to extend Manager Dulac's contract from that June to the following May, with a substantial increase in pay — Counsel Cram had suggested it. At his end of the table, waspish Chester Cram smirked sweetly. Dulac had been on the job for four months and had only recently been awarded the customary Annual-Meeting-to-Annual-Meeting contract. Each year, action on the manager's contract had been the new board's first order of business, but Cram, making no effort to disguise the Dulac raise as anything but an award for him and a slap at Cohen, said his thinking was that new boards should have time to work with the manager a while before voting, hence the proposal to extend the contract until three months after the next elections. This change had some debatable merit, but in context it was an abrasive action. My meeting notes were full of exclamation points. Winston knew he'd been set up. He argued lamely, but the others summarily outvoted him — Dulac didn't even bother to leave the room.

Transfused by the cheering of his own conspiratorial cabal, Herman Cohen was undergoing change. He began to relish his ombudsman image, chuckling with the point of his tongue between his teeth during his weekly visits, indiscriminately collecting disputatious material and expanding his field of battle to any official action that could be remotely construed as accommodating the business community, school department, land developers, or anyone whose interests could be called "special." He attacked the plumbing inspector for granting borderline permits, the assessor for granting abatements, the School Board for approving capital improvements, the water district for wanting to raise rates, or any department at all for spending money on anything.

Cohen the inventor worked out a system for refuse compaction and forced the town to study it as an alternative to the selectmen's dump expansion plans. Cohen the authority on combustion attacked the School Board's proposal for increasing boiler capacity and offered an alternative plan that he forced to an expensive, time-consuming study. Cohen the zoning authority attacked every observation of the Planning Board. Cohen the engineer objected to town equipment choices and maintenance procedures. Cohen the lawyer raised hell when town equipment was used to remove roadside elms whose branches overhung Establishment-infested Summer Street, but whose trunks were on private property. He learned enough about Dutch Elm disease to argue against every proposal by the tree warden. Cohen the hair-splitter attacked the business people whose signs overhung the sidewalk.

All committee work, meaning the course of government, came screeching to a halt while Cohen led discussion contentiously from the floor. His constituents were around him, ready to object if the chair failed to recognize him, or tried to silence him or table debate and turn to other matters. There were demands for posted meeting agendas, and many points of order were raised. Meeting-goers challenged everything, arguing heatedly among themselves while the chairmen helplessly gaveled for decorum.

That first year of his rebellion Cohen lost every skirmish except the Town Meeting vote to repair Kimball Lane. Cohen's "little people" had no power but the vote. No Establishment member or official group would entertain a Cohen proposal, foolish or meritorious. If he said white, the echo came back BLACK! If he said halt, MARCH! came back. But every decision had to be defended — Cohen could not be overlooked. The school boiler matter occupied 20 people for four months, the refuse compaction study many more people for much longer. The elm tree debate involved town meetings and cost $60,000. Instead of being a force for progress, and in spite of his growing proletarian sympathy, Cohen was wrecking every program he supported.

Any governmental department has flaws; every action can be legitimately questioned. Aided by nearly total recall and the special insights of his boosters, Cohen probed the soft underbelly of every committee, found the tenderest part, and kicked it hard. By June he had gathered together enough talking material and tried to rent Town Hall for a Second Coming. The selectmen stalled him until August, when he ordered another large *Star* ad to plug attendance at his extravaganza "dedicated to the protection of the taxpayers and to breaking the grip of the Establishment on the Town." The ad copy was sprinkled generously with the provocative slogans of his letters ("disinfect Town Hall," "riding on the backs of the working people").

The selectmen were damned if they were going to spend the $3,900 raised at Annual Meeting for repairs to Kimball Lane. I was calling for an end to their stalling, being both anxious to redress a wrong and laboring under the delusion that if Cohen could gain this victory he'd loosen up. The school year was over, and his granddaughters had returned to their parents, so bus service was no longer an issue. But Counsel Cram and Manager Dulac had thought up a hooker for the Board of Selectmen, and Chairman Bowdoin did the honors. Flanked by his three jovial huntsmen on the one hand, and by Winston advertising his discomfort on the other, Bowdoin announced the selectmen's dilemma. Before spending money on Kimball Lane, he said, the selectmen had wanted to make absolutely sure it was a public way. They had searched town records in vain for evidence that the road had ever been accepted by the voters. This turkey was rehashed with more stuffing by Chester Cram, wearing his mock-turkey smile to disguise the prevailing Town Hall glee. Particularly in view of Mr. Cohen's elm-tree-removal thesis, Cram explained, that public money should never, never be used for private benefit; the selectmen shouldn't *dare* spend money on Kimball Lane.

Like most Kennebunk roads, Kimball Lane had existed before Maine seceded from Massachusetts. Probably none of the older roads had ever been formally accepted, but if they had been, the records had been lost in a fire before the turn of the century. Money was periodically raised to maintain all of them. I called this ploy another example of the hypocrisy that underlay the whole Cohen brouhaha and exhorted the selectmen to get on with carrying out the stated will of the voters. They continued to stonewall with pious insincerity, carrying their charade to the point of farce by asking the town historian to conduct a search for the will-o'-the-wisp "acceptance" of Kimball Lane.

Cohen's theme all along had been that favors and favoritism guided the conduct of Kennebunk's affairs to the benefit of the influential and at the expense of the "second-class taxpayers," who were increasingly following his banner. A single week of questionable events brought the pervading bitterness to one of its early climaxes.

That week, the selectmen awarded a road-paving job on the strength of a single, rather high bid. Cohen started yet another row that forced the selectmen to spend virtually their whole regular meeting angrily defending themselves.

A man named Roger Lovejoy, who delivered papers to our news-stands, was hauled in that same week by the police and fined for obstructing other part-time sea-moss gatherers from collecting washed-up Irish moss on Strawberry Island. The island was owned by a reclusive old lady who had sold Lovejoy exclusive rights to gather moss on her island, and Lovejoy had his receipt.

Also that week, Cohen had been prevented from tape-recording the selectmen's meetings, even though Chairman Bowdoin was trying to trap Cohen, and me, by recording the meetings on his own machine.

That same week the Board of Selectmen followed the Budget Board's recommendation and sold the no-longer-used Washington Hose Company fire station, with its landmark bell cupola, to the *lowest* of three bidders, a man named Joe Riley, himself a voting member of the Budget Board. Riley had bought a small market next door to the venerable fire station. His plan was to raze the building and pave its tiny plot for customer parking. The next-higher bidder was an out-of-state man nobody knew. The high bidder, who should have won, was a skinny, balding man in his late thirties who lived with another youngish man in Wells, where the two operated an antique shop and a rather decadent eating club that had a theatrical clientele. This man, Russell Leonard, had wanted to preserve and remodel the fire station into a summer rental. It was generally understood that the budgeteers and selectmen had rejected the Leonard bid partly because of Leonard's style and partly as a favor to Riley. Leonard, a *Star* reader and occasional advertiser, was insulted and came to me; then he sought an audience with Cohen. Following his Cohen meeting, he retained a lawyer to take the selectmen to court.

That same September week the Zoning Board of Appeals heard a request from erstwhile selectman and plumbing contractor Ralph Curtis, attended by his Kennebunk Establishment lawyer, Thomas Reagan, for a permit to build four six-unit apartment buildings on High Street. Curtis had bought a Victorian mansion on ample grounds, razed the building, and subdivided. He had anticipated Zoning Board approval and started roads and water mains leading into what he confidently expected would be Kennebunk's first apartment complex. Neighboring High Street residents objected to the metastasis of their quiet residential neighborhood. They and Cohen, in his rumpled khaki uniform, were in the audience, confronting the Appeals Board as lawyer Reagan explained the Curtis plan.

As they studied the scale drawings, the Appeals Board members asked their pro forma questions. Ignoring the glares of loathing from the officials assembled around the drawings, Cohen rose and ambled forward. He pulled a steel tape measure from his pocket, applied it to the plans, then returned to his seat, drew a copy of the ordinance from his rear pocket, studied it briefly, and, without waiting to be recognized, began to speak.

What Cohen had learned with the aid of what he would often afterward refer to as his "unstretchable" tape measure, was that a goodly portion of the subdivision spread beyond the residential zone into "farm and forest," where three-acre lots were the minimum and where apartment buildings were prohibited. What remained within the residential zone would support only one six-apartment building, not enough to justify Curtis's investment. How come, Cohen wanted to know, no one had caught this "mistake"? Had Curtis himself never bothered to measure? How about his attorney, Reagan? The bank lawyer must also have seen the plans. The Planning Board's very first act should have been to find out what zone they were talking about. And here was the Appeals Board, with the plans on the table . . .

The embarrassed Appealsmen, caught with jam on their faces and no place to hide, quickly adjourned the hearing.

Next evening at the selectmen's meeting, Cohen again ambled up to the head table and picked up a document from it, a quit-claim deed to Joe Riley, the successful low bidder for the Washington Hose Company building. Town Manager Dulac, who sat at the table, snatched it from Cohen's hand. When Cohen protested, Dulac told him to "be quiet!" Chairman Warren Bowdoin, his well-known temper detonated, lectured the stolid Cohen and threatened him with permanent expulsion from future meetings. Cohen's letter that week again referred to Town Hall as a "cesspool of moral bankruptcy."

In a long editorial, I wrote that Cohen might have erred in specifics and by overreaction, but there was reason behind his basic charges. The native insider's sense of smell had been conditioned by custom and chauvinism. The outsider was saying, "Phew!" The locals knew that septic outfall and rotting fish contributed to the odor, but, they argued, this was the way all tidal estuaries smelled when the tide was out.

> . . . Cohen, of course, represents no danger to anything but their positions of privilege. What do the Cohen-haters fear? Are they afraid he'll seize control of government? Or are they afraid that Cohen, in his rummagings, may turn up the corners of the rugs, and that what he finds there may lead to a revision of local privilege?
>
> Cohen is a political reformer. Like most, he starts with a sense of being on the short end of the political stick. He starts with damage to an ego sensitized by successive contusions. A last-straw incident sets him off. His opposition stiffens, and pretty soon you have a good brawl going.
>
> The reformer has the initiative — he's attacking. The Establishment tries to reassert its initiative by finding a skeleton in the reformer's closet. When nothing turns up, it fights from its privileged position, getting more and more recklessly incensed until whatever truth there is to the reformer's charge becomes unavoidable. In his zeal the reformer usually overstates his case. Living so close to his mission, he sees drunks behind every bush. He hears a laugh and calls it drunken laughter. He sees a stumble and calls it a lurch.
>
> The mediator, if there is one, tries to keep the reformer from excesses, and the Establishment from overreaction. Mostly, like us, he fails. His primary duty is to see to it that if reforms are in order, reforms are accomplished. We have been asked why we don't criticize Mr. Cohen. We do. But change in the tactics of the reformer is less important to the people than improvements in government.
>
> This week we invite you to sample the Kennebunk fish. . . .

I went on to recall and comment on the events of the week, asking rhetorically at the end of the accounts of dereliction:

. . . If the government ignores the rules, who protects us from the government?

. . . If the police ignore the law, who protects us from the police?

. . . If the officials are immune from regulation, who protects us from the officials?

. . . If our appointed Boards ignore their duties, who protects us from our neighbors?

The editorial concluded:

All these are isolated examples, each, by weight, perhaps insignificant in the balance. We are going to say that in most other towns a Herman Cohen might uncover as many or more examples of official transgression. The fact remains that they exist in Kennebunk, and that Kennebunk would be better off without them.

But in all these cases of official transgression, who protects us from the transgressors? In Kennebunk the answer is plain, if unpalatable: Herman Cohen and the *York County Coast Star,* and we make no apology for the association.

★ 38 ★

Modern Press, Old Memories

In early December I introduced a new partner. The Bishops had agreed to sell their shares for $60,000. John Wood's opening telephone remark was a caveat — he had only $30,000. During our refreshing conversation I learned that he was 40, six years my junior. As an undergraduate at Harvard he had met Pamela Holley at Radcliffe, whose middle and last names became Holley Wood. Their four children ranged in age between 3 and 17. John claimed Maine roots back to Revolutionary War Captain John Wood, who had settled in Lovell, Maine, after marching with Benedict Arnold to Quebec. John had started his journalism career during college vacations and had gone on to successive editorial, sales and business positions with three of the largest U.S. dailies, after which he and Pam had bought, and for three years published and edited, a small California daily. They sold it when John joined the early Kennedy administration, first as a press information officer in Chile, then as director of the Regional Technical Aids Center in Mexico City. Anxious to return to journalism, he had been in Washington when he saw my ad.

The Woods were congenial, enthusiastic people. We came quickly to terms. Using a share formula similar to the Bishops', the Wood share was 16 percent. We had a deal when Bob Stinson persuaded his bank directors to expand our notes by $30,000 to retire the remaining Bishop shares to treasury.

John would be copublisher and business manager, devoting his prodigious competitive enthusiasms to improving efficiency and sales. He was tall, with a strong torso and a slight limp from early polio. His speech was varied in timbre and rather breathless, the sentences of great lineal range and tumultuous pace, words tumbling out as though he were filling a bin with them against a stopwatch. He walked purposefully, head forward, mixing everywhere in the classless *Star* community. His constant exhortations were followed with an air of conspiratorial fun, and he injected us all with a vigorous optimism.

John became the fourth man on our advertising team, selling over the phone, handling the drop-in trade, masterminding promotions. His government publications background was useful for our major printing customers. Sales of all kinds leafed and stretched. I had a hard-working partner during the day, and the Woods became the Brooks' constant off-hours companions. We were not only going to produce the best weekly, which John agreed was the first priority, but we were also going to make money doing it. I began to think of my work as adventure again, not the lonely, plodding, Sisyphean effort of so many prior years. John accepted the continuing Herman Cohen controversy with light heart and got along well with our relentless visitor.

When Kathy Pulkkinen, who reported Wells and Ogunquit, left in April to have her first child, I was fortunate to replace her with Harvey Elliot, a man with a workman's construction and a dark head, from whose wide mouth and lantern jaw came gentle speech and infectious chortle. He and Bryan Chernack worked together with audible enjoyment in the room over the office I now shared with John, because by that time, glory be, I had retired yet another apartment at 1 High Street.

John's ebullient sales efforts propelled us into extra pages, straining our mechanical capacity. By June we had come to a heady decision: we would take the plunge to photo-offset newspaper production — if the bank would let us. Back we went to Bob Stinson. Bob had observed with no little wonder not only our survival, but also our ability to expand rapidly under back-breaking debt. After he studied our financial statements he listened to our lament that heavy use was wearing out the obsolete equipment. Offset was the wave of the future — we asked for yet another $30,000 for down payments on about $85,000 worth of equipment, including three web-offset press units and a folder, a cold-type typesetting system, camera and darkroom paraphernalia, light tables, a platemaker — essentially what Bud Wright had been installing in Rochester to print the three Alta Group newspapers when I'd bought his Duplex — and more money to cover interior renovations and start-up costs. When all was added, our long-term debt would be upwards of $160,000, meaning an annual payment increase of about $24,000. The year before, 1968, Star Press had lost $11,000. Well, Bob said when he agreed to recommend our proposition to his directors, he might as well be hung like a goat as a lamb.

George Pulkkinen's job at the Intertype machine was phasing out just when he faced fatherhood and a one-paycheck income. He was taking night courses in marine biology, but matriculation was a year and a half away. From his keen interest in community affairs and from setting our stories, he knew the towns better than any reporter, and the tools and styles of writing. I took him aside; when hot metal goes, how about reporting sports for the *Star* until you finish your courses? After brief cogitation, George said, sure, he might be able to do it.

George and Kathy Pulkkinen lived in Arundel, between Kennebunk and Biddeford. We had covered the little community haphazardly until George started reporting. As he gained confidence, George eventually took on Arundel and North Berwick as well as sports.

John and I chose a Goss Community press and an IBM magnetic-tape typesetting system that produced justified proofs for pasteup. Completed pages would be photographed, and the negatives burned into plates for the press. As equipment began arriving, Ellen Stevens started training on the IBM, and we hired a trainee for ad pasteup. For camera and darkroom work we found Dana Mayo, broad, bluff, humorous, and highly skilled.

There was a terrible intensity to those days and nights that blurred the economic realities. Like most other publishers who had "gone offset," we had been aware that we were getting into a more expensive process, but hadn't guessed how much more. Offset gives the weekly shop a more attractive product and a greater capacity that some day, when the investment is retired, can make greater profit possible. But almost no home-printed weekly that adopts offset is so big it doesn't have to grow into it.

The response at Star Press to our expanding horizons was heartening. By the time the press units arrived we had shaken down the other equipment. The week before our first offset newspaper was printed from our own negatives and plates, I recalled the old days and old presses in "Hebdomadal Persiflage," my personal column:

> A machine comes to have its own character, like a person, but the machine's character develops more slowly, and when it does, it is usually ornery. Like ornery old people, old machines can be lovable, in their way. This week, almost immediately after our old Duplex newspaper press falls silent, a faithful, ornery old machine will have dropped into memory for us all. With the Duplex will go one old Intertype, one old Scan-a-Graver, one Teletypesetter, one small process camera, one small platemaker, and almost all the rugged old composing stones and benches that have carried the metal type for printing the local news since before there was a *York County Coast Star,* before there was a *Kittery-Eliot Star,* or a *Wells-Ogunquit Star,* before present ownership, before, perhaps, the old *Eastern Star* became the *Kennebunk Star,* for all I know before the first *Star* was born.
>
> This is not the time to hail new toys — that will come later. It's the time to remember old tools. The memories are bright in reproduction, and often tender in sentiment, but there is a dampness of mold about them, and a clutch at the heart these chilly, dark October nights, as I think back. The memories are of days of unrelieved work and worry, of vanishing youth, waning health, no relief time for old friends, no time for anything but a snatch of mad forgetting, here or there.
>
> I remember vividly the old two-page Whitlock press, and feeding it, sheet by sheet, 1,200 page-impressions an hour. We soon outgrew it, so I bought a Premier, four pages up, and faster. Three years later the Duplex that replaced the Premier printed eight pages up, at twice the speed. We needed all of that. By this summer even the Duplex was too slow. When our three-unit "Community" begins to roll we'll be printing 152,000 page-impressions per hour, a heady speed, one we may never outgrow . . .
>
> Meanwhile, during the time of night in bed, just before sleep, as my mind unwinds in the dark, and the old house creaks in the wind, and the old tendons relax — the old presses roll. On them and

around them I see figures, some oddly youthful, others naturally youthful because they were gone from my view years ago. I see them on the feed platforms flipping the pages, setting them into the cylinder-grippers, watching the turning rack fly, feeling the hydraulic shudder underfoot as the flatbed plunges back and forth. They are surrounded by the shrieking of the gears and the flashing of the shadows and the lights, as the ornery old machines ground out their lives in my service. I remember one form particularly, and one face, and two arms at the stack, and one foot on the impression plunger — and what makes that form so vivid is that it lives on in another dimension, a whipping at the fingers, a dribble of sweat down the small of the back, an ache in the instep, and a frenzy in the mind.

When the Community was together and tested, we were off and running. We now had two more employees, much greater materials expenses, and all that added debt on the heels of our 1968 loss. With no cushion for our bloated bank and finance company payments, we simply had to find more typesetting and press work. Advertising volume and rates would have to rise radically. To pull even again, we'd need annual sales of $400,000, and we were starting at $260,000. I was counting on paying only interest on the Ocean National notes — Bob Stinson had said if we were hurting he could remake them, quarter by quarter.

The new process saved a lot of press time, and the transformation in the looks of the paper was thrilling. Offset illustration was inexpensive, so we used more of it. We all carried cameras and started using the cellar darkroom Jerry Robinson and I had carved out for George Stevens. We sold spot color ads, and experimentally printed our first process-color ad by doubling the web back on a single unit and registering the yellow in reverse. We printed our first 34-page paper December 3, then two 36-page issues back-to-back with Christmas advertising, and even 26 pages Christmas week.

It was toward the end of the year that the *Biddeford-Saco Journal*'s advertising manager, Fred Tebbenhoff, left the *Journal* after a row with Publisher Paul·Cassavant and started a short-lived weekly alternative called the *Biddeford Weekly News Review*. He published it for only a few months, found himself losing money, and offered us his dinky subscription list for a dollar. We weren't ready for more territory, God knew — even if Paul Cassavant didn't — particularly York County's two small cities, which meant daily territory to boot, but we didn't want to knock opportunity when opportunity knocked us. We retired the *Weekly News Review* and sent the *Star* to its former subscribers. We started a

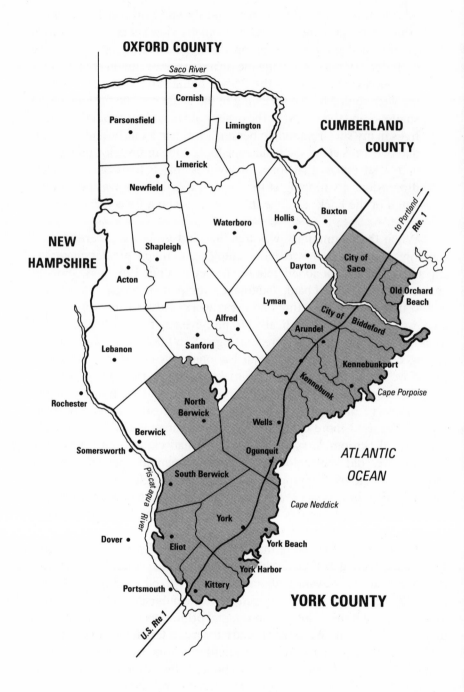

correspondence column offered to us free by *Journal*-hater Ted Dyer, a former *Press-Herald* reporter, covered some of the biggest Biddeford and Saco stories ourselves, and began selling the *Star* on city news-stands. A *Journal* reporter told a *Star* reporter that Publisher Cassavant had gone into an inverted spin by stalling out upside down.

★ 39 ★
Democracy Victorious

The Kennebunk Revolution and the efforts to gag or punish Herman Cohen and me were to continue through 1969 at a rolling boil, with the Establishment swatting at its gadflies in unnatural frenzy. No longer willing to endure the ostracism of his fellow board members, moderate Selectman Ed Winston resigned, leaving a vacancy on the five-member board and leaving the field to what I called the Unified Foursome, or UFO. The assessor and building inspector was fired for a minor breach of etiquette, and a full-time assessor hired. Donald Dulac himself was appointed building inspector, a dubious sideline for a town manager. He proceeded recklessly, committing egregious favors that antagonized the conservationist moderates. The Washington Hose case stretched out unresolved in interminable delays. At a special meeting called expressly for the purpose, the selectmen tried to brand Cohen a liar and me a troublemaker, then planted their minutes in the *Biddeford-Saco Journal*. Cohen sued the selectmen for malicious conspiracy, and this case, too, ran its oft-delayed course.

Cohen's original irritant, the School Board, recommended a school district to replace the school union, a move primarily designed to gain additional state subsidies to build a new high school. Cohen and his antischool coterie fought this proposal tooth and claw, and almost won. The affirmative margin in Kennebunk was only 17 votes. When Cohen petitioned for a ballot recount, the selectmen brazenly decided to judge the contested ballots themselves and in private, and then, without explanation, announced that the district had still won. Cohen was furious and began a 12-year litigious delaying action against the district and its building plans that was to cause even more Establishment fury than his fight with Town Hall.

The school building studies brought me together with a splinter of the super-parent bloc, opposed on the one hand by the costive anti-spending bunch behind Cohen, and on the other by the coalition of Cohen and Brook haters that included educators, middle-class parents, and run-of-the-town Establishment members in rare agreement. The newspaper was the arbiter constant in school and government wars, the battleground for both, and the heavy gun. All factions fought with letters to the editor, and I wrote the editorials that kept the score and called the hits, misses, musters, misters, and Mrs. I was free-agent competition for both Cohen and the Establishment in the school wars, but was Cohen's major confidant in the government struggle.

There was, meanwhile, developing evidence of disillusionment with Town Hall. In the March elections, *Star*-supported candidates Heber Smith, the Cohen collaborator, and James McMahon, a moderate with reform leanings, both won — Smith against incumbent Richard Brown, and McMahon against three Establishment candidates for Winston's unexpired one-year term. The remaining Majority Three worked swiftly, always united, to defeat all motions by the new men. They reelected Bowdoin as chairman and reappointed Chester Cram town counsel, assuring continued disharmony. I wrote:

> Harmony must now wait. Meanwhile there is a fascination in watching the tigers of government running in circles, each with the other's tail in its mouth, and foreseeing the familiar ending when they all turn to butter.

The selectmen's meetings were sullen confrontations, every one — taunt and invective from gavel to gavel — mobbed by partisans who cheered their respective champions and hurled insults all over the room.

Cohen continued to run unsuccessfully for Town Meeting moderator, causing cyclical panic in Establishment ranks. To muzzle him, Clarence Crosby, the Kennebunks' state representative and a rabid Establishmentarian, quietly dropped a seemingly innocuous document in the legislative hopper, proposing an amendment to the municipal enabling act to provide for the annual election of moderators for full municipal years. I heard about it and told Cohen, who surprised Dulac, Crosby, et al. by appearing at the hearing, where he successfully transfixed the legislators with a scathing argument against the bill, which he characterized with epithets familiar to *Star* readers.

Throughout 1969 the Majority Three continued to commit indiscretions in the form of favors to friends and recriminations against Cohen and the Minority Two selectmen. Manager Dulac, as building inspector, compounded his earlier ordinance violations with a permit that caused the new moderate Planning Board chairman to sue to rescind it, and win. The incident was a symbolic turning point for the moderates. With hatred everywhere and the tide turning, Counsel Cram resigned, a serious blow to the Majority Three. Rather than appoint a new counsel, they decided to use the sympathetic legal arm of the Maine Municipal Association.

Little by little the least partisan among the Establishment, by now recognizing that the reforms being offered by Smith and McMahon represented no less than responsible government, were getting uncomfortable with the people they were supporting. Dulac, the flamboyant hired tiger, with his freewheeling machine attitudes, was becoming rather ridiculous. His bosses, Bowdoin, Bibber, and Googins, were encouraging him in discredited political ways. Those would-be town leaders who had been grandly riding the caparisoned horses that pulled the bandwagon of hatred for Cohen and Brook began to look as foolish as they were ineffectual. The good burghers of Kennebunk, who would once have risen as one to shout down a Cohen motion to assist the blind across Main Street, were beginning to praise Cohen with faint damns. A new elite was responding thoughtfully to my editorial arguments. In short, the warmth of public skepticism was in the air, though the entrenched Establishment was too hot to feel it.

Outside the ramparts of Town Hall the revolution had already succeeded. Kennebunk had become the most alert town in America. Democracy was fiercely protected; privilege and class were no longer acknowledged; campaigns were aggressively waged; boards and committees were ethically and legally rigid.

In January 1970, the Majority Three selectmen voted once more, over strident objection from Smith and McMahon, to give Manager Dulac a generous raise and extend his contract prematurely for the year and a half that would take it out of reach of the next board. My first editorial that week was called "The Tale of the Selectmen's New Clothes, or We've Been Workin' on a Railroad." The extension had to be viewed as an extraordinary act of benevolence to Dulac, and because it could only heighten bitterness, I marveled at it. The Majority Three, I wrote, had presented Smith and McMahon

> . . . with a "fait accompli," an old railroad term. . . . At this point things get so transparent as to be laughable, like the Emperor's new clothes. No apologist for Kennebunk today wants to be the first to laugh as the Big Three walk down Main Street in their moral underwear.

I went on to recall 23 of the more flagrant bits of official funny business, and concluded:

> The people of Kennebunk reject the knowledge of contamination in their town. The light has been shining into the obscure corners of small-town psychology, and, lo, it develops that the pillars of society are weak, the smart are dull, the educated are self-deluding, the good are bums, the admired are not admirable — rather among the scorned and derided and spurned you will find the honest and upright and true.

That January Vincent Mason, a sound man of quiet humor, was persuaded to challenge Chairman Warren Bowdoin in his reelection bid. McMahon, whose one-year term was up, filed for the other three-year seat. On March 11 my headline was a banner. McMahon and Mason had both won, to join Smith, leaving a reverse Minority Two of Bibber and Googins to protect Dulac. I was jubilant — the weight of public opinion had moved another notch on the slide, and the balance had shifted.

The new board's first cantankerous meeting lasted far into the night. There was a thrilling expectancy in that room. I wrote that week that the manager's new contract was a toothless document — it failed to mention salary. Until Dulac left there could be no peace at Town Hall.

There followed an electrifying week of ferment all over town. Dulac, given the opportunity to resign, vowed angrily, "I will remain in office," and half his audience shot to its feet clapping and cheering. A temporary manager was appointed by the new majority, and a week of scuffling for the manager's office ensued, ending with a court restraining order obtained by Dulac's attorney to prevent the temporary manager from serving until the case was settled.

At the next selectmen's meeting it was the new majority's supporters, led by Herman Cohen, who arrived early to pack the room, while the Establishment milled about angrily outside behind the closed door, shouting demands that the meeting be reconvened upstairs in the big hall. I could hardly hear what new Chairman McMahon was saying over the din in the corridor. Dulac left the room momentarily to return briefly to confer with Bibber and Googins. Suddenly the three were pushing for the door and leading a surge of their supporters upstairs, yelling epithets over their shoulders as they went.

Upstairs, in a hubbub of cheering, the rump session, two or three hundred strong — the Sore Losers Club, I called them — unanimously approved a motion for recalling, or removing from office, McMahon, Smith, and Mason. Several, brandishing copies of the *Star,* were roundly applauded when they roundly denounced it. A Recall Charter Committee was chosen amid shouts of "Let's pull together!" and "I think we can settle this right now!"

But these people were deluding themselves: there were no provisions for recall in the enabling act that was Kennebunk's authority to govern itself, and when the Sore Losers Club met again its members were chastened, having learned to doubt the legality of their petition, now with nearly a thousand names on it. Most, however, were not ready for moderation and wanted to "get rid of what we don't want in town," pointedly including the *Star*. One man suggested foxily that the "best way to starve a horse is not to feed it."

Judge Wernick heard the restraining order testimony against the temporary manager and the new majority and deliberated. At last he decreed that Dulac should remain manager, but went on to explain how a manager could properly be removed "for Cause." I wrote that I interpreted the words as an invitation to fire Dulac properly — there was plenty of "cause" to fit the description. Dulac must have thought so too, because that week he took the opportunity to resign on a triumphant note, still on the job.

That was late April. In late May, Bibber and Googins, seeing their own support losing interest, decided that they too had had enough and resigned. The new majority, now in complete command, named Herman Cohen, scourge of the developers, not only plumbing inspector, but building inspector as well. The rout was complete.

I couldn't resist a triumphant editorial. I called it "When the Going Gets Tough, the Tough Get Going."

> Stripped of non-essentials, they are quitting because they are outnumbered. They could dish it out, but they couldn't take it. . . . So, they have resigned. Chester Cram resigned. Donald Dulac resigned. Warren Bowdoin and Richard Brown were defeated. The last members of the old inner circle are gone. What is going to happen now?

I suggested some possibilities: the Sore Losers Club would pounce on any mistakes, doing its best to persuade the voters that a breakdown in government was imminent. Then, with three seats open the following March, they would rally behind three Establishment candidates chosen from among

> . . . their recent support phalanx, whose activities during the period of tension just past will be recalled for you by this newspaper when that time comes. They will again lose.

Observing the dignified conduct of the men who had been described to them as power-thirsty despots, the remaining moderates came around. The Establishment's Recall Charter Committee fizzled and died. When the time for elections came again, none of them, not even Dulac, had the heart for an uphill struggle.

Cohen himself was to win a selectman's seat he would hold obstreperously for two three-year terms.

Herman's wife died in 1974, and about six years later Herman died too. The news of his death two years after I had left the newspaper came unexpected to me almost as relief, but one of the saddest things I'd ever heard.

I'd love to tell you the rest of it, how the Cohen influence both directly and subtly affected town government all over York County and beyond, how town officials all over Maine, from selectmen to tree wardens, were made to rethink their methods. Cohen won few of his battles, but he challenged everyone and everything, basking in his prickly reputation as the dangerous man of law and science from La Mancha.

I know and respect some people who still call Cohen evil. He was vain, yes, given to excess, unforgiving, intractable, and many other things we are taught to deplore. But he was a vulnerable, tragic figure too, a man of unfulfilled dreams, of fatal human flaws and no little sentimentality. He changed the way government is conducted in Maine as much as any of his contemporaries did, I think, with no greater title than the one he gave himself at the bottom of his letters to the editor: "Herman Cohen, a Citizen of Kennebunk." He was proud of that title, which he properly regarded as the highest that can be bestowed in a democracy.

Plenty of newspapers make more or less vigorous passes at their governments, but few in America know the drama of a fight to the death with them. Almost none get into the risky business of calling their readers names, particularly not the influential majority that includes many of their advertising and printing customers.

Without the Cohen experience I might never have known what my newspaper could do, and so might never have sorted out my true responsibilities to it. The Kennebunk Revolution honed my political insight. It broadened my understanding of the forces at work in society, by which I guess I simply mean people. It revealed the guts and gizzards of grassroots government to me as nothing less could have done. But Herman's greatest gift to me was what he called second-class citizenship, which few people with the means to defend it ever attain. For the weekly man with his very personal product, such drama is keenest by far.

★ **VII** ★

★ 40 ★

Letters to the Editor

Letters to the editor were the best free copy we got. Sometimes their authors were self-promoting, but most were merely seeking an outlet for personal expression. From the editor's point of view, the most satisfying addressed issues raised by the paper. Whatever the motivation, a healthy letters column is proof of stimulated readership.

You'll find no kook letters in the *New York Times*. Large dailies get so many letters that they publish only well-written, thoughtful comment on current affairs. The weekly paper can publish them all and usually does, because they add a significant dimension to its vitality, a window on the panorama of local opinion.

Unless the newspaper is lively, the letters it receives will be almost exclusively promotional, mildly or markedly self-serving. Early in my experience I was too apt to exercise my editorial advantage by adding footnotes in boldface type. The advantage is unfair — the letter writer has to wait a week to reply, and so should the editor. But when the critical letter writer is making known misstatements of fact, particularly when a vote on his issue will take place before the next week's edition can carry a correction, the misstatements shouldn't be allowed to settle into the public consciousness unanswered.

Humorous letters give the editorial section a pungency beyond the success of the humor itself. Best of all are the funny letters that aren't meant to be funny. When the writers are inveterate out-of-state correspondents, the weekly editor can have some fun denied proper daily editors.

Every weekly gets letters sprinkled with Bible passages chosen to support the writer's views on the general depravity. These letters tend to wander off in unreadable convolutions. When local people write them it constitutes a kindness to return them with apologies, but proselytizers from beyond are fair game. I remember Eugene Changey. From the first of his letters I was surprised to learn that Eugene Changey was God

Himself, writing to me over the signature of His Son. Changey wanted nothing from any of us except publication and attention. He made no appeals — his letters were just friendly expressions of cheer and hope for readers whose faith wavered. I couldn't resist comment:

> It had to happen: as readers last week noted, I have heard from God Himself, Eugene Changey of Maple Heights, Ohio.
>
> From time to time I have heard from Him, but never before so directly. Back in the early 60s I heard weekly from a man whose outpourings of evangelistic fervor slopped from inside his letters all over the envelopes. He wrote particularly to me — he was a subscriber from Massachusetts. He wrote the words he heard from God, but didn't claim kinship, only special consideration. The letters were sources of wonder also to the postal employees, who had to filter around among the afterthoughts on the envelopes to find their delivery instructions. The thrill of receiving the letters was muted by the fact that the spelling was less than perfect. Let me not mince words — the spelling was lousy. The writer was in ferment and cared little for accuracy. The messages called on me to repent — I never did change my ways.
>
> But Eugene Changey is Something Else. Copies of his letter went to other editors, for all I know all of us across this land. I wonder how often the words were published last week, and if Eugene Changey knows. He may be unaware that we did. I like to think he knows.

I also remember Chester Rudnicki, a man of less benign purpose. I heard from him the same week and was again moved to share my delight — and his innovative grammar and spelling.

> A letter addressed to "York County Coast Star, Star Press, inc., Pub," arrived the other day from Presidential Candidate Chester Rudnicki of East Boston. Like the lawyers, I prefer "Bar" to "Pub," and was prepared to cast the letter contemptuously aside when curiosity intervened. Mr. Rudnicki was not a Democratic candidate whose name I recognized, and since the envelope was addressed in longhand, with Republican President Eisenhower's image rated 8¢ upper right, I stayed my casting hand and took a second look.
>
> There were two sheets, one reproducing a letter from Richard (Dick) [sic] Stone, Florida Secretary of State. Incidentally, he signs his name "Richard (Dick) Stone," his secretary types his name that way, and his printer does the same on his letterhead. These friendly

orange-juice people. The letter from Stone (Dick) to Rudnicki couldn't have been more cordial. Apparently Rudnicki is not only a candidate for President, but also for Vice President, and qualifies for both, Stone observes.

The other sheet is the "Mr. Chester Rudnicki, 2nd Announced Democratic Presidential Candidate" platform announcement letter to the media. It is dated January 10, 10972, but Mr. Rudnicki either decided that was too late or too early, because that date is scratched out and "February 9, 1972" handwritten beside it. It is addressed "to all news directors in TV broadcasting facilities," and the salutation is "Dear News Director and their staffs." Here is what Chester Rudnicki has to say to the news director and their staffs, if he are so inclined:

Chester Rudnicki being a 2nd announced Democratic presidential candidate and who resides at 5 Shelby Street, East Boston, Mass.

on December 27, 1971, the candidate was notified by Mr. Richard (Dick) Stone, Secretary of State for Florida that pursuant to the Florida law concerning the Match 14 presidential preference primary. This office has established a press clipping file which indicates that you are a possible candidate for the presidential nomination.

CANDIDATE'S PARTIAL PLATFORM: That Blue Cross and Blue Shields should be non profits medical insurance but it isn't so based on profits they have made in the year og 1970 of about four billion dollars. This profits should be returned back to the insured.

JUSTICE: Based on Mass. state and judicial system which is the worst corrupted judicial system in the country and perhaps there are more in the United States. In Mass. State judicial system the court cases fixing is a natural habits on part of Mass. State court judges and such acts are criminal under thr Federal Criminal Code as well as being violations of Federal Civil Rights Act Statute. Laws must be complied with, even by Mass. state court judges.

UNEMPLOYMENT: As to decrease the unemployment problems in United States is to reduce Social Security retirement ages from 65 up to 62 years of age. The work week should be reduced to 32 hours week with full compensation for 40 hours week. These two would be the only help as to reduce the high unemployment conditions in United States.

PRESS AND NEWS MEDIA BLACKOUT: Candidate is being blacken out by Mr. Yhomas Winship from Boston Globr newspaper, by Mr. Samuel Bornstein from Boston Record American and by Mr. Wayne Thomas from WNAC TV station, by Mr. Arthur Smith with WEEI radio station, and by Mr. Paul Robbind with United Press International. All of said persons are great violators of Federal Civil Rights Act Statute dealing with elective franchise as is mentioned in United States Constitution.

Mr. Rudnicki will not be blacken out by the *York County Coast Star,* or its Pub, Star Press. Perhaps Mr. Rudnicki's faith in the Fourth Estate will be somewhat restored by this knowledge, and we are tickled to be the ones to restore it.

Beyond that, I must say I agree with most of what the candidate has to say. For non profits Blue Cross to make four billion dollars in the year og 1970 is a hell of a note. I am furthermore four-square against court cases fixing as a natural habits on part of Mass. State court judges, as he is. He has a pretty clever answer to unemployment too — I'm surprised no one has thought of it before. It stands to reason that if you cut everyone's workload by one-fifth and reduce the number of workers by taking three years off their working lives, if I understand what Mr. Rudnicki means by "reduce from 65 up to 62," you can't help but create enough jobs for the unemployed who want to be employed. And if they all make as much money as they did before, who's the loser?

I don't really give Mr. Rudnicki much of a chance, with all those news people blackening him out, and that's as good a reason as any to follow the plan to give all candidates the same amount of money from taxes and let them all start even. Otherwise, where does a working stiff figure to get an even break? But give him his share of the $20,000,000 . . .

While I'm on the subject of correspondence with the great, I was fortunate to have another letter from God this week. It was nearly a year ago that I told you about my first letter from Eugene Changey. The salutation itself in this new letter makes me warm all over.

My Dear Mr. Brook: As Almighty God, I greet you.

As you may already know, the newspaper media is My prime and only access to let the world know that I am Truly Alive and do Exist in this Dimension of Time and Light. My Son and I have been affiliated with the newspaper industry for the past ten years.

Most letters We received have been *for* Us. But as Time

rotates, there have also been a few mongrels *against* Us. So you see, My Light is made to shine on the just and unjust alike.

I can assure you, Mr. Editor, there is absolutely nothing to fear to keep this letter from being published in your newspaper. I am the ONLY True and Living GOD in this generation, as also in the past generations. There is NO other God ABOVE Me!

As this letter may also have its rebuttal, I deal out Justice to the just and unjust alike! I love a challenge!

My Son and I have come a long way in these past ten years. This letter is being widely read in newspapers all over the English-speaking world, as well as in many foreign newspapers.

As Time must slowly come to an end, I now close this Blessed Letter which I, YOUR Living GOD, has dictated to you through My Loving Son, who wrote down My Very Sacred Words. Time will never alter My decision not to have My Holy Name written on any document. My humble Son will sign this Blessed Letter to alter fear of destruction!

Prayerfully yours,
Eugene Changey

It is encouraging to hear that God can still rise to the challenge of mortal rebuttal, and to know He and His Son are still plugging away, and have been getting somewhere during the past ten years. But it is with a sense of vicarious pride and satisfaction that I read that Eugene Changey and Junior have been affiliated with the newspaper industry during these ten years of their special progress, from which I may be pardoned to infer that my line of work has been in some small way responsible.

Three years later both of these valued sources of editorial-page copy wrote again, and again I shared my good fortune:

Eugene Changey writes letters for publication. He has an affinity for editors because he himself was once an editor. Quite a few editors fancy themselves to be God Almighty, but so far as I know, Eugene Changey is the only one who has the guts to sign his letters that way. Anyway, it is always nice to hear from the Almighty.

The latest letter from Mr. Changey, I am sorry to report, is full of signs that he is getting on in years, and getting tired. He seems to be turning things over gradually to His Son, and taking it easier. The responsibilities of his position must be vast — I myself have marvelled that one man could handle them all. It appears, however, that the Spirit was willing.

Mr. Rudnicki, on the other hand, is still going strong. His letter of 1972 was full of scathing declamation against the political commentators and editors who were ignoring his bid for the Democratic Presidential nomination. Candidate Rudnicki's platform was difficult to follow, partly because of its cavalier attitude towards the elements of grammar, partly because of its free-falling ideas.

Rudnicki's latest communication is starkly simple, being a mimeographed copy of a Massachusetts legal form. From it I gather that he is suing a bunch of big corporations for ignoring him. Apparently acting as his own lawyer, he "respectfully requests for permission to file" his motion. As far as I'm concerned, he can file it till doomsday and it will never be any sharper than it is today.

> Petitioner's ex parte motion for final decree and judgement (he respectfully submits), in this case being a partial in form.

> Now comes the petitioner in above entailed action, and requests this honorable court to issue a judgements of decrees in partial form in this case. Chester M. Rudnicki seeks a sum of 5 billion dollars agaist each of the following:

("The following" includes 7 radio stations, 4 TV stations, 11 metropolitan dailies, 2 wire services, 8 broadcasting companies, and 3 companies owning mixed electronic and wire service facilities.)

> This is for damages caused to petitioner by all said companies, stations with interference with elective rights of petitioner seeking a national office as Democratic Presidential Candidate in 1968, 1972, and for 1976. At Suffolk Superior Court all have received great protection in the case, in violations of equal protection of law clause under the 14th Amendment to the U.S. Constitution. Wheretofore, Chester Rudnicki prays that this requests is granted according to the law.

O.K. That is the statement of a man who has sustained $170,000,000,000.00 worth of damage to his reputation by being ignored. At a lousy 5% interest the income on the money Mr. Rudnicki will receive each year if the court grants his request would be $8,500,000,000.00. You won't catch this newspaper ignoring his third try for the nomination next year, on that you can rely.

Then there was an irresistible letter to the editor of *Clue,* our humorous summer magazine. I began my column by explaining that Peter Agrafiotis wrote most of the zany stories in it. That year, however, Peter had run short of copy, so at the last moment I had filled it out with a

few humor pieces of my own, one of them a blatant spoof with prepos-
terous events and figures lifted from a *Star* anniversary–April Fool
edition. First the April Fool story:

Salmon Run Starts
in Local Tidewaters

The salmon are back! Earliest run in history has been reported this
week in local rivers. First report came when Henry Armitage,
worm-fishing for blackbacks in Branch Brook, saw his bobber go
under. He knew that no blackback could pull that bobber below the
surface.

He leapt up from under the tree, picked up his pole, and tried to
set the hook, without success. But the poison in the bait soon took
effect, and the small salmon, for such it turned out to be, floated to
the surface, belly up.

After that, reports came thick and fast. Salmon were seen passing under the Mousam River bridge, small at first, twelve or
thirteen pounders. Then lobstermen at Government Wharf saw the
tell-tale gleams in the water on the flood tide. In the Josias River
young Peter Ramsdell waded into the icy water and headed off a big
one in the tidal shallows, pounced on it, and dragged it up the sand.
Until Tuesday noon it was the biggest landed between York and
Biddeford Pool, weighing in at 43 pounds, 7 ounces.

The big ones came with a rush that afternoon. The streams were
so crowded that some of the bigger fish, gasping for water, kept
choking on the smaller ones that got in their way. In this condition
they were easy prey for the club-fishermen, who beat the water
constantly, stunning a great many fish. Biggest salmon caught as
we go to press is Amy Worthing's 109-pound Chinook. While Amy
used a tuna rod and reel, Bob Scully caught another in Mill Creek
that weighed in at 103 pounds dressed and was thought to be a
bigger fish. Bob used a whole codfish for bait and caught his fish
handlining from the Route 9 bridge. His was a landlocked salmon.
So far the Pacific salmon caught in this run have been small — 35
pounds and under, but the big ones that feed on them are always
about a week behind.

Hundreds of fishermen lined the riverbanks the first day, but by
now most of them are arm-weary and the riverbanks are deserted.
All local freezers are full, and salmon is selling for 3¢ a pound in
local markets. The streams are so crowded that some of the old-
timers who remember the runs of 1904 and 1911 are saying that the
fish are so stacked in the streams that they won't have room to turn

around for their return trips to the sea, and that next year might be a lean one if too many of them keep leaping up onto the mud to die.

One *Clue* reader from Haverhill, Massachusetts, took the trouble to write the following letter to the editor of *Clue* on lined yellow foolscap. He signed it "Mr." and then his name, so I assume he was an irate adult male.

Dear Sirs:

I recently picked up a copy of your magazine. In this magazine is a story utterly improbable. The story is about the big salmon run in local tidewaters. This ridiculous story tells about 109 lb. chinook salmon and 102 dressed out landlocks. There was nothing said in the newspaper about this "fairytale." The landlocked salmon in your story is the most unbelievable since the present day world record is only 22 pounds 8 ounces. The landlocked salmon in your story was supposedly caught in Mill Creek. This is completely impossible because landlocked salmon do not migrate to the sea. They live only in lakes. This story is completely and utterly ridiculous and disgraces your magazine to have such garbage in it. It also happens that chinook are not found in the Atlantic Ocean. I can't understand how you could let such a fraud be printed. I would like to know who wrote this article so I can write him the same as I told you.

Yours untruly

I got a sheet of *Clue* stationery, grasped a pencil firmly in my left fist, and snapped off the following reply:

Deer M. F.,

You got one hell of a nerve. What dose any body in Haverhill know about salmon. We got bigger fish in our sewer pipes than you got in the whole Merrymack River.

Yourn

I glued a stamp to it and sent it off. I wish I could have been a fly on the wall when he opened his mail.

★ 41 ★

"Number One"

The three-year Kennebunk Revolution and the much longer school jeremiad, during which I served on contentious committee after committee — both superimposed on our expensive conversion to offset printing — had a devastating effect on our treasury. Devastating because so many of our customers were Kennebunk Establishment people, but not fatal, because now we were regional. Inflation had pushed forward our theoretical break-even sales figure from $400,000 to $470,000 by 1971. Actual volume had grown faster — from $260,000 to $420,000, but even so leaving us still losing money, still adding people.

By mid-1970 major payables were where they were before Bill Bishop — six and more months delinquent. We were back to the assorted horrors of stalling creditors and pacing the collection circuit on Fridays to cover payroll. In August, two weeks before an Ocean National quarterly note payment was due, Bob Stinson called me to say that interest payments would no longer suffice; the bank was calling in an $8,000 demand note. I reacted with shock — if we wrote nothing but payroll checks for two weeks we couldn't put half of that together.

I sensed trouble behind Bob's uncharacteristically terse replies. Was it the effects of the Kennebunk Revolution on his directors, or knowledge of our desperate circumstances? Or was the bank itself in trouble? I never knew which, but it may have been mostly the latter, because in two months Bob himself would be gone.

Alarmed, I called Canal National, a much larger statewide institution whose recent branch opening had given Kennebunk a second commercial bank. Eager to overcome Ocean's home-court advantage, to my immense relief Canal ignored our peril and agreed to assume Ocean's notes and mortgages, even advancing us additional cash in return for our payroll and checking accounts.

Canal's apparent faith revived my shaken self-confidence, but John saw things more starkly. Even with Pam's high school salary, the Wood bills were mounting. Late that month John pulled a chair up to my desk.

He'd been offered a good job in Washington and had to take it. He'd keep his *Star* stock, hoping to return some day. His family would remain — he'd be a frequent visitor. He did his best to buttress my sagging spirits — the newspaper and printing volumes were both growing fast; maybe in a year or two volume would pass the break-even point. Meanwhile, I wouldn't have to pay his salary.

The September 2 issue was John's last; I staggered forward with sinking heart. Again I took George Pulkkinen aside: I'd need blocks of time I couldn't find; he knew the people and the process, and was a first-class newsman. How about being managing editor? George said yes.

Before John left we had started setting type for and printing a small tabloid weekly and an Air Force Base paper, both in New Hampshire, and several high school papers, all marginal short-run jobs for the web press. We had also found some advertising flier jobs with longer runs. We were filling the Heidelbergs with books, pamphlets, and state printing jobs, bidding low to build a printing base beyond York County. What we desperately needed was at least one big, regular, long-run job to keep the newspaper web press rolling.

Milliken-Tomlinson was a food supplier for the eastern supermarket chain IGA. Once a month they ordered slick advertising fliers from a giant Chicago printer. No one was then printing process-color fliers on small newspaper presses. When I asked the shop people if we could hold color registration for a long run on our Community press, Dana Mayo and Bezo Bissonnette, the cameraman and newspaper foreman, were optimistic. With no little trepidation I asked ad manager Kai Suhr's successor, Dick Roberge, to approach Milliken-Tomlinson's Portland ad agency for the chance to quote on printing their Maine–southern New Hampshire fliers, including the typesetting and pasteup they had been doing themselves, even including the distribution.

Our prices and our promise of one week from rough layout to delivery, instead of Chicago's three, finally overcame the agency's skepticism, and after months of Dick's lobbying, the agency prevailed upon Milliken-Tomlinson to give us a trial.

Here was our big, precarious opportunity, the job that might save us. I crossed my fingers and put my faith and hopes in my crew.

Our schedule was bottle-tight and carefully planned. Monday we received rough layout. That day and Tuesday we set type and pasted it up during our heaviest newspaper schedule. Wednesday morning the Milliken-Tomlinson man checked our proofs, gave us last-minute prices, stayed till these had been set and pasted, then left. That afternoon Dana shot, stripped, and burned plates, working into the evening. After printing the last sections of the *Star,* Bezo, Larry Hill, and Bob

Kinne cleaned the press, filled the ink fountains with color, and re-threaded the web over our three press units — one short of four-color process — doubling back on the last unit to the yellow fountain to accept the reverse-burned plate Dana would prepare. They left the shop about 9 P.M. and returned at 6 A.M. Thursday to find Dana's plates, clamp them to the cylinders, and adjust the color and register at slow speeds.

As they revved up for production a small gang of the Wednesday evening collators returned to jog, count, and bundle for Roger Lovejoy, whose truck was backed up to the door. By noon Roger rolled off with his first load on the southern run, returning Friday morning. By Friday evening all fliers were printed. Roger loaded that night and delivered to the northern newspapers Saturday morning and early Monday for Tuesday inserting.

Nothing could go wrong; a press or truck breakdown could cost us everything — as could illness, or undetected pricing error, or bad color register. All of our processes were slower than Chicago's, but we were close to source and delivery, and we were the whole show. Our quality surprised everyone. Market sales volume traceable to response to our fliers printed on newsprint was essentially identical to that from the slicker Chicago fliers, and total expense for participating IGA markets was about half. As the weeks went by and Milliken-Tomlinson's confidence in us grew, more independent IGA owners began to come aboard, and pressrun and frequency steadily increased. Eventually we were doing a flier almost every week, with pressruns of more than 320,000, a $150,000-a-year job — but not that year, or the year after.

Several months after our first IGA flier, Shaw's markets, bigger locally than IGA, observing IGA's success, decided to try us. I financed another unit for the press to make process color printing less risky, and incidentally to give us a 16-page section capability for the *Star*. When the two fliers coincided, we went double-shift with the same crew. Shaw's started with 230,000 fliers once a month, and over the next few years increased the run to 410,000 and the frequency to 40 times a year. Other printers with similar presses, seeing what we had done, grew bolder and started bidding — unsuccessfully — for our jobs. Associated Grocers also joined us for a time, and others occasionally, until by 1976 our web press business exceeded half a million dollars.

There was one other bright spot in 1971, but only one. Almost all respectable American weeklies and most dailies are National Newspaper Association (NNA) members and enter its annual contests. I had joined the year before, in 1970 — the year under judging review for 1971 awards, and Kennebunk's sesquicentennial year. In the *Star* I had celebrated the sesquicentennial with a supplement about town history done in antique format, an expensive labor of several months, 160 tabloid pages in nine sections. It had won first prize for Special Editions in the New England Press Association competition, and I chose to send it to the nationals as well, whose results would be announced in June 1971.

As in the New England competition, most of the NNA prize classifications were open to all newspapers, daily and weekly, but General Excellence was judged by circulation class. With our 1970 circulation average of 6,600 we were competing with about 1,500 other weeklies in the second largest class (6,000 to 10,000).

On the Wednesday before the awards gala, an NNA bulletin arrived by mail. In it was the news that we had won second prize for Special Edition, outscored only by a Florida daily, and first prize for General Excellence in Class 2. The judges' comments were reproduced in the bulletin:

> What's with the editor of the *York County Coast Star*, anyway? Didn't the guy ever go to journalism school? Hasn't he read Ed Arnold's books on how to put a newspaper together? Doesn't he know that you aren't supposed to have dinky little heads — or worse still, no heads at all to crown all that type running to the top of the page? And what's with all the Down East flavor, and the essays and features on unexpected subjects? Does the *Star* have to print every blessed thing about every blessed person in every cove and cranny along the coast?
>
> Ah, yes, the *Star* is so different from every other weekly in the country that it stands out like the sparkling gem it is. The editor is obviously too contrary to do things properly, but we'll bet his readers are waiting at the gate every Wednesday, because he understands them, and his newspaper is beamed right at them.

My editorial that week was called, of course, "Number One." After describing the contest results, I commented defensively:

> To be sure, a different set of judges might have decided otherwise — probably would have, in view of this set's comments — but the award gives us courage to say we have as much right as any to call ourselves the best weekly newspaper in America. In the wild time we all had in the shop Wednesday evening getting the *Star* to bed and in the bags, we were all saying we might as well call ourselves the best weekly in the world, maybe in the whole blushing galaxy.
>
> Our critics, bless 'em, see a great many things wrong with the *Star*. They detect factual errors, misspellings of names and places,

typographical errors, grammatical ones, stories or photos missed that should have been written or taken, stories crowded out and published a week late, advertising errors — whatever mistakes can be made in this business, we have made them. If we had the money and manpower available to many of our competitors, we might be more nearly perfect.

So we say to our critics — and we number ourselves among that ornery bunch — if we can win with all our faults it must be because it's hard to publish a newspaper with fewer faults, and we hope you'll accept that excuse for not giving you something better.

No matter what comes after, nothing will equal the spirit, and very few will equal the spirits, with which the thirty-four regulars who have a day-to-day part in Star Press celebrated the news that they were Number One. That, friends, can really break a man up.

★ 42 ★

Flirting with a Sale

Before our offset operation turned profitable, the financial horrors of the year and a half after John Wood left took their toll. Beyond that, years of recuperation would follow, years of paying off debt and bringing current payables down to manageable proportions. I was plunged backward five years into the old frenzy of round-the-clock, round-the-week work. My own journalism turned perfunctory as the business beast tightened its grip.

I was 49, tired and disheartened, running scared. Unable to hire more help, I was spending weekends on job-work composition, the side effect of an encouraging spurt of business from Boston and Washington, where John was doing what he could to help. It was all slow pay, though, and the Boston people, our biggest job-work customers ever, left with a bad debt that turned our modest loss into a bigger one.

I did the quoting on our bid jobs, manned any machine the printers were too busy to mind, did the management chores John had been doing, yo-yoed from customers to personnel to maintenance to money problems.

I ate, slept, and worked with a monkey on my back whispering in my ear. Failure haunted me by day, numbed me by night. I couldn't even seem to read any more — my eyes jumped and wandered.

The thought of selling out completely, or of finding a majority partner, had been an attendant specter for 13 years. Now I felt drawn to it, as to a dark corner. Maybe an impersonal corporate partner could drag Star Press from under its stifling carpet of debt. I yearned for normal work weeks, vacations, time to revive myself and my marriage. The kids were 15, 17, and 19, reared in a dangerous decade. There was no one to talk to any more, even at home — after too many years of dashed hopes, poverty, and working strain, Anneke and I were arriving at the divorce conclusion.

But maybe I could save everything yet. It took all my resolve to act. In early 1971 I told Anneke what I had in mind.

Jean Gannett Hawley was chairman of the company that owned the Portland, Waterville, and Augusta dailies, and the Portland radio and television stations. I called to see if she and her directors might be interested in owning Star Press. Mrs. Hawley was away; talk to the financial man, I was told. On appointment day I dusted off my best pre-Kennebunk suit and drove up to talk to him, a man of about 60, neither cordial nor otherwise. He asked the usual questions and looked expressionlessly at my financial statements.

I talked — the talk flowed from me. Here was the deal: his company could own the best weekly in Maine. Sure, it wasn't profitable, but that was because it was underfinanced and had grown too fast. We covered half of York County — the rest belonged to the *Sanford Tribune* and *Biddeford-Saco Journal*. We already had a toe in Biddeford, Saco, Old Orchard, Sanford, Alfred, and Lyman, as well as solid readership in 11 other county towns. The remaining 9 tiny hinterland communities had no newspaper allegiances. With Gannett money and prestige we could blast into the Sanford-Biddeford-Saco areas before the sluggish Alta Group woke up and blow the *Tribune* and *Journal* right out of the water. We'd beef things up, maybe lose money for the year or two it would take to put the competition to rout. Then we'd go daily, but daily with the *Star*'s interests and format. The same people would still buy the *Press-Herald* for state and world news and the syndicated stuff.

In great detail I had set out cost and income projections. A circulation of 25,000 was an easy early goal. We already had sufficient press capacity, but in my prospectus I included a second four-unit Community press, a new typesetting system, a fleet of delivery trucks — the works. Using modest ad-rate figures, I came to an annual gross of about

$3,250,000 for the newspaper alone. Profit came in at nearly 40 percent, current quality maintained. I would come reasonably, myself, for a long-term contract. The foundation had been laid: I had the central location, the shop, the people, the county experience, the newsstand distribution mostly in place. What about it?

Very interesting, the financial man allowed. He'd be in touch.

"I think they'll go for it!" I told Anneke. "They'd be chumps not to."

I was wrong, at least about supposition one, for reasons I didn't suspect. The man called me. He had presented the deal to his board members, and they had turned it down. He started with confetti: they felt my figures were too optimistic. Maybe we could do it with so few people, but they couldn't.

But, I argued, wouldn't half the profit I had projected be enough? There were other savings I hadn't even mentioned.

Well, the man said, let's face it, they didn't need us. The standoff between us and the other county papers was fine with them. They were content with their York County circulation and comfortable with the *Journal* there, stagnant, in Biddeford.

A few days later *Journal* publisher Paul Cassavant called me. Cassavant was the nephew of a former publisher who had chaperoned Paul up through the business ranks. He was rather tall, with eyeglasses and a small, moist mouth. Over the phone he wasted no breath in banter. He had heard I might be wanting to sell. How about talking in his office next day?

Cassavant's office was unadorned and uncluttered. He greeted me without expression, and we got right down to fence and parry. Within minutes I had reaffirmed my resolve never to work in a situation that called for recurrent contact with Paul Cassavant. Nor, I felt, did Cassavant have any thought of recommending purchase to his principals. Either someone had told him to talk to me, or he was just trying to find out how much I was hurting. I was the enemy in the water without a life ring, while he leaned on the taffrail watching the water widen between us. The interview produced nothing, not even a follow-up call.

These two discouragements melted what starch remained in me. I became dead weight, a drag on Anneke's once plucky and cheerful spirit. My dark, silent moods, after all those years of making do, led to increasing anger and recrimination as her divorce convictions strengthened. I was too hurt and too proud to do anything but urge her to take the final steps.

Dave Strater represented me in little Saco courthouse — I did not appear. Anneke would have our Cape Porpoise home, a modest monthly alimony and child support check, and half our possessions. I would have the other half and my Star Press shares. It was autumn, the off-season, so I rented a small, winterized cottage at Wells Beach where I could feed unobserved on my despairs and lick my bachelor wounds in isolation.

I decided to play my last gambit. Again I advertised, this time offering a majority interest with an option to buy all remaining shares. The likeliest of the replies came on a Chicago letterhead from Steven Boynton, working partner at a small firm offering advice to buyers of stocks and bonds. He was really a journalist, he wrote, who wanted to redevote himself to newspaper work. He had enough liquid assets to make the down payment specified, and a readily salable home that would bring him the balance needed to buy 51 percent of my stock. He had access to other money, too, he assured me, to buy the other 49 percent over a reasonable period of time.

Boynton flew east, and we talked. He was about 42, dark-haired, straight-featured, from the middle southwest, friendly, with sober deportment. His body was rather large and heavy, his face once good-looking, now with a soft fullness under the chin. He was a teetotaler, an ardent member of the Church of Christ, Scientist — he had ascertained that there was a Kennebunk chapter and looked forward to regular pilgrimages to the Mother Church in Boston. Dress was imitation Madison Avenue, speech heartily confidential, motions slow.

Well, so what? I was in spiritual purgatory and business extremis.

Boynton said he'd decided he didn't want to buy stock, after all — he wanted assets, an outright sale, for depreciation purposes; full ownership, with a promissory note to me backed by Star Press assets. I wasn't enough of a man of finance to know the implications, tax and otherwise. I hesitated, but agreed — I didn't want to lose him. Boynton said he'd keep me on, at least for a couple of years; I would guide him aright.

During his three-day visit Boynton typed out what seemed like an innocuous document and asked me to sign it. The earnest money and down payment he could get immediately, but if he were to sever his current business ties, sell his home, and move himself and his family east, he'd have to have this letter of intent before returning to Chicago — fair enough. With the letter he'd raise the immediate cash needed while he went about liquidating his own assets. The letter we both signed merely said that I agreed to sell the business to him at a specified price, down payment specified, note at 7 percent, closing date no later than a date specified, about two months thence.

Throughout our discussions I had repeatedly insisted that the down payment should be his own money, not borrowed, not venture capital, no phantom partners. The man who ran the business should take the risk. God knew there were easier ways than weekly newspapering to make money, we agreed. But before he left for Chicago I had begun to suspect that his only motivation was money.

Soon Boynton was back with his family. He rented a house and started arriving midmorning at the plant to occupy John Wood's former desk in my office and to wander around talking to people. I explained to my employees that Boynton was a possible investor. When stories began coming back to me from the street that he was introducing himself to local businesspeople as the owner-to-be, I had to allow that we were discussing it.

Finally I sat him down and closed the office door. He had been there a week now; where was the escrow money? Oh, he replied, he didn't have his separation money yet. His house was on the market, but it was taking time to liquidate his securities. He was getting his family settled, enrolling the kids in school. He would return to Chicago soon to close out his affairs, and we could get things moving when he returned. The deal, he assured me, was "golden."

He had wanted to get the feel of the business, he added, and had some ideas about making it more profitable. I listened aghast. He thought he'd split it into two companies, a holding company by another name, and the old operating company renting quarters and equipment from the holding company. He'd sell the printing business and machinery to raise capital, and might even sell the real estate and newspaper equipment with a lease and a contract to print.

Hold on! I couldn't agree to that! What would back up my note? What about the Star Press printing family?

He dropped the subject but, I was sure, not the idea. I began to see dangers everywhere. Once I had the down payment and he had the assets, he could do as he pleased. In my paranoiac state I had recurring visions of Granville Rideout and his oceanographic college.

I drove him to the Portland airport for his Chicago plane. He said he'd keep in touch by phone, but I wouldn't be able to reach him, because he'd be moving around.

A week went by before he called. Things were moving, but slower than he'd hoped. He might not have all the down payment by closing date, but we could complete the formalities, and the rest would follow shortly. I insisted that we keep to our original agreement. All right, he said, no sweat. He'd find the money, even if he had to borrow from friends.

Wait! That wasn't our agreement! It had to be *his* money. He backed off again, but when I reread the letter we'd signed, I knew I couldn't make that stick, either. If he made the down payment before deadline, he'd own the company. Then, if he chose, he could sell the real estate and equipment, pay the money to himself as salary, pay no bills for four or five months, and declare the company bankrupt, leaving me with a worthless note. I had signed a loose agreement that bound only me. The more I thought about it, the crazier I got.

Two weeks remained till closing date. Several days later I heard from Boynton again. From Chicago the voice was cheerily confident. He was hot on the trail of the money — should have it in a few days. He had friends who were going to lend it to him. I reasoned that he could have mortgaged his home by this time, if he hadn't already sold it, withdrawn the savings he'd spoken about, and sold his securities. He must be looking for venture capital.

I prayed constantly that I wouldn't hear from Boynton again until our closing deadline was past. The midnights kept coming, one by one. When the final midnight of the deadline sounded, I let off steam like a tired donkey engine and sat down with a fifth of whiskey to congratulate myself into a stupor from which, finally, sweet sleep came.

Four or five evenings passed before the phone rang. Boynton's bouncy voice was asking me how the weather was, up there in Maine.

Fine.

Well, he said, he hadn't quite put the deal together yet, but things were on track. The deal was golden. "It'll fly!"

I stopped him there. No, the deal was grounded. His deadline had come and gone. I was disenchanted, and had other plans. I was sorry he'd gone to so much trouble. I had lived up to my end of the bargain; for whatever reasons, he hadn't lived up to his. My mind was made up.

There was a long silence at the other end of the wire, then a surprisingly calm voice said, OK, if that's the way things were, no hard feelings. I had been prepared for protests, and pleadings for more time.

Boynton sued me and Star Press for breach of contract. He took nearly a year to do it, and another half year to bring his case to court. He wasn't suing to buy the company, but for damage to his career. The figures on the suit document seemed extravagant, but that was the going legal philosophy. He retained Roger Elliot, partner in Charles Smith's Saco law firm, which was known for its antagonism toward me. A sense of this and other ironies colored my thinking about my certain defense expenses and possible ruination. Dave Strater's new law partner, Frank

Hancock, betrayed no confidence of winning. I was incredulous —
I had scrupulously honored the only document, drafted privately by
Boynton and signed privately by me. I, more than Boynton, had
been damaged in lost opportunities. How could I have sold as specified
if he couldn't buy? Shouldn't I countersue? Why couldn't Hancock
persuade the judge that the suit was baseless? Anyway, why a jury
trial?

Hancock's responses were that Boynton was exercising his right to
trial by jury in a criminal case; the judge couldn't predict what form the
argument would take; and countersuing would be expensive and of
dubious outcome.

Hancock and I drove to the Saco law offices where Roger Elliot
took my deposition. I felt sure enough of my facts and my innocence to
be long-winded, getting everything on the record. Hancock listened
nervously while Elliot fidgeted — Boynton's legal-fee meter was spin-
ning. "I've got all afternoon," I told Elliot when he pleaded for
brevity — he had asked the questions.

Our presiding judge was Sumner Goffin. Lawyer Elliot, armed
with my copious deposition, was baiting me on the stand. Aha! he
exclaimed triumphantly, but only once. How did I square what I had just
answered under oath with my answer to the same question in my
deposition? He read from the deposition, then called on the court
stenographer to read back my answer. When I pointed out that the
answers were identical in meaning, and nearly so in wording, I was sure
the jury took notice.

In the gracious old county courthouse Boynton sat expressionlessly, his body facing me and the judge, but his eyes on the tabletop in
front of him. Elliot made no case for bad faith and had no surprises. The
informal letter was the only exhibit, and it favored me. When Judge
Goffin charged the jurors, he said merely that one of us was lying; their
job was to decide which.

While the court recessed and the jury deliberated, Boynton approached me in the nearly empty courtroom, smiling palely with his
hand out. "No hard feelings," was what he offered. I ignored the hand.
Whichever way it went, I told him, he was an opportunist and a liar, with
a phony suit designed to make him some money and ruin me, and he and
I had nothing to say to one another.

The jury must have felt unanimously as I did. I heard later that
Boynton had moved to Florida, where he was doing something in the
condominium line. I paid Hancock $2,500 for his time and went home
smarter.

★ 43 ★

Personal Storm Clouds

A year and a half before Boynton's suit against me was settled, as soon as I had told him that our deal was grounded, I had advertised again. I didn't want another down-payment-for-assets deal, certainly. This time I asked for a partner who would agree to hold a minority interest at first, but who would be willing to buy all remaining shares owned by me and long-absent John Wood according to an agreed schedule.

Robert Brigham was the likeliest among seven men who answered my ad. He was ten years my junior, prematurely white-haired, very tall, quick of speech and mind, assured, reserved, a successful journalist in tweed suit and vest. He had grown up near Gloucester, Massachusetts, where he had done some boating and commercial fishing. After college he had taken an editorial staff job with the daily *Gloucester Times,* then had gone to *Life* magazine, where he had spent 14 years as photographer-writer in prestigious company, serving as Paris correspondent, Moscow bureau chief, and finally as the junior member of *Life*'s two-man editorial-writing team. He was tired of suburban living on the New York Central's Westchester line and wanted to do something on his own. The *Star* and its territory appealed to him — he, his wife, Becky, and their two young daughters would be happy in Kennebunkport.

Bob had $60,000 to invest immediately, this time to pay me personally for shares of mine rather than buying treasury stock, as John Wood and Bill Bishop had done. Bob would have five successive annual options to buy more from me, up to 51 percent of Star Press. Then, when I would be 55 and John Wood 49, Bob, or Bob and others, would buy all remaining shares. He would concern himself primarily with business duties. I would remain president, publisher, and editor until he owned a majority interest. We agreed to pay ourselves $15,000 apiece per year, a pittance for him, but half again as much as I had been paying myself. He would also have his substantial *Life* pension.

Once we had established philosophical rapport and concurred on aims and ambitions for the newspaper, we discussed job printing.

Neither of us relished managing that part of the business or had strong faith in it, but I told Bob I wouldn't agree to drop it. Aside from my loyalties to so many employees, the irrecoverable capital investment it represented and its value to any future sale of stock or assets made dropping it unthinkable.

Bob told his lawyer to subdue his natural lawyerly instinct for the jugular and write a fair document. I would use a lawyer only to check his contract. I insisted that even though John Wood had broken his contract with me when he left for Washington, he should receive the same considerations, short of payroll status, as Bob and I.

The three of us met on a snowy February weekend in my Wells Beach pad. First, we negotiated value per share. Gross volume for the previous 12 months had risen by that time to $550,000. To decide where, between half of base and base plus 20 percent, Star Press should be valued, we next counted our blessings: proud, integrated communities; working populations no longer dependent on a few dominant industries; area attractive and recreationally diverse; high caliber of company staff; growing, enthusiastic readership; suitably modern equipment; history of rapid business expansion; owning our own plant; rising potential for ad rates and printing prices; 97 years of uninterrupted publication; quality product.

Then we listed the minuses: several other, fringe-area publications and radio stations, and one internal weekly, in York; sharp seasonal sales fluctuations; no large advertising centers; low per-reader income; high rural costs for most essentials; high cost of sales, news coverage, and distribution due to our small-town, centerless territory; printing a substantial part of gross; history of losses and marginal profits. When we balanced it all out, we assumed a base of $500,000.

Next we deducted current and long-term debt, then added receivables, and arrived at a value for all shares of about $400,000. John's shares had more than doubled in value; mine were worth $340,000. When he paid me $60,000, Bob would own about 15 percent, compared with the Woods' 16.

Among the safeguard paragraphs we carved out during that snowbound weekend was one that would prove significant to the point of terminality. It was designed to protect the interests of the two minority shareholders, first Bob and John, and then, if Bob exercised his stock-buying options during the subsequent five years, John and me. We agreed that if one shareholder wanted to sell, the other two would be offered the seller's shares in proportion to their own share interests at the time, at a price per share governed by the same formula we had used to arrive at current market value. If either one would not buy, the other could buy all offered shares. If neither would, the company itself would be obliged to buy.

It would transpire that the growth momentum of the prior years would continue in force, that our formula share value would rise beyond Bob's financial expectations, and that he would exercise no further options.

With my own writing involvement waning, before Bob arrived I had called Peg Hendrick, once the one-person *Star* advertising department. Peg had spent several years at home before launching a new career as gem of the otherwise lack-lustre *Biddeford-Saco Journal* reporting staff. *Journal* Publisher Paul Cassavant was moving into the Kennebunks to counter our mild northward intrusion with the remnants of Fred Tebbenhoff's *Weekly News Review*. Peg came home joyously to take on most of my Kennebunk-Kennebunkport beat, responding to every reader request, no story too humble or too difficult for her. Her audience, fed up with my school and town government fixations, reacted warmly.

My initial gambit into Biddeford, Saco, and Old Orchard Beach had been to hire a young man named David Déspres to split his time between reporting and selling, extending our coverage — thinly — the full length of the York County coast. Déspres was a writer of only modest, promotional talent, but while he stayed he did a job that served as a wedge to be driven deep by his successor. His few stories, and the free correspondence column offered by Ted Dyer, constituted no more than a leaflet-drop into the *Journal*'s territory, but they were viewed by Paul Cassavant as a *Journal*-istic Pearl Harbor.

Déspres lasted less than a year. Before he left, Bob Brigham and I decided to hire a full-time reporter for the twin cities. Our choice was Myron Levin, who started resoundingly in high gear, going head to head with the B.S. *Journal*.

Half the money Bob paid me I invested, and another $5,000 went into my checking account for an alimony and child-support cushion. The rest I set aside and began a three-month search. Sailing had been a passion of my youth in Maine and a factor in my return. Anneke had learned this passion, too, in the succession of little old boats we had found and anchored in our tidal cove in Cape Porpoise. Now I could have a bigger one. What I found moored in a New Jersey harbor in May was a lovely 36-foot auxiliary sloop, raced in those waters by its owner, which I rechristened *Crazy Horse*.

Relieved of the day-to-day frustrations of life together, Anneke and I had begun seeing each other again, reinvigorating our courtship of long standing. On three successive spring weekends, while I expanded like a bullfrog, I and some friends, Anneke and Art Hendrick among them, sailed *Crazy Horse* northward to a mooring I had dropped out beyond all the others into the waters near the mouth of broad, island-rimmed Cape Porpoise Harbor. I rationalized my extravagance by calling *Crazy Horse* home during the warmest six months, when rents in our resort communities rocketed beyond the altitude in which my wallet could breathe repeatedly.

Until the November weather drove me ashore, I rowed each morning to my pickup truck by the distant pier, and each evening back to *Crazy Horse* after work, often late at night. I'd cook and eat my supper and drink my rum standing in the hatchway in solitary contemplation of sky, islands, and wind-stirred water. In November, when I sailed over to winter storage, I moved back into the old Cape Porpoise home, Anneke's now, for another test of our tolerances. We managed to stick it out together through the winter and spring, by which time my tenant status and our ingrowing habits and preferences had rubbed the old wounds raw. Too many things had been said that could no longer be unsaid. In the spring I left again, and withdrew again, and licked my wounds on *Crazy Horse,* till once more we would begin again with dinners out, then move closer again, as of old.

By now our children were nearly grown. Only Eben remained at home with Anneke, but that summer he left too, and I moved back in for what turned out to be only a few months. The old aggravations were still there, but closer to the surface and deeper into the gut than ever. So when that summer ended I once more left the home I loved for what we agreed would be the final going. We divided our belongings, and from my share I carted the things I most hated to leave to the bottom half of a little rented house at the head of Cape Porpoise Harbor, where I settled into my future alone, disconsolate, in the autumn of 1974. I felt beaten, and poor, and unfulfilled, without enthusiasm even for my work.

I had written every story more than once, and editorialized on every recurring theme. I was stretching for new ways to say old things, and my writing turned flabby. I could no longer bring myself to work so hard or produce anything spirited from my tired mind. I relinquished my writing assignments to others and turned my attention to our galloping business expansion, in the process losing much of my zest for local affairs.

I had never supplied the conventional staff direction, preferring to encourage by example. Now I no longer had an example to offer. Managing Editor George Pulkkinen became more and more the force that moved the newspaper forward, and drove it to the barn Wednesdays. George, himself driven, was much admired in the abstract but not universally loved by his crew. He was a taskmaster, as a managing editor should be. Where I had grown weak, he was strong. However hard he drove others, he drove himself harder. When snow threatened to buckle the Star roof, it was George who was out there all day with me, shoveling.

One day in January John Wood, still a close friend and absentee partner, called me from Washington. He had mentioned me to his friend John Upston, then assistant secretary of state with responsibility for UNESCO affairs. The United Nations Educational, Scientific and Cultural Organization had set aside some money to launch two weekly population-control newspapers, one in Arabic for the Arabic-speaking nations of Africa and the Near East, the other in French for French-speaking Africa. Would I consider going there, finding editors and printers, and arranging for distribution? UNESCO would supply most of the copy and photos for the papers I'd start.

I had taken only two widely separated weeks away from work in 16 years. Upston's offer had caught me in the grip of a deep melancholy following what seemed a final estrangement from Anneke. I yearned to get away alone, and I needed the extra money. Bob Brigham had learned quickly, and others could fill in for me operationally. I promised myself I would complete my mission in exactly one month.

My first stop was Paris, for consultations at UNESCO headquarters — five wasted days — then a day in Rome en route to Africa, wandering about that lovely city where Anneke and I had strolled during stopovers to and from my India job in the first years of our marriage. A desperate nostalgia overtook me and grew in my solitude all the rest of that journey.

During eight days in Cairo I was manipulated and flattered by Egyptian bureaucrats keen for the UNESCO dollars I represented. I remember crowded, inefficient offices, cup after cup of sweet mint tea, and a dinner with the son and daughter-in-law of Foreign Minister Ismael Fahmy. I was turned over to President Anwar Sadat's press boss, who introduced me to the editor of *El Aram*, and escorted me to the *son et lumiere* spectacle at the great pyramids and afterward to a lavish belly-dance nightclub nearby, the paying "guest" of a dashing young empty-headed government greeter. Lonely and longing as I was for my return and the reconciliation I fantasized, the glitter and sweaty sensuality repelled me. When I left Cairo, a publication, of what sort I had to take on faith, was scheduled to be born, probably blue.

I spent my next nine days in Dakar, Senegal, a pleasant city, clean and industrious. There I found my editor, Abdou Cissé, a clever, young-ish, semicultivated man of good humor who spoke fluent English as well as French, and who would later become Senegal's minister of communications. If he could make a bit more than I could promise him in salary, at least UNESCO would get an honest publication. This time I avoided all but a few government officials, tentatively engaged the services of Dakar's only practical printer for my job, arranged a newsprint quota and a rather complicated distribution system, and generally felt that I had control of things, as I most decidedly hadn't in Cairo.

With five days of my month left, I put my editor friend Cissé on standby while I flew to Lagos, Nigeria, to compare the practicalities in that other French-speaking capital. In those early oil-rich days, Lagos was a city of stark contradictions: glitter and squalor, riches and abysmal poverty, bustle and sloth, and, it seemed to me, promise and hopelessness. After a few days spent shuttling ineffectually from bureaucrat to politician to printer to prospective editor, finding almost no one who could both understand my project and take an interest in it, I reconfirmed and energized the Dakar arrangements before boarding a plane home, my mind cleared, mission accomplished, body rested, brimming over with renewed strength, hope, and dreams of a new life with Anneke.

I hadn't written or phoned, and had no reason to expect anything but the former finality, but I had the conviction of hope born of change, in attitude as in absence. Back in Maine I was stunned to learn that she was seeing someone else. The final drop from so high a lift sent me into a tailspin serious enough for medication. But I wooed again, and won again, and we were together again by summer.

My trip home from Africa had been directly to Cape Porpoise. A couple of weeks later I gathered my notes together for a trip to Washington for my report to Upston at the State Department. I arranged to stay overnight with John Wood at the apartment he kept there. Two days before I arrived, John had developed intestinal pains acute enough to send him for a complete physical checkup at a Washington hospital, so I spent my night in Washington without his jovial companionship.

A few weeks later John learned that the source of his pain was an inoperable malignancy. He was flown back to Maine Medical Hospital in Portland, where, visited almost daily by his family, and by Anneke and me, he weakened steadily, suffering the indignities of radium and chemotherapy, determinedly cheerful, interested, and plucky to the last. I remember vividly my profound sense of anger at whatever caused John to die that summer, a gaunt, gray shadow of the ebullient, laughing man we had all respected and loved.

★ VIII ★

★ 44 ★

Dailies and Weeklies

Modern technology has made the world immediately available to giant news-gatherers, and they dispense it wholesale to the retailers, meaning the smaller TV and radio stations and the lesser dailies. From such vast source material these retailers pick and choose world news highlights and stories of regional significance; the Iowan sees and hears the same world news at the same time as the Mainer. Only the local newspaper is interested in the local scene, so it must gather those stories itself, a comparatively costly and exhausting process.

Before I left it, the *Star* contained between 60 and 84 broadsheet pages a week devoted exclusively to what was happening to 50,000 residents of 15 communities. The *Times,* New York City's newspaper of record, devoted perhaps 4 or 5 of its daily pages, and more on Sundays, to the most sensational crime and government activities of the 10 or 12 million residents of its city and environs — call it 40 pages a week. Our page size was one-fifth larger and our advertising percentage one-fifth smaller, so it all translated into more than twice the news space for one two-hundredth the population. If the *Times* had recorded the doings of New Yorkers in as great a detail as we recorded those of Yorkers, each day it would have contained about 2,000 pages and weighed more than 25 pounds. Put another way, our news was 500 times as trivial, or (another way) we were 500 times as truly the local newspaper of record. A moderately active Kennebunker could expect to find his name repeated hundreds, even thousands, of times in the *Star* during his lifetime. In his local library's bound volumes were all the highlights of his life and the community events that shaped it. The average Brooklyn resident never, all his life long, finds himself mentioned in the *Times*.

The *Portland Press-Herald* was a small metropolitan daily. One mustn't judge such papers by the standards of the greatest dailies, which keep large professional staffs and compete for news on a world scale. Most second-level dailies like the *Press-Herald* highlight local sports, civic, and social news gathered in-house. But after skimming the major world and national stories from the wire services and scheduling their syndicated charts, comics, columns, puzzles, weather reports, and financial pages, they have precious little space for local news, and their staffs are thin as twigs. Even readers of the most geographically isolated of all such newspapers are so conditioned to rich servings of external affairs that they are beyond bobbing for apples. The supermarket of reports available to the editors of these papers is risk-free and inexpensive. For further economy the editors plump out their pages with mail culled from the deluge of thinly disguised, free promotional copy that arrives daily from all manner of indefatigable public-relations people. Did you think *they* wrote all that stuff?

Although the weekly may sometimes prevail upon town officials to meet only a day or two before its publication day, it is in the nearby dailies that many of the routine stories and larger happenings appear first. The common reader's admiration for news scoops and his assumption that size and wealth are measures of influence combine to bestow on the small dailies, with their rather trashy potpourri of in-house offerings, an Oliver Hardy sort of authority.

To overcome its six-to-one newsbreak handicap the weekly must try harder. To overcome its glamour handicap — being denied the luxury of lacing itself with spicy national and international items, titilating bits about celebrities and beautiful people, sensational crime, war, sports, and features available to all dailies from the common international talent pool — the weekly must do better with its local news. To interest readers enough to buy their product, weekly people must add other dimensions to their appeal, and these are all personal. They must do only what they can do best, and that is to touch readers where they live.

If the weekly is worth its newsprint, its editor assumes personal responsibility for the health and integrity of the communities it serves. Its reporters give their readers as much of the whole truth as they can learn. The whole truth isn't found in official releases or self-promotional statements; it is found under rocks. It is gathered by digging and questioning, by discovering what is often the closely held secret of people who want it kept hidden.

Before the *Star* began embarrassing the nearby dailies with the energy of its local coverage, their major common mission was to operate in the black. Their common editorial condition was pretty close to stasis. Their stories about our communities were almost exclusively taken from meeting minutes or police blotters, constituting little more than outlines of actions taken. "The selectmen decided to delay bridge repairs and advertise again for bids on an altered plan," or "Lacking a quorum, the School Board tabled a vote on the proposed band uniform purchase," or "According to a report filed by Chief Burns, 12 cases of breaking and entering were investigated during the month under review."

Until they read the *Star*, local people weren't aware that the reason the selectmen had tabled the bridge-repair vote was that the only bid they received was from the contractor cousin of one of them, and they didn't know who voted which way on the motion to table. They didn't know the humorous reason that the School Board lacked a quorum, or about the bitter behind-the-scenes wrangle over band-uniform style between the Band Boosters and the Athletic Boosters, or the names one board member had called another in the corridor after the meeting, or what the editor thought they ought to think about it all. They didn't know that the break-ins reported by the chief included three at the same corner store, or that the chief was pretty sure he knew who was doing it, and so was everyone else in the neighborhood. These were things they learned on Thursdays.

The big-news reporter writing about famous people doing things in familiar contexts doesn't have to remind his readers what those people look like or how they feel about things, or what their attitudes are toward one another, or what problems they face. When we wrote that Wells Budget Board member Smith had told Selectman Jones that Town Clerk Brown had failed to submit a properly detailed accounting, too many readers lost interest if we failed to tell them what these people looked like or neglected to remind them of Smith's recurring feud with Brown, or what Jones had said when he heard Smith's accusation, or what was behind Brown's apparent delinquency.

The daily's interest in the outback where the weekly lives is as a source of readership for the head count it gives its advertisers. So it acts merely as a scribe. It doesn't probe for the story behind the story, because that can be dangerous — and why bother? It doesn't wage community service campaigns or investigate outback official shenanigans, because so what? It doesn't waste editorial breath on outback improvement, because who cares?

The daily that wants readership in the weekly's area is competing with other dailies, not the weekly. The Kennebunker either bought a Boston paper or the *Press-Herald* in the morning. When he chose the *Press-Herald* it wasn't for variety or excellence, but because he wanted Maine rather than Massachusetts news, or wanted to know immediately, before the *Star* came out, which of his townspeople had died, what local decisions had been taken, or what was for sale in the nearby city. No matter which daily he read, he never felt comfortable about his own town's news, or knew what goods and amusements were available in town, until he got his *Star*. Then he learned the thousand other things that made his town useful and interesting, and made him part of it.

★ 45 ★

The News Team

From top to bottom, the value range among weeklies is far greater than among small and medium dailies. Page for page, the weekly can soar with the best of them. Or it can plumb the journalistic depths, like the old *Kennebunk Star,* to creep about with its blind brethren on the ocean floor, feeding on what filters down from above. Reporting only local news, the best weeklies will explain, illustrate, quote, include byplay and amusing incident, fleshing out and bringing to life the bland creatures scooped by the dailies. They can do this because these stories are their primary offerings, their big deals, not just items competing for space with flashy purchased news. Living where its news happens gives the weekly insights denied to its competition. The weekly reporter's intimacy with his newsmakers provides him with tips and observations that make it easy for him to anticipate the dailies on nonscheduled news, to spot human interest stories and features, and, above all, to comment.

The weekly reporter writes about people he'll meet face to face in the post office or around the ends of supermarket aisles. He among all news people takes the greatest personal risks and has most to lose. And there he sits, with the most personal product. The weekly reporter knows things about reaction to the printed word that the others will never know.

For the same reasons, the weekly's readers are more affected by the news of their communities. Each event reported in the weekly involves people they know, or has a bearing on their lives. They all know at least a few of the staff people, and this familiarity sharpens their reactions to what they read. They write letters to the editor when the spirit moves them, and the letters are published. Such things help explain the weekly reporter's satisfactions. He is the expert in the thick of things. Reaction to what he writes is instantaneous.

The weekly reporter is hired to do everything, to work a whole territory, to follow the leads he finds himself, and to write in a variety of styles to suit his material. He takes his own photos, writes his own captions and headlines. A daily may have already reported the bones of his major story before his weekly goes to press, but he can't ignore the story. His must be rounder and better and longer, or what's the point of writing it at all? He must rise to that challenge no matter how unassuming his subject may be. I have employed several superlative reporters who failed as weekly journalists, because in squandering themselves on their big stories they disregarded their minor ones. The children's walk-athons to raise money for a local cause bored them, and their reports, if they wrote any, showed it. They failed because they fancied that most community news was beneath their notice. Readership stagnated, and resentments formed. Wasn't what the kids did important enough for the *Star?*

When I interviewed reporter prospects I looked for strong and appealing personalities. I judged my prospects more on their language and comportment than on the story clips they showed me. Who knew how much editing had been done on these stories that had been chosen from among who knew how many others? Only occasionally did I check references — these too were suspect. When I interviewed reporters I was also looking for editorial writers. I watched reactions as I rehearsed what would be expected of them at the *Star*. I looked for people I thought I'd like to have as friends, assuming that my coworkers would enjoy them too. Morale and spirit, in the newsroom as throughout the plant, were my uppermost concerns. Training and former newspaper experience were the undermost. The person who spoke well and gave evidence of a strong approach to his work would be trainable, by me or by the example of other reporters.

The first thing I told the prospects I interviewed was that, if hired, they would be Mr. or Ms. *Star* in their communities, expected to live in the towns they covered. They should form local loyalties and understand local feelings, sense local currents beneath the surface, grasp the subtleties of local traditions, know the ingredients of the local decision brew. Such knowledge matures slowly, so I didn't want short-term people looking for professional credits to peddle to the dailies. Living where they worked meant *Star* writers were personally affected by the events and decisions they reported, so they reflected their towns' respective cachets. Their local friends saved them from false assumptions.

To infuse each reporter with a sense of the worthiness of the job, he or she was given exclusive responsibility for the news of one or more communities. As soon as I thought reporters had established a grasp of that news, they were made assistant editors, required to write editorials, and encouraged to write personal columns inspired by their working experience. A reporter was hired to be a Compleat Journalist, totally unspecialized, reporting at all levels, doing features and reviews, covering sports and local history, human interest, schools, government, social and entertainment events, business and industry — everything. He mustn't overlook the farmer who had grown the biggest turnip, or the woman who had hooked a commemorative rug, or the neighbor who took uncommon trouble to bring moments of pleasure into the days of the folks at the nursing home. The scope might be narrow — a wounded gull saved, rather than a bison herd — but our readers found greater enjoyment in knowing that a girl in their daughter's school class had found a gull with a crippled wing on a familiar beach and nursed it back to health than they did in reading that some group in Wyoming was trying to return the bison to the prairie.

The *Star* people were the only ones writing into fluid situations. They could discuss and review and rewrite as their stories developed, then turn in thoughtful, balanced products that our readers could compare with the cardboard skeletons that often (though not as often as you'd think) appeared earlier in the dailies. They were the authorities with the editorial options. Each, individually, could change the climate and conditions of life in his or her own territory. They felt the elation of participating in campaigns waged by an elite corps in a profession of utmost importance. No second-level daily reporter could make more than a dent — or a welt. If *Star* reporters fulfilled the promise I chose them for, they became their towns' most knowledgeable and influential citizens. There is nothing more inspiring to a journalist than striding out on top of things, where the action is, carrying the burden of responsibility for the success or failure of community endeavor.

Star reporters were to be, in effect, editors of smaller weeklies inside the large one. I wanted attractive personalities, because they would be the major *Star* presence in the communities they covered. My interviews were informal, characterized by minimal inquiry into background, mostly just discussions of whatever came to mind. I wanted substantial people, because they would lead public thought as well as report it. I wanted them to be sound of judgment and analytically alive, because they would devise and promulgate solutions to local problems. I wanted people with the integrity to defend their views, popular or unpopular. I didn't want radicals, with their atrophied peripheral vision. I wanted critical people, but not rigid ones. I wanted self-starters —

there wasn't time for routine supervision. I wanted subtlety of thought and style. I wanted good humor, meaning perspective.

The young reporter who transfers from the weekly to the metropolitan daily may congratulate himself on financial advancement, but not on his new assignments. He becomes a police reporter, or a court reporter, or chases ambulances, until he is lifted to another narrow shelf. He will never write a column or an editorial, no matter how long he remains a reporter. He'll be lucky, at first, to write a published feature or to be assigned an exciting story. These he will have later, if he makes the grade.

The daily editor can pay more for reporters, so he hires the pros who write to formula. Their copy is as simple and declarative as they can make it — the terse synopses the editor thinks the readers want. They write much as the editor did when he was a reporter. Their sharpest concerns about the areas they cover are as vehicles for employment. The editor himself, being one step removed from the action, drops naturally into an adversarial role with his writers.

When *Star* reporters wrote editorials, they wrote from personal observation developed from their own involvement. The editorials in the lesser dailies are of a different stripe. The people who write them are usually instructed to save most of their breath for subjects of nationwide interest. They have no greater intimacy with these subjects than the rest of us have from our own readings and listenings. The resulting distillations, parading under such banners as "In Our Opinion," are plainly unequal to the task of satisfying sophisticated minds, and only sophisticates are likely to read them. Each editorial will please some and irritate others but will propel none to horseback.

I don't fault the small daily's editorial writer — it is the task that is hopeless. Unlike his counterparts in the most prestigious newspapers, the unspecialized small-city-daily editorial writer, working without benefit of research staffers, is expected not only to assume the mantle of reigning expert on local affairs, but also to comment on the liveliest current world affairs, however remote from his experience. Even the local news comes to him secondhand, from the reporters. He chats with them on the rare local subject he chooses for comment, and does some telephoning. From what he hears he makes up a mind equipped, it is to be hoped, with a filter of former reporting experience. His approach to his writing is neither red-eyed from sleepless anger, nor hoarse from cheering. His editorial mouth is unflecked with foam. He sits cogitating in an air-conditioned office with a mug of coffee at his elbow, weighing his editorial options. His piece must be short (his readers won't read the long ones), so he can't get far into his subject. He chooses one facet of it and makes a single point. He mustn't carry on, or indulge in oratory, or use words that shock or challenge. As a representative of a respected business in his city, his tone must be soberly forthright, his message simple, straightforward. He's not going to squeeze literature out of that bag.

No such constraints inhibit the weekly publisher-editor, who writes many of the editorials himself on pretty much whatever moves him. He can be humorous, satirical, angry, sentimental, reasonable, eccentric, or nostalgic. He can hammer away on a single subject to his heart's content. He can be emotional, and should be, in ways that are intolerable in the dailies. He writes exclusively about things he knows as well as anyone else does. If he runs an exciting newspaper, his editorial staffers do the same.

The weekly editor is the senior member of a collaborating news team. I never had time for nearly as much collaborating as I wanted. Mine mostly took the form of short discussions about aspects of stories or editorials I questioned, or explanations of my editing, or questions about the validity of a conclusion, or my playing devil's advocate to check the thoroughness of the research. It wasn't the more constructive collaboration of participating in newsroom discussions, or of taking reporters aside to analyze their stories or to suggest sequels, although I did some of this too. I didn't praise enough — when I did it came as a noteworthy surprise. I was too shy to praise effectively, and too busy. The best I could do was to edit completed writing and set the tone and standard in what I did myself, and in these ways to exert a positive ethical force. With the two *Star* hometowns as my special beat, I felt constrained to turn in more than my share of copy. Involvement was what I wanted from my staff, so involvement was the example I set.

★ 46 ★

Taking on a District Attorney

The day after New Year's Day, 1975, aging but still legally nimble Biddeford lawyer William Donahue was elected York County district attorney. Donahue was a rather big, jowly, gray-haired man, upright of bearing, in vested suits, a bit rumpled, schooled in the rough-and-tumble of Biddeford politics. His professional manner was domineering. In demeanor he reminded me of President Richard Nixon's old law partner and campaign director, Attorney General John Mitchell. Like Mitchell, Donahue privately sported the mischievous twinkle of an old pol.

Donahue's first choice as assistant DA was a fellow Biddeford lawyer named Theophilus Fitanides, known as Tuffy. Fitanides was about 55, of medium height, with a well-knit body, direct of gaze, macho, looking much like G. Gordon Liddy of Watergate burglary fame. For second assistant DA, Donahue chose a man in his thirties named James Martin Dineen, who had joined his father's law practice in Kittery, where the two carried on a combative form of law for people who felt mean. District Attorney Donahue and his assistants shared a bull-in-the-china-shop approach to the games lawyers play.

In those days America's temples of journalism were buzzing with the Watergate developments and the post-Watergate enthusiasm for investigative reporting. The *Washington Post* reporters who had helped pry open the Watergate can of worms were the idols of young reporters. Among their admirers were two of the *Star*'s staff, Tom Heslin and Myron Levin, both in their middle twenties. Both sported beards and mustaches, which parted frequently to discharge infectious laughter. Both were casually, nay, sloppily dressed, but their craftsmanship was neat, and both were intrepid interviewers. They shared a liberal outlook, a mistrust of business and privilege, and a spirit of fun. The *Star* newsroom was buoyant with esprit de corps. We campaigned on all fronts in our 15 communities and countywide, fighting sleazy subdividers, industrial polluters, questionable budgets, shoddy government, white-collar crime, environmental mistakes. In those days newsrooms were glamorous places to be, none in weekly newspaperdom more so than ours.

One day very early in 1975, Tom Heslin was in the county seat, Alfred, researching a courthouse story and incidentally acquainting himself with the practices of the new district attorney and his assistants, not yet a month in office. Tom's attention was arrested by what looked to him suspiciously like legal prestidigitation. It seemed that DA Donahue had decided not to prosecute 31 of the 38 cases he had inherited. Among the dismissed defendants were at least 3 of special interest to Tom: he had learned that these defendants were private clients of Donahue, Fitanides, and Dineen. Suspicious, Heslin wondered how many of the other 28 defendants were also their clients. When Heslin asked Donahue why he had dropped so many cases, Donahue's answers included: prosecution too costly, witnesses hard to find, police work poorly documented, evidence flimsy. Back in Kennebunk, Heslin discussed his suspicions with Levin, who covered Donahue's home territory, Biddeford, and then talked them over with me and Managing Editor Pulkkinen. We all agreed that dismissal of so many inherited cases was either irresponsible or, if many other cases involved clients of Donahue and his assistants, it represented blatant self-interest. Heslin and Levin would team up for a more thorough investigation.

When they returned to Alfred and asked the clerk of courts for the records of other cases dismissed during the early days of the Donahue administration they were told that the records had been locked up and were no longer available — the so-called Expungement Law, which shields from public view the records involving defendants who have won acquittal or whose cases have been dismissed before coming to trial, forbade access.

Faced with the Expungement Law roadblock, Heslin and Levin changed their request. Arguing that expungement was designed to protect the defendants, not their lawyers, they told Donahue that they didn't care to know anything about the cases except the names of the defending attorneys. Again rebuffed, they sought advice from two experts in the offices of the state attorney general in Augusta, Joseph Brennan. Both lawyers agreed that DA Donahue was bending the Expungement Law out of shape.

Like Richard Nixon with his National Security blanket, Donahue wrapped himself in the Expungement Law and stonewalled.

The mere suspicion of conflict of interest was an insufficient reason for the state attorney general to investigate county affairs. But as the Heslin-Levin sequel stories appeared, including one about a Fitanides scuffle with a police officer and another about the defense by the elder Dineen of a client being prosecuted by his son, they settled into the lap of Attorney General Brennan. No longer able to ignore the swelling hoorah, Brennan ordered a formal investigation into Donahue's professional conduct.

After reviewing the results, Brennan agreed with the Heslin-Levin conclusions and summoned Donahue before Maine's Governor Longley and his seven-member council. They heard 32 witnesses weave together a tapestry fragment of political strong-arming, attempted intimidation of police, expungement of records, conflict of interest, and freewheeling, arbitrary justice during the first few months of Donahue's administration. In the end they deadlocked, four to four, with the governor voting for acquittal but with a motion to censure. The tie went to the accused, and Donahue returned to his Alfred office in jocular triumph. I called the case our Watergate East, wondering at the decision and deploring the fact that Peter Rodino, chairman of the House Judiciary

Committee during the impeachment hearings, had not been there in the governor's place.

Attorney General Brennan had questioned DA Donahue's activities in terms of his fitness to hold elective office, and Donahue's assistants, Tuffy Fitanides and James Martin Dineen, had been tangentially exonerated when Donahue won his tie vote. But the attorney general had simultaneously launched a parallel investigation into the professional activities of the young Kittery lawyer, Dineen, during the years prior to his Alfred appointment.

Some of my earliest *Star* recollections are of lawyers complaining about our handling of the complicated legal advertising they ordered. Among the complainers, earning special status in my memory for his sarcastic appraisals of our collective intellect, was a Kittery lawyer named James H. Dineen, a tall, conservatively dressed, late-middle-aged man whose face and form are now inextricably confused in my memory with those of an unsmiling Spiro Agnew. His son, James Martin Dineen, acquired a law degree and joined his father's practice in Kittery, where he learned the trade from his old man. First the father, then the son, earned a reputation for high-handed use of the legal advantage. Dissension seemed to surround and nourish them.

In their investigation of the actions of Donahue and his assistants, Heslin and Levin had pieced together the details of quite a number of questionable past legal exploits of the younger Dineen. And so it transpired that at the same time they reported the news of the Donahue investigation, the two reporters could write a companion story whose headline was:

Dineen Tactics Eyed by Attorney General

The Attorney General's office has launched an investigation into alleged misconduct by York County Assistant District Attorney James M. Dineen in a series of civil suits extending over the last three years. While spokesmen for the Attorney General refused to discuss details, it is known that investigators are looking into incidents in which Dineen allegedly:

• Seized a $25,000 Boston sightseeing tour bus carrying 35 passengers when the bus arrived in Maine, claiming that the bus company owed him $245 in expenses and back pay.

• Sent York County Sheriff's deputies six times to take money from the cash register of a York store, on behalf of a client who had sued the storekeeper to collect an alleged $2,491.35 debt.

• Helped a divorcee break into the Massachusetts home of her ex-husband after a judge had awarded the husband the house in a divorce settlement.

• Advised a male defendant in another divorce suit to remove furniture from his home, but after the house had been stripped, denied that his client had taken items from the house.

The Attorney General's office began its probe of these and other incidents after details were furnished by the Grievance Committee of the Maine Bar Association. The bar committee had known of the cases through complaints filed by the parties and attorneys involved.

When the investigation is completed, prosecutors in the Attorney General's office may ask the Maine Supreme Judicial Court to take disciplinary action against the young Kittery attorney. If the Court were to rule against Dineen the penalty could range from formal censure to suspension or disbarment.

There followed about 50 inches of copy explaining the circumstances of the 4 cases known by the reporters to be material to the investigation and ending with a paragraph hinting of other cases not yet made public. That story would lead James Martin Dineen later to sue the *Star* for libel.

Before he entered law practice, the younger Dineen had driven a bus for the Gray Line Sightseeing Company. In 1972, now an attorney, he sued Gray Line for $245 he claimed the bus company owed him in back pay and expenses — and for $9,500 more in damages. Without proper authority from the court, he had then had a sheriff's deputy attach a Gray Line bus in York Beach while passengers moseyed around. Over the phone a bus company official agreed to pay Dineen $1,500 to release the bus and call off his suit. Dineen kept the bus impounded until he received the check next day.

But Gray Line had stopped payment. The check bounced, and Gray Line counter-sued. When Judge Rubin heard the case he directed the jury to reject Dineen's claim and ordered Dineen to pay the bus company $2,000. Supreme Court Justice Sydney Wernick, reviewing this part of Attorney General Brennan's complaint, agreed. In his summation, Justice Wernick, his sarcasm showing, wrote that "this court need not go to the extreme of disbelieving [Dineen's] sworn testimony" that he could properly hold the bus for ransom, or that punitive damages were available to him, but that certainly this belief could not have been held "with rational conviction."

In the Boyle v. Share case Dineen had represented Howard Boyle, who claimed that Samuel Share, owner of Carroll's Cut Rate store in

York Beach, owed him about $2,500. Dineen prepared to attach Share's property, whereupon Share gave Dineen $1,200 as partial payment. When Share delayed further payments, without court authorization Dineen had sheriff's deputies take money six times from Share's cash register. After Share appealed a Judge Danton ruling that he should pay Boyle the balance, Judge Rubin reversed that ruling, finding that Dineen had acted illegally by failing to petition the court for permission to send the deputies. Dineen countered with a fruitless appeal to the Maine Supreme Court. Afterward, Dineen's retaliatory view of the law led him to sue Share's lawyers for calling his actions "outrageous." This libel suit too ran its unsuccessful course.

When Justice Wernick reviewed this case for Attorney General Brennan, he again expressed himself as prepared to "lay aside [his] sense of reality and take [Dineen] at his sworn word," and called the actions improper, taken with "reckless abandon" without "authority in law."

Judge Wernick also found that Dineen had acted improperly in several other cases by acting as attorney for a man in a land dispute against another client of his, prosecuting people as Assistant DA against whom he had taken private cases, and others in which conflict of interest was "actual or apparent."

Brennan dropped the Frechette v. Frechette divorce case, in which Dineen's role was questioned in a client's improper removal of furniture. Brennan could not pin witnesses down to specific times and dates.

In the Shedd v. Shedd divorce case, Dineen was attorney for Mary Shedd in uncontested proceedings. Clifford Shedd was awarded the Shedds' Charlton, Massachusetts, home by Judge Danton, and Mary got their York Harbor home and $120 a week in child support, $90 less than she had asked for. Within days, Dineen had filed papers appealing Danton's monetary awards.

A short time later, Dineen allegedly accompanied Mary Shedd to her former husband's Charlton home while he was away and helped her remove some furniture. While there they called friends of Clifford Shedd's who were storing his antique auto. In a complaint to the Maine Bar Association Shedd complained that he was told that Dineen had driven the auto back to Maine and kept it as partial payment for his services to Mary Shedd.

Shedd also charged in his complaint that five months later a police officer told him that Dineen, Mary Shedd, and two men had arrived at Shedd's home with a U-Haul trailer. Dineen had shown the officer his attorney's card, saying he had a court order for possession of certain property. However, Shedd said, his attorney told him that no such order had been issued. Shedd complained that the four had entered his house by breaking garage windows and then forcing the house windows open. He said they had broken cabinets, ripped off closet doors, pulled hand-rails off the stairway, broken bathroom and plumbing fixtures and two storm doors, removed a built-in stove from the kitchen, and ripped a phone off the wall. Shedd added that the four had taken items purchased after the separation, even some borrowed mason's tools. He wrote that the police officer had told him that Dineen had personally helped the others carry things from the house.

Clifford Shedd claimed also that while the original divorce order had called for $210 a week in child support, later reduced to $120, Dineen had then brought action against him for $1,320 in back payments, the difference between $210 and $120 per week for the period the matter was being adjudicated. That case had been dismissed in District Court. Then three months later Dineen had filed an identical motion, now for $2,490, this time subpoenaing all Shedd's financial records, even though Shedd had never claimed inability to pay the $210. Again, the case was dismissed.

When Dineen heard that Shedd had complained to the Maine Bar Association, he sued Shedd for libel, $200,000 in compensatory damages, and another $200,000 in punitive damages.

Shedd v. Shedd was, in fact, one of eight cases submitted by Attorney General Brennan to Supreme Court Justice Sydney Wernick after investigating the legal conduct of James Martin Dineen, but one that Justice Wernick decided later was either weak or hard to prove.

It was after Dineen had been suspended from four months of law practice and had appealed his suspension, but before the appeal had been considered and rejected, that he filed his libel complaint against the *Star*. The senior Dineen, as his son's attorney, restricted his complaint to the news article's discussions of the Frechette and Shedd divorce cases, which had dropped from view of the Supreme Court.

The Dineens were apparently counting on the fact that some of the detail in the *Star* story had been difficult to demonstrate and hadn't been reviewed. They made the lateral argument that while young Dineen had been a public figure when the story was written, he had been in private practice when he'd handled the cases.

Our attorneys filed motions for summary judgment supported by the depositions of Heslin, Levin, and Gordon Scott, the assistant attorney general who had prosecuted the disciplinary action against Dineen. In his brief, *Star* attorney O'Leary argued that there was no question of the accuracy of our story, and that no damaging facts were revealed in the depositions.

Even if all the incidents reported were defamatory, there was no question of their truth, nor did Dineen offer evidence to the contrary. What was more, there was no issue of malice. A public official must show that the report was written with knowledge of its falsity or with serious doubt as to its truth. Anything regarding the fitness of a public official to perform his job is relevant.

Arguing for summary judgment, O'Leary pointed out that libel action subjected us as the defendants, and other newspeople generally, to unwarranted, expensive trial procedures offensive to the principles of the free press because of their chilling effect on public debate. Levin's and Heslin's inquiries had been thorough. Much time had been spent uncovering the information, many people had been interviewed, confirmations were obtained from many sources, and several unsuccessful efforts had been made to communicate with Dineen prior to publication. The reporters' notes supported these contentions.

Justice Wernick did, indeed, issue summary judgment, dismissing the case before it came to trial. Later Dineen's appeal of that decision, too, was dismissed. It had taken a long time, more than three years from publication date, but we were clear.

On April 16, 1980, about two years later, the *Star* carried another Dineen story on its front page: "Dineen Suspended for Three Months Over Illegal Writ." This time it was the elder Dineen, James H., whom the Supreme Court had suspended from the practice of law. The chief justice wrote that Dineen's actions in completing a writ of attachment of property other than real estate and then stating that the attachment had been approved by a judge (when in fact the judge had dismissed the petition for attachment), "constituted a plain violation of the ethical standards demanded of a member of the legal profession. . . . Suspension," the justice continued, "will serve as a warning to the 70-year-old respondent to guard against unethical breaches during his remaining years of practice."

Only a few weeks later the *Star* was to report that James H. Dineen was being investigated by the Board of Overseers of the Maine Bar Association. Judge Donald Alexander had complained that action taken by the senior Dineen in what he called a groundless York easement dispute that had been dragged through the court system for five years, had not been maintained in good faith, but rather had been "frivolous, vexatious, and intended for harassment of the Defendant." This description, I am sure, applied also to the suit against us.

The elder Dineen had been brought before bar grievance committees of yore, but never before penalized. The Supreme Court's actions, and the *Star* reporting that gave them birth, may just have put some starch in the legal fraternity and a crimp in its buddy system in Maine.

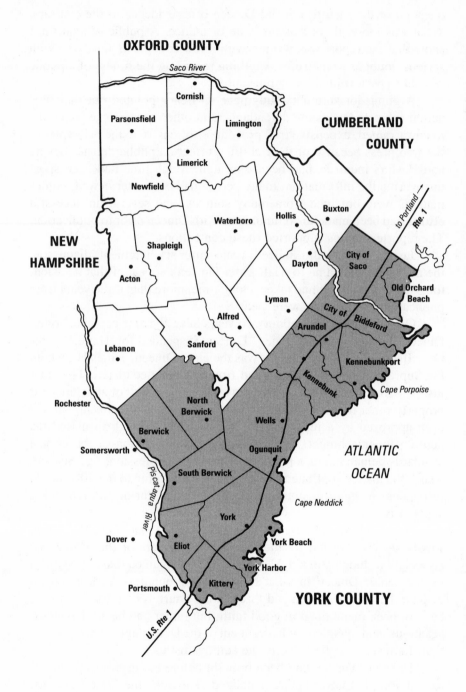

OXFORD COUNTY

Saco River

Cornish

Parsonsfield

Limington

CUMBERLAND
COUNTY

Limerick

Newfield

Waterboro

Hollis

Buxton

to Portland →
Rte. 1

NEW
HAMPSHIRE

Shapleigh

Dayton

City of
Saco

Old Orchard
Beach

Acton

Lyman

City of
Biddeford

Alfred

Arundel

Kennebunkport

Lebanon

Sanford

Kennebunk

Cape Porpoise

Rochester

North
Berwick

Wells

ATLANTIC

Somersworth

Berwick

Ogunquit

OCEAN

South Berwick

Cape Neddick

Piscataqua River

York

Dover

Eliot

York Beach

York Harbor

Portsmouth

Kittery

YORK COUNTY

U.S. Rte 1

★ **IX** ★

★ 47 ★

Monkey on My Back

Average circulation topped 7,500 in 1972, 8,500 in 1973, and 9,500 in 1974. Page count went to 38, then 48, then 56. There were 10 on the editorial staff, 10 in sales and the front office, 35 more in production, and many part-timers. Sales volume had gone over the million-dollar mark, and by 1975 our growing readership strength to the south and north had pushed us to an average circulation of 10,800, with 60 to 80 pages and half a dozen more people.

The three "community" dailies that nibbled at the flanks of our circulation area were smaller and lesser newspapers than the *Portland Press-Herald*. Like the two New Hampshire papers, the *Portsmouth Herald* and *Foster's Daily Democrat* in Dover, the Alta Group's *Biddeford-Saco Journal* subscribed to a junior wire service and ran comics and puzzles but no financial news. It employed a couple of editor types who oversaw local news gathering, monitored the wire service, and coordinated content; a couple of city reporters, and two or three correspondents in outlying towns, who made minimal effort. But regardless of their respective merits, on the pole of the public mind the weekly is always one totem below the daily. That bulge you see under the shirt on the shoulder of the weekly newspaper person is a permanent chip. Carrying larger editorial and sales staffs per page, selling small ads to a gaggle of small business owners rather than scooping up bigger, ready-made ads from larger customers, the large weekly charges less for its space and gets the same price per copy for double the bulk of the community daily.

In 1975 the Alta Group decided to fold the smallest of its encircling papers, the controlled-circulation weekly *Somersworth-Berwicks Free Press,* with which they had flooded the Berwicks when I bought the little North and South Berwick papers. We exulted briefly, hired another reporter, and spread into Berwick.

The Alta Group's *Rochester* (New Hampshire) *Courier* on Berwick's western flank remained insulated and apparently prosperous, but the other two Alta papers, in Sanford and Biddeford-Saco, were hurting. The *Sanford Tribune* was on the down escalator, living on its fat, losing readers, cutting editorial expense by substituting a syndicated feature service for local reportage. We were locked in an ideological struggle with the *Tribune* on the issue of a threatened oil refinery in Sanford — they promoting it, we alone of all Maine newspapers in strenuous opposition. Our Sanford advertising and circulation were growing, without our even having correspondents there.

For decades the *Biddeford-Saco Journal* had let itself decay. Finally, alarmed, the Alta Group principals in Boston decided to do us battle. They built a modern plant in Biddeford and transferred to it an oversize offset press and ancillary equipment from their Massachusetts daily. An enterprising young editor was hired who expanded his city reporting staff and opened an office in Kennebunk a block away from us, giving more editorial emphasis to the Kennebunks than to his home cities. Design and typography were radically improved.

But Biddeford and Saco readers were unimpressed with the transformation. Advertisers failed to respond. Spending all that money had merely gained the *Journal* some readership in the Kennebunks at the *Press-Herald*'s expense. It was too late for the Alta people to turn back, however, even if that would have helped. Publisher Paul Cassavant was fired. Publisher Bud Wright left Sanford — I was told he was given another Alta job.

Meanwhile Star Press was gaining on its finances, but barely. Instead of the usual small losses, we made small profits each year from 1972 to 1974, and grew on our depreciation. By 1975 our annual gross had swollen to $1,250,000, and that year we made a profit of $100,000 — about 8 percent — not grand, but five times as much as the business had ever made before. With that profit we reduced our payable arrears to major suppliers from six months to three, while receivables, being a constant percentage of gross, grew by $40,000. The remaining "profit" went for new-equipment down payments and increased principal payments, so we still kept the same precarious checkbook balance.

In 1972 we had won only three minor awards at the New England Press Association's annual Better Newspaper Competition, while our bitter rivals in Sanford were annointed with third prize in our General Excellence class for a product we all agreed wasn't a patch on the seat of our pants. The Nieman Fellows no longer judged the competition; awards were distributed, not won. Next year the *Tribune* again got third prize, and again we came away unmentioned. By then we were in NEPA disgrace, following a Boston ruckus when two *Star* reporters tried to press the membership into endorsing their antinuclear manifesto, and I grew belligerent in their defense. We continued to send in our dues checks, but we stopped entering the contests and never again in my time attended what we now called the "Annual Horrible" in Boston.

We did continue to send entries to the major contests of the National Newspaper Association, assuming higher judging professionalism. By 1975 our circulation of 10,800 put us in the over-10,000 class of the nation's largest weeklies. In October 1976, when the 1975 results were announced in Wisconsin, they gave it to us — first prize for General Excellence.

I noted in my banner story that week that the news of our triumph was greeted by the *Star* staff with a blend of modest restraint and unprofessional raucousness, which was half true. After proclaiming our happy circumstances and reminding readers of our similar 1971 triumph in the next-smaller class, I wrote that we had called ourselves best then, even while nursing the doubt that somewhere out there among the giant weeklies of America there might be one or some that could be called better. But now we were the only newspaper ever to have won a top prize twice, and we'd done it in the two largest classes.

My late partner John Wood's widow, Pam, still held a sixth of Star Press stock — by 1976, quite valuable. She was still teaching at Kennebunk High, and had reported for us during summer vacations. With two college-age daughters, another in private school, and a son entering high school, she was renting out the Wood home and living in a remodeled barn extension. Much of her financial worth was in nonincome, nonliquid Star Press stock, and she needed money.

Late the year before, Bob Brigham and I had consulted Pam about a major expansion, presenting the following arguments: The summer *Star* was averaging 70 to 80 broadsheet pages a week, with five pressruns of more than 14,000 each. Our grocery-chain flier business and other web work was into two shifts, and growing. Our four-unit Community web press was aging with the strain — a breakdown would kill us. We were overloading two computer typesetting machines fed by seven electronic keyboards, all thermostatically neglected and in constant trouble. Nine pasteup people were scattered all over three buildings. Our darkroom and camera room were seriously outgrown. Space problems had sent our orbiting sheet-fed printing out of control. The Occupational Safety and Health Administration was after us about noise levels, exits, fire prevention. Employee autos had overflowed parking space front and rear, inconveniencing customers. Delivery and shipping were hair-raising, warehouse space totally inadequate, even for work in progress, and we were renting roll and flat storage space a mile down Route 1. Either we stopped growing, or we added space. Add space, Pam had agreed.

We laid plans to start building early in 1976, a steel structure a quarter of a mile away down Water Street. All printing, binding, warehousing, and shipping would move there. The shop space on High Street would be partitioned and renovated into air-conditioned typesetting and camera rooms, and a consolidated pasteup area. On the ground floor at 3 High Street would be stripping, job-work preparation, the offset darkroom, and the printing offices. Advertising, editorial, and general offices would have all 13 rooms at 1 High Street. We'd buy a second, larger offset camera, light tables, automatic negative developer-dryer, a computer billing and bookkeeping machine, and add four more, higher-speed web press units, a heavy-duty folder, and other equipment to our production facility at Water Street. To finance it all we'd have to consolidate our existing notes and mortgages, and borrow one-fifth of a million dollars more, a frightening proposition.

We took our 1975 profit figures to the bank and popped the question. After a lengthy negotiation with no, the directors carefully said yes, at decent terms, with all our corporate property as collateral. We were warned that for the foreseeable future our credit was stretched drum-tight. We ordered the new equipment and hired our builders and renovaters.

But Pam Wood was worried. The thought of ten more years of added risk to her nonproductive capital oppressed her. Her fortunes would rest uneasily on the continued health and vigor of her two fellow shareholders, Bob Brigham and me. Several months after we had made our commitment, and as we were nearing completion of the new building, Pam came to a reluctant conclusion. Following the terms of our old contract, but knowing we couldn't buy, Pam first offered her shares to Bob and me. Her prescribed next move was to demand that Star Press buy them. That, too, was impossible — the original Wood investment had grown by a formula factor of seven. With the help of a local mediator, we negotiated. Pam agreed to wait, but only for a while.

In September we started moving in at Water Street. Business continued to boom — gross would top a million and a half that year, with another quarter-million built into 1977.

The same formula that had improved the value of Pam's shares had barred Bob from increasing his share interest. While inflation had eroded the $15,000 salaries we continued to pay ourselves, Bob's savings had dwindled. Waiting for Pam's other shoe to drop, Bob came to a similar conclusion. He was dreaming of buying a commercial fishing vessel before his capital ran out. I, ten years older at 54, divorced, without a home, with no assets at all but the remnants of Bob's purchase money, a boat, and my Star shares, tired and fighting the business, saw the same years stretching out ahead. Ten years — 15 maybe — was what I had left to make the *Star* into an influential countywide paper, and that wasn't enough.

The old monkey settled again on my back. Maybe I, too, should turn my shares into money and sell my services to a new owner. Then, in easier circumstances, I might get back together with Anneke again in my old home and have time for things I still longed to do. Anyway, burdened Star Press couldn't buy the Wood and Brigham shares.

That summer, shortly after we had moved the shop, Pam made her move. Bob countered by offering his shares to the company.

OK, I said, I'll have to call my options too, so now we don't have a buyer. We don't even have a company. Either we put the business in receivership, or we sell it.

I can never forget that day.

★ 48 ★

A Negotiated Sale

We called newspaper broker Robert Bolitho, who rushed to Kennebunk from Kansas City the next day to get the drop on the competition. Shadows from the racing late-September clouds swept across our rattling windowpanes as we talked. Bolitho was a long-limbed, urbane man who played a humble-pie hand in a table-stakes game. After he had heard our story we did the High Street tour and then drove down to the nearly completed Water Street plant where our second four-unit Community was being erected.

Yes, Bolitho allowed, we had a property he could sell quickly — but not to just anybody. We had outgrown individuals — like it or not, the newspaper chains were our customers, and they were in the market with all feet. Bolitho shepherded us into an asking price of $1,650,000, less the difference between debt and receivables, or a net of about a million and a third after Bolitho's cut, almost identical with the formula figure that had forced us to sell. Once he had pronounced that exciting sum, Bolitho effortlessly got our signatures on his agency contract and flew home to Oklahoma.

Even the wrenching thought of trading the *Star* for lucre had only half my attention. Within days of Bolitho's visit, after five years of divorce, Anneke agreed to marry me again, and we rushed this announcement through the Star Press job process:

This is a marriage with a history — a history that needn't be repeated to friends. All that bears saying about it now is that it started long ago and had its ups and downs, like all marriages. The ups were better, and there were, on balance, many more of them. We never really gave up, certainly never both at the same time.

So, after twenty-six years of marriage and divorce, children and play and work, here are two people who have come to a decision short in the making but long in the re-making, and who have reached it with as much certainty as any of us can have, and more than most, that their love and affection and need have not only survived, but have grown strong enough to re-commit after all these years of inspection and introspection.

While purchase offers pulsed daily Maine-ward in short waves from Oklahoma, at noon on a brilliant Indian summer day, Anneke and I and about 35 old friends rowed, paddled, sailed, and motored to the outer end of Bass Island in Cape Porpoise Harbor. The scent of wood smoke from shore chimneys and the rich half-tide odors of sun-soaked island kelp and rockweed mingled with the bouquet of bloody Marys poured from jugs nestled in ice-filled washtubs flanking driftwood planks groaning with delicacies. A purple, green, and yellow flag, sewn with a magenta heart lettered with the *Star* slogan, T.H.W.T.B., a creation of our daughter Megan's, fluttered behind Justice of the Peace George Pulkkinen, and Eben gave his mother away to his father. The sun was dropping, bright yellow, toward the shore horizon before the martial hullabaloo of a small-boat flotilla weaving back to Nunan's Creek was heard from the land. The celebration at our old home lasted beyond dawn — a landmark, world-class party.

Once you've made the decision to sell, that's it: there's no turning back. You want to end it. It hadn't been my wish or my idea, but once the decision was made, I wanted it over. I couldn't buy, so I had to sell. Here I went, down Prosperity Road at last, the road not taken.

I think the number of eager bidders surprised even Bolitho. He passed along to us only the names of successively higher bidders. First came a sight-unseen million-dollar offer from a perennial midwestern bargain-hunter. This we grandly ignored. Next came better terms in the same range — some said it was a fat pig; Bolitho, he said nay. There followed Jock Whitney with a better proposition, but Whitney Communications dropped out early. Others, too, came and lost, and went. Bolitho helped us whittle the finalists down to two who had almost simultaneously raised their offers to our full asking price. We stopped shuffling and started to deal.

The one of the two we liked best was a low-key man in his middle forties who owned and operated a small fleet of community dailies and large weeklies in and around Pennsylvania. He was proud of his newspapers and wanted another feather for his cap. The other suitor we did not meet till after our negotiations. We were told that Joe L. Allbritton had started his meteoric business career as a California bank lawyer who had parlayed a group of troubled West Coast funeral parlors into the nation's largest undertaking undertaking. He went on to buy an insurance company and three or four banks, started a real estate holding company with large properties in downtown Houston, later got into the "media" with several big-city radio and TV stations and the *Washington Star*. In the nation's capital he occupied a penthouse overlooking the White House; it was only one of his five staffed residences. Courtly and dapper, in his early fifties, Joe L. flew around in a private jet with his young wife. Allbritton's emissary was a very young Texan named Dean Singleton, who estimated the Allbritton net worth at upwards of a billion dollars.

Not long before we met him, Singleton had negotiated Allbritton's purchase of a small Massachusetts daily and had been rewarded with the title of publisher. Until I complained to Singleton about dealing with someone I hadn't met, Allbritton never spoke with any of us. Then he called me once at home and delivered himself of ten minutes worth of meaningless platitudes.

The Pennsylvanian dealt exclusively for himself. Because his newspapers kept him too busy to be tripping back and forth to Maine, we saw him only once. He talked mostly with agent Bolitho, as we preferred. Allbritton worked otherwise. He left all the contacts and legwork to Singleton, who divided his time between the Massachusetts paper and the Sea Spray Motor Hotel at Kennebunk Beach. Singleton knew Bolitho pretty well from some unspecified prior cobrokerage experience, and pretty much ignored him, preferring to park on our doorstep and do his dealing direct.

During his initial visit to Kennebunk, Singleton insisted on taking Anneke and me to a dinner from which she and I drove home in total harmony: anyone who sent a stripling like Dean Singleton to represent him shouldn't own the *Star*. But maybe Singleton was just the advance scout who would vanish after the preliminaries. The *Washington Star* was a venerable institution. Singleton was merely an overweight 23-year-old dressed in cowboy boots, starched white shirt, and polyester knit suit cut in "Edwardian cowpoke" style. From the neck of this sartorial anachronism rose a smooth head with a delicate nose. His mouth was a tiny cupid's bow, hair light brown, skin alabaster-smooth, speech high-pitched Texas drawl with a decided lisp.

Business and Allbritton were Singleton's only themes. He told me that his three years of newspaper experience included buying a small, isolated weekly in the Southwest, which he had sold for a quick profit, and investing the proceeds in another paper with similar results. Somehow he had strayed into Allbritton's magnetic field and had stuck. He seemed to enjoy his employer's contract imprimatur within a broad framework, being able to confer personally with Allbritton at any hour of day or night.

Singleton was inescapable. He called constantly when he was away, and when he was with us he hung around and talked. He knew how we were swinging all the time. He accommodated us in ways that would make it difficult to brush him off when we came down to a dead heat. I think Allbritton must have told him to pay as little as he could, but to bring home the paper.

Terms took time. We thought we should get at least $200,000 down, so when we were offered $150,000 we said, Gee, we were figuring $200,000, minimum. Our Pennsylvanian wouldn't rule it out — he'd have to consult his accountant. Singleton, seeing us stiffen, said $200,000, and Bolitho went back to the Pennsylvanian, who matched it.

So we moved on to the next part, the "covenant not to compete." Bolitho had warned us not to expect a contract with less than a fifth of the net offer in this form of payment. We were trying for a ten-year note pay-out, and wanted to keep the noncompete payment down to $200,000 with the same completion date. Noncompete payments are taxed as income, representing salary to us for not doing something, in our case doing no printing, publishing, or newspapering within 50 miles of Kennebunk. For the buyer this salary represents business expense.

"That's a lot of money tied up that way!" we protested when the noncompete was proposed at $350,000 over 15 years. Haw would say, "Hem." Hem would say, "Haw! You sure are hard bargainers!" Back would come $300,000 and 11 years from one, then from the other. Finally one suitor agreed to our $200,000, and the other followed suit.

In succession we agreed to a ten-year note at 7 percent, all payments monthly, balloon at the end to be discounted after one year by the total amount of all remaining uncollected receivables. Both bidders agreed to include the new Community, not yet accepted, and to honor all other term obligations and current payables. The new owner would pay the first $5,000 of any legal bill for unforeseen suits or claims that materialized after title passed, a sum that just covered our $4,950 libel defense costs when Dineen sued us a month later. I'm sure the bill would have been higher if our agreement with Allbritton had been higher.

With all demands met and two identical offers, we had run out of negotiables. Bob and I called Pam and told her where we stood. Go with the Pennsylvanian, we all agreed. That evening we called Bolitho and asked him to get the Pennsylvanian to write us a contract. It had been a long sweat in January.

Next morning, before Bolitho could call Pennsylvania — or was it? — Singleton rang us. Since we had reached agreement on everything, he was saying, he assumed we had a deal. So he had stayed up all night with three packs of cigarettes and two six-packs of coffee, putting a contract together, and now he was in his Cadillac on the road to Kennebunk with it. Would I book him a room at the Sea Spray? How deep was the snow up there? Come down for drinks and dinner after work for signing and celebration!

I had to hand it to him. Well, I said over the phone, sure. There might be some other things we hadn't talked about yet, but let's see what you've got.

Bob and I drove down in the snow to the Sea Spray, synchronizing our thinking. We'd look at Dean's contract, then get one from Pennsylvania, compare the two, and make up our minds. We were both thinking that maybe we should have asked for more. Too bad we hadn't asked for a stock sale instead of an assets sale, but that had always seemed out of the question. In terms of seller's gain and buyer's loss in lesser depreciation for future tax savings, asking for a stock sale was like asking for another hundred grand up front. The buyer preferred assets, which would let him start depreciating everything all over again as new. It was too big a hooker, though, to toss into the mix at this stage of the game — too bad, we thought, on the way to the Sea Spray. But we had a good deal — no sense in crying over spilled milk.

Singleton was already seated in a corner of the lounge when we arrived. We ordered drinks and waited for him to begin. After floating a few conversational balloons, he produced his copies of the contract, and we began our study, finding no fatal flaws. Singleton had a pen poised. When neither of us grabbed for it, he began sniffing the air.

Oh, we said, we couldn't sign anything that night. Someone else was drafting a contract very like this one, and we owed it to him as well as to ourselves to take a look at it. Dean could only agree, but his gears were churning. We ordered another round of drinks before trooping off to our table. When coffee came, Dean could stand it no longer. Look, he had worked hard to get this contract together — been up all night. Joe L. expected him to bring one home tonight. Wasn't there some way we could wrap things up? Had he missed something? Joe was waiting for his call.

Almost casually, Bob mentioned the stock sale. Would Joe agree to this? He could check, Dean allowed, but he didn't want to. He'd only dare ask if he could assure Joe of a contract if he agreed. He'd retype the pages himself that night if we would sign and go to bed.

First we wanted to talk with our accountant, John Cummings. Bob left the table. When he returned, he motioned me into the lobby. Cummings had been home, but would drive to his office and do the calculations. Bob said Cummings had been flabbergasted. Did we really have a buyer for that amount of money? And maybe a stock sale too?

Cummings called us back in less than an hour to say a stock sale would be worth about $120,000 more to us in saved taxes than selling assets. OK, we told Singleton when we sat down again, give Uncle Joe a jingle. If he agreed, we would sign that night.

With success so near, Singleton went off to call Allbritton. Half an hour later he returned, smiling. Sure, no problem — no difference to Allbritton, stock or assets. No telling whether he'd need losses or gains in 1977. Let's get to work.

We borrowed a hotel typewriter and a private conference room. Shortly after midnight we had a new document, and, with a toast to the future, made it three-quarters official. We'd get Pam's signature next day and arrange a closing in Portland a month later.

How about that!, Bob and I said to each other on the road home in the darkest hour of the morning.

★ 49 ★

Life With New Owners

Following a complicated legal pas de deux douzaine at the Portland closing, Bob and I returned to Kennebunk and went back to work. Bob was still copublisher. I had lost the title of president to Allbritton but remained publisher and editor. Bob would stay on until his new gill-netter had been launched. I promised a year, if they wanted me.

Dean Singleton's first order of business was to sit down with me to get our pecking order straight. First, he said, Allbritton had made him vice president of Star Press, his title also at Joe's Massachusetts paper. I'd get my instructions from him — he was my boss.

I hadn't expected that. "You're not my boss," I said. I'd listen to suggestions, but while I was there I managed the show. If that wasn't OK, Joe could tell me to leave. I hadn't asked for a contract. I was there because none of them knew how to run things yet.

Dean was silent for a moment, his small mouth set. He couldn't fire me yet, but he had to nip this sort of thing in the bud. Oh, yes, he was my boss, he said. He did the talking with Allbritton — I talked through him. Was that clear?

I understood the words, I told him, but when I felt like talking to Allbritton, I'd do it, and I assumed that if Allbritton had anything special to say to me, he'd say it direct.

Singleton glared, and pushed on.

He didn't think the job printing made money — did I?

No, I didn't, I told him, and that was why he didn't. But it didn't partly because we had run it as a sideline. It would be foolish for Allbritton to drop the printing without giving it his best shot. He'd paid a lot of money for it, and if he ever wanted to sell Star Press, he'd lose a lot of money by not having it. With proper attention, printing could make money. We'd been looking for an experienced printing manager — had even made an offer to one, too late. Get a printing manager and tell him to make money at it. Let him bill the newspaper for production and leave the rest to the publisher. Then get an accounting firm to separate the two parts of the company books and apportion overhead. We'd looked into that too.

Singleton said he'd think about it. Why did we need such a large editorial staff? The Massachusetts paper operated with half our people, and it was a *daily*.

What *kind* of a daily? I countered. Two-thirds of its 70 pages a week were filled with bought copy, and the rest was 65 percent advertising. Its staffers operated from a hub, reporting on a third of our coverage area. Our sheet size was larger, and we ran 50 percent news copy, so our 11 reporters had to write twice as much apiece, in tougher territory.

Allbritton had inherited years of groundwork, I went on, years of chicken-and-egg tooling up to reach current potential. We were at the chicken takeoff point, and he was talking about clipping our wings. Give it three years and Joe would have a paper twice as big, worth three times as much, with many times the money-making possibilities, one that could be turned into a 24-page county daily, or whatever else he wanted. If I'd had Allbritton's money we'd have been there long ago, and he wouldn't own the *Star*.

I was talking to a man with a tin ear for my kind of music. Singleton wanted to be able to drop a handsome profit into Allbritton's lap the first year. York County wasn't Joe's war, but a bush skirmish. He hadn't made a billion dollars soldiering. He wasn't in the printing business, either — printing was too slow.

Before I'd fire the printing staff, I told Singleton, Joe would have to fire me. That subject, too, went on simmer.

Weren't the ad rates awfully low?

Yes, I agreed, they were. But we were strung out along a competitive coast, and this was Maine. We couldn't justify higher rates in our southern territory yet.

Why bother with the southern end at all, if it lost money? Cut coverage, Singleton argued, reduce costs, and concentrate on where we could make money. Plenty of weeklies were making 40 percent.

His argument made sense in his philosophy, and his was in fashion. Leave the uphill struggles to other people, the reorganizations and turning things around. Don't throw good money into product therapy. You won't be around long if you don't show the directors a profit. Your job is always on the line — the bottom line. Here we were, country journalist folk, plugging away with T.H.W.T.B. for a motto. The hard way's for guys who finish last.

But my heels were dug in deep, so in the end Singleton said he'd take my thoughts about a printing manager back with him, and meantime let's see a few monthly statements. He'd work up some figures himself and take a hard look at them.

Two days before the end of each month Dean would call. "How're we dewin'? Have a good week, linagewise? How's that compare with last year? Next week lookin' good? Your figures ready for the accountant?"

Not yet. The way we billed, we had to wait for the last issue of the month before measuring ads, and then it took a week to bill and tally up. It took the accountant a couple of weeks beyond that, so we were ready for the next billing before we got the previous month's statements back. Anyway, he wouldn't learn much from one statement — he'd have to see trends. Wait till the weather warmed up and our annual rate increases took effect.

Couldn't we go up more than 10 percent this year? he'd ask, and I'd go over it with him again.

The day after we delivered our figures, Singleton would be on the phone to the accountants, urging them to rush. When they were done, he'd get the bottom line before we did, and my phone would ring again. I hated that.

The figures weren't good in February, and they were worse in March. Singleton was approaching hysteria. Why the big phone bill? How come newsprint was so high this month?

I'd check the phone bill, I'd tell him, but I was glad his calls weren't in it. Toll calls were part of our territorial problem. Newsprint came in as we needed it, and we just happened to get an extra shipment last month.

Everything but the loss was explainable.

By mid-April Singleton was developing business hives. I was sure my continued presence was being discussed in Washington. Meanwhile, somebody had to get to me. Maybe Dean just had a personality block with me.

One day Dean called to ask me to reserve a room at the Sea Spray for Wilmot Lewis, known as "Bin," who would be up to get acquainted so he could share Dean's absentee supervision role. When I met Lewis I breathed easier. He was 53 or so, a long-time Washington journalist of temperate speech. I thought he, Bob, and I got along well. By the time Lewis left I was feeling better than I had in months.

Maine's daily newspapers were agitated by the Allbritton invasion, speculating that he might plan to take the *Star* daily. *Star* staffers were picking up the beat of Biddeford-Saco council drums and likening the humid *Journal* atmosphere to cold sweat.

The Boston accounting firm Charles Jesson & Associates administered the affairs of the Alta Group papers. After having closed the free-distribution *Somersworth-Berwicks Free Press,* Jesson had decided a year later to revive it artificially, sending it, free, to a wider audience than before. To our astonishment, he had also turned the 6,000-

circulation weekly *Rochester Courier* into a controlled-circulation free paper.

The Alta Group's troubles went even deeper. Now, not long after its efforts to improve the *Biddeford-Saco Journal* had backfired economically, it was threatened by the presence of an acquisitive billionaire in the lair of its chief tormenter. I imagined the *Journal*ists twitching nervously around the panic button. In April they heard that Allbritton had bought two fair-sized New Jersey dailies. Singleton and Lewis were in New Jersey for the reorganization. Allbritton was looking for other Maine newspapers — he had even, in fact, extended some feelers *Journal*-ward, as I had been urging.

By then the Alta Group's Sanford *Tribune* had shrunk to about two-thirds of its former size and circulation. Faced with the shrinking about a year earlier, by some strange logic Jesson had elected to publish twice weekly, Mondays and Thursdays. The *Tribune*'s banner slogan, "Maine's Greatest Weekly," had been changed to "Maine's Greatest Biweekly," which was more logical — it was Maine's *only* biweekly. By 1977 the Monday edition was half the size of Thursday's. Advertisers who ran in both were given bumper discounts. The golden profit era for the *Tribune* was over. We had nibbled away its circulation wherever we had gone, even in Sanford itself. Shortly before Bob, Pam, and I had made the decision to sell, we had been approached by a delegation of Sanford business people disillusioned with the *Tribune* and pledging us their advertising if we started a Sanford edition of the *Star*.

All this we had told Singleton, but he hadn't listened seriously. He wanted minimum risk, meaning a smaller, profitable, uncompetitive weekly. Money was Allbritton's bag, not journalism, certainly not York County heroics. While I was resentful, I was also loyal to the newspaper. Allbritton was paying my salary, and I still wanted the *Star* to grow and be successful.

In late April, less than four months after the Allbritton purchase, rumors of impending changes in Alta Group operations reached my ears. Even so, the May 2 announcement came as an electrifying surprise. The *Journal* and *Tribune* would merge into a single daily newspaper called the *Journal-Tribune*, with three editions, one for the Kennebunks and Wells, one for Sanford, and one for Biddeford-Saco. A brand-new weekly shopper would be delivered free, in a manner unspecified, to every one of the 25,000 combined-area households, "reaching" upwards of 80,000 "readers." A complicated four-way rate structure would permit advertisers to choose one or any combination of these four publications. Rates for the shopper, particularly in combination with other editions, were so low that when I worked out costs of printing and distribution in the numbers promised I could see no chance for profit.

Bob and I held an excited conference, then got on the phone to Bin Lewis, who arrived with Singleton the next day. Here was an opportunity they couldn't refuse, we told them, to start a weekly *Sanford Star*. Readers and advertisers in the town that had long boasted its own weekly would resent an edition of the daily they despised, headquartered in their rival commercial center. The shopper would flop.

A minimal investment was required, maybe $15,000, mostly just carrying money till advertisers had been billed and had paid those bills. We'd need a Sanford office with a couple of telephones. We had more than enough production capability. We were already dropping bundles of *Stars* to every Sanford newsstand and to many in its outlying towns. Sanford advertisers knew us — a *Star* salesman was there every week. We could run our attractive classified section, now up to four full pages, in both papers, with a modest increase in rates. We could sell combination display ads at attractive prices to many of our regular customers who already advertised in both *Star* and *Tribune* for nearly twice our suggested combination price. We'd do the billing and bookkeeping in Kennebunk. Management overhead wouldn't increase. We'd be filling a vacuum rather than competing. Sanford would have a better weekly than it had ever had. We presented some educated guesses of cost, net income, and increased company gross. If all went well, Allbritton would have a new product worth half a million dollars for a temporary carrying investment.

This time Lewis and Singleton couldn't avoid the logic and quickly gave us their blessings. In due course a start-up expense check for $15,000 arrived by mail.

I called former *Star* reporter Tom Heslin at his New Hampshire daily, and Tom accepted the managing editorship of the *Sanford Star*. Pam Wood agreed to give us part-time reporting till school was out, then full-time till fall. We hired two more reporters, a part-time photographer, a receptionist-bookkeeper, and a sales helper for our Sanford salesman, Bob Lawson. On June 7, five weeks after the Alta Group had made its fateful announcement, the new *Star* was born with 16 pages. In a *York County Coast Star* editorial I pulled my oar in the Singleton puddle, tweaked the beard of the Alta Group, and patted our own backs, all at the same time:

We might not have chosen to start a Sanford *Star* from scratch, although we've often thought about it, because scratch might have been the only result. But with the County base we've already built,

OXFORD COUNTY

Saco River

Cornish

Parsonsfield

Limington

CUMBERLAND
COUNTY

Limerick

Newfield

Waterboro

Hollis

Buxton

NEW
HAMPSHIRE

Shapleigh

Acton

Dayton

City of
Saco

to Portland
Rte. 1

Old Orchard
Beach

Lyman

Alfred

City of
Biddeford

Lebanon

Sanford

Arundel

Kennebunkport

Rochester

Kennebunk

Cape Porpoise

North
Berwick

Wells

ATLANTIC
OCEAN

Berwick

Somersworth

Ogunquit

South Berwick

Cape Neddick

Piscataqua River

York

Dover

Eliot

York Beach

York Harbor

Portsmouth

Kittery

YORK COUNTY

U.S. Rte 1

with more than the nucleus of experienced sales, editorial, and production people already on hand, the opportunity provided by the Alta Group's decision to move up was irresistible. With our new *Star* the people of Sanford will have a first-rate publication of their own, right from Word One.

We have going for us a growing, prosperous, receptive community, suddenly without its own weekly newspaper. We have late spring, with its apple-blossom promise. We have the enthusiasm and capability to succeed. Whether we do or not is in the hands of the gentle readers of Sanford. Long may Sanford wave, and long may our banner wave back.

Within months the *Sanford Star*'s circulation reached 4,500, and page count, 24. Our two *Stars* were selling about twice as many copies per issue in Sanford as the *Journal-Tribune*.

The Alta Group's shopper sold its advertising on the promise that it would "reach" the total population in the *Journal-Tribune's* three-edition area, a figure probably about four times its pressrun. Rather than mailing it to every home, a costly affair, the Alta Group hired a small army of housewives who sped down the main thoroughfares once a week with their children in the backseats scaling rolled-up shoppers onto lawns and driveways as they went. Many landed in bushes and were claimed by rain. None of the motorized dispensaries ever came down our dirt road, where ten families lived, and only half a dozen copies a year graced my mother's lawn on Cape Porpoise's best-settled street. Alta's claim for anticipated "reachings" may even have been made in semantic good faith, but it shouldn't have taken the circulation manager long to suspect inaccuracies. We waited in vain, though not breathlessly, for a disclaimer. Hardly read at all, the shopper languished on in diminishing circumstances, and finally ceased to loop lawnward.

The new *Journal-Tribune* fared poorly. The Sanford edition was eclipsed by our *Star*. The Kennebunks-Wells edition trudged forward without improved sales. All the Alta Group had accomplished was to deliver the coup de grace to a once-proud weekly newspaper.

★ 50 ★

Off Again, On Again

Dean Singleton and Bin Lewis followed our advice, and we were permitted to hire an experienced production manager, George Cogswell. When Cogswell arrived Bob Brigham gave his notice and slipped away to his new commercial fishing career. The cost and quality control measures Cogswell planned to initiate would be slow to show up in the profit and loss statements. Start-up expenses for the *Sanford Star* and our production transfer to Water Street were clouding the picture, and Singleton wanted quick results — we continued to show losses in May and June.

"What's goin' on up there?" Singleton's voice was a whinny. Where were the profits? I had told him to wait for summer — it *was* summer. "What are you guys doin' up there?"

Working, I told him resentfully. No one's throwing money around. Things were growing all over. If he was so eager to save money, how about some of the labor-saving machinery I had been promoting, like the flier-and-newspaper-section collator? This machine had been in our plans all along — we just hadn't bought one before they bought us. I had written a long prospectus and sent it to Bin Lewis, and hadn't heard a peep from anybody.

But Singleton's mind was on something else. I was told about Richard Morin in early September, after he had been hired. He was a real find, Singleton assured me. He'd been top man at the *Kennebec Journal,* one of the dailies in Gannett's Portland communications family. Morin was experienced in everything we did, Singleton said, with a strong background in accounting. He'd be arriving the first Monday in October.

The *Kennebec Journal* was two things: a small daily for the state's capital of Augusta, and the largest printing business in Maine. Both sounded bigger than they were. Isolated from competition, the newspaper squatted at the hub of state government, threadbare of political influence and devoid of journalistic merit. The printing plant fed mostly on the stream of documents gushing from the divisions of government. I reasoned that Allbritton must have offered him a substantial salary, and my job when I left, maybe before I left. I had already made up my mind not to stay beyond my Ides of March twentieth anniversary. If Morin knew his stuff, fine. I hoped he'd be strong enough to keep my *Star* dreams alive.

In mid-September Morin called me to invite himself down to see Star Press and get acquainted. During his visit our talk was mostly about his cost reduction and personnel management successes in Augusta. I gathered that his work had been keeping track of money and delegating authority. He didn't mention journalism.

At noon on Friday, September 29, I was sitting alone in my office, feeling insulted by the thought of Monday, when Morin would report for work. The week was almost over. Most of the others were gone to lunch or were eating at their desks, like me. The day was warm, not much going on — end of the week sort of thing. My phone buzzed, and Bunny Sampson told me that Dean Singleton was on the line.

"Hullo, Dean."

"Sandy, you remember once you told me if I ever got dissatisfied, I should fire you? Well, I'm firing you."

"I said Allbritton, not you. Is Allbritton firing me?"

"I'm firing you. I want you off the premises by five this afternoon."

"I see. I think I want to hear it from Allbritton, so I'll call him." The anger was taking hold.

"No, you won't. He doesn't want to talk to you. I'm firing you."

"All right, I'll be out by five. But first," I told him, "I've got a couple of things to say. One, you're making a mistake. I don't think you've got the right man for the job, and he's coming in cold Monday. The other thing I've been thinking about — you have a serious personal problem, Dean, and it's got a name. I think you ought to see somebody about it."

I hung up and rose from my chair. I walked to the window and stared out for a few minutes before the tears started. I walked to my office door and shut it, then back to my chair between the worktable I'd built for myself and the old rolltop desk behind me that had been in the office at Garden Street when I'd bought Star Print, Inc., not quite 20 years before. My pickup was in the garage that day, so I called Anneke. "Can you come get me? Singleton's fired me."

"No! Can he do that?"

"He's done it. Can you be here in half an hour? There's nothing much to collect, so I'll be ready. Don't bother to come in — I'll be watching for you. I'll call the Star people from home."

I stood again, and stuffed a few things in my briefcase. There was a

knock at the door, and reporter Jim Martin came in. He started talking about how he wanted to handle a story about a power plant across
the Piscataqua that was converting to coal, and what it would mean to
the people of Kittery and Eliot when the smoke drifted into Maine on the
prevailing westerlies. I listened for a minute, then stopped him with my
hand.

"Jim," I said, "I can't concentrate. Singleton's just fired me."

Jim's mouth was still open from talking. I repeated what I'd told
him. "My God," he said, "what can I do?"

"Just leave me alone for a bit. Anneke's coming for me."

"You sure? OK." He turned and left the office, closing the door.
Soon I could hear excited buzzing, and through a window I saw some-
one run over to the take-out place next door. Then I saw George
Pulkkinen striding back with his head down. He knocked.

"Jesus," he said. He was going to make some phone calls.

He left, but was soon back. Singleton had already left to catch a
small plane to Sanford. George said he'd meet him there. The whole Star
company was streaming in and milling around in the pasteup area.
Everyone had quit work. They'd locked both plants and were preparing
wholesale resignations. Police Chief Frank Stevens, alerted by a pass-
erby to the strange seethings on High Street, had even driven over to find
out what was going on, and then left. There was blood in their eyes,
George said. He'd call me to let me know what happened.

Anneke arrived. I slipped quietly out of my office and into her car.
Down toward Kennebunkport we passed the lovely old mansions of
Summer Street, and the cemetery, and the woods, and the old hollows in
the riverbank where the sailing ships were launched long ago. A large
modern home was being built for an out-of-stater, incongruous among
the little native buildings — like the new *Star,* I thought. The new
money would raise the values and taxes of the old homes, the old-timers
would sell to newcomers and move out, and the flavor of the little
community would change. People with old values couldn't keep what
they'd built, and others like them couldn't afford to buy.

At home the tide was coming up Paddy Creek. I greeted the cats,
and carried some wood in for the stoves. Anneke and I talked some
about the future. I told her George would be calling later about Singleton's visit, but it was all over. I regretted not having said my good-
byes to the people or written a farewell editorial. Anneke fixed us
drinks, and we let the autumn afternoon shadows settle into the corners
of the room. I had nothing to regret, Anneke assured me, except that
day.

George called at about half past five. He had picked up Singleton and pulled off the road by the blueberry plains for briefing. When they had arrived at High Street they'd walked into a hornet's nest. Singleton had tried to talk, but wasn't permitted to. People were yelling at him, making short speeches, calling him names. He didn't have a company any more, they shouted. Not a single employee but Dick Morin would show up Monday morning.

The hubbub lasted till Singleton broke down. I could have my job back, he had told them — it had all been a bad mistake. After his ordeal, stunned, he had followed George back to my office where George had advised him that if I didn't return he would have a wrecked operation. And he shouldn't call me himself — get Lewis or Allbritton to do it, George had said.

Bin Lewis called me about an hour later. Would I go back to work Monday, please? A mistake had been made. There would be no more firings, and no more scenes. Dean had been impulsive; it was the continued losses, and my attitude. With Allbritton's blessing, he, Bin Lewis, was asking me back.

Yes, I said finally, I would come back. I wouldn't be around long, in any case. I was coming back because I wanted to leave with dignity. We could work out a suitable date.

Dick Morin arrived Monday morning. He wanted to talk to me privately. Morin was 45, ten years my junior, of medium height, trim but not robust, with olive skin, thick eyeglasses, and coarse, curly hair. His voice was studiedly resonant, his manner unoriginal. After 15 minutes of small talk, he got down to cases. He was now president of Star Press. His direct boss was Singleton. He wanted to work closely with me, relying heavily on my guidance until he learned his way around. He was my boss but hoped I'd feel free to talk plainly with him.

I did. First, I told him, he was not my boss; we were coworkers, like everyone else there. I was prepared to like and help him, which included telling him everything he wanted to know. I sincerely hoped he'd do a fine job and have a pleasant stay. I think Singleton had told him to be tough. He tried, briefly, but when things got heavy he stopped. He was a friendly man who didn't like confrontations.

Sharing an office would be awkward, I said. He could have mine when I left. All other rooms were full, but for the time being I'd clear out a back room upstairs, find him a desk and a movable partition. It wasn't first-class, but it should do temporarily.

Morin told me that for a while, at least, he'd be commuting from Augusta, an hour and a half each way. He could do a lot of the work he did with figures at home. They were renting him a car.

For a month or so Morin spent most of his time commuting and

arranging his personal affairs. The rest he divided between filling elaborate sheets with figures taken from our monthly statements and wandering about the two plants talking with employees. He'd arrive between 10
and 11 each morning carrying his briefcase, and leave about 4. For one
reason or another he spent only about four days a week in Kennebunk.

He began introducing little housekeeping measures, safety codes,
company policy memos, a suggestion box, a bulletin board, informal
voluntary plantwide weekly discussion get-togethers with employees —
all introduced with interminable preparation and joyous fanfare. I concluded that Morin must be following, page for page, some handbook
from a night course in business management.

Morin professed an interest in journalism, but our discussions
never got beyond how to make money at it. He never mentioned the
contents of the newspaper to me; I was sure he never read it. He seemed
to have little interest in, or knowledge of, production or machinery. In
Augusta he had left the job estimating and graphic design to his department heads. While he must have been familiar with accounting funda-
mentals, his unfamiliarity with production processes led him into
allocation errors. I spotted and corrected overlooked expenses, overlap-
ping functions, misapplications of supplies and employee time. His rows
of figures were leading to no conclusions evident to me.

I told myself that Morin was probably a suitable manager for a
more structured company, a sincere, uninspiring, reasonably intelligent
man. I was horrified to think that leadership of the newspaper would be
in his care. I attributed his functional disabilities and evident discomfort
to our awkward working relationship and the unfamiliar casual democracy at Star Press. The tension of our first frank discussion eased,
replaced by a self-conscious cordiality. I began to feel sorry for him,
working away in isolation in his back room upstairs, or wandering
around aimlessly in coat and vest.

Singleton was relieved to have his own man in Kennebunk. He
hadn't visited us since my firing and no longer called me. However, as
week followed uneventful week, he grew fidgety again. By mid-
November his calls to Morin were becoming abrasive. Noticeably agitated following these calls, Morin would descend to say we had to get
things moving together, profitwise, and would solicit my thoughts on the
subjects of Singleton's concerns.

During one of these sessions I told Morin I thought a newspaper
section collator could save us money and increase efficiency. Attentive,
he asked me to put some figures together for him. I said I would — and
that in fact months ago I had sent Bin Lewis a long letter about it, but
hadn't heard boo from anyone. I told Morin I thought Lewis must have

dropped the letter into a file drawer and forgotten it, if he had ever read it. I pulled a copy from my files, boiled it down to essentials, and gave the result to Morin. A few days later he descended for elaboration. I could see that my rather technical analysis was beyond him, so I painstakingly explained again, correcting misunderstandings, convinced that I was talking futilely. Finally Morin said the whole thing sounded good to him. He'd take it up with Singleton — we'd get some action on it, one way or another.

Two days later Morin wanted me to see a copy of his letter to Singleton before he mailed it. Between opening and closing paragraphs it appeared to be essentially a copy of what I had given him. My name wasn't mentioned. Morin had studied the matter, he wrote, knew that such collators were being used to advantage elsewhere, and that the make and model he was proposing was most suitable for us. He urged prompt attention to this cost-saving item.

Well, I thought, maybe it was best if Singleton didn't suspect my hand in it. Anyway, the letter would probably die on his desk. He wouldn't understand it, any more than Morin had.

But it didn't die. Singleton passed it on to Lewis, asking him to talk to Morin about it. Lewis called me. Wasn't this the same collator I had written him about? Lewis said he'd be in Kennebunk in a couple of days, and we could talk then. He asked to speak with Morin, and I had Bunny Sampson buzz him.

A few minutes later Morin was in my office. He had just had an encouraging call from Lewis. Bin would be up in a few days, and among other things he wanted to discuss was this collator thing. Morin thought all three of us should be together for that talk, so I could help him fill Lewis in.

When Lewis arrived at 9:30 he stopped first in my office. I told him Morin hadn't arrived yet. Lewis said he'd address his questions to Morin and preferred that the answers come from him. When Morin arrived he greeted Lewis heartily and excused his lateness with a description of heavy traffic and weather conditions between Augusta and Kennebunk. When that was over, Lewis pulled out Morin's letter and began his questioning. Morin would answer in a few general words, then turn in my direction, but I'd be riffling through my morning mail. Morin would stumble on. Lewis would stop him — wasn't that different from what he'd written? How had he arrived at this figure? What was the expected downtime? How many sections per hour per person did we now collate by hand? How many stations could one person mind? What were our current costs per thousand? Did the machine stack the inside sections in the cover section, or was each inserted into the last? Flustered, Morin would guess at the answers, or refer to his letter, talking in circles. Lewis knew the answers already. At last he turned to me — did I think this purchase had merit?

Yes, I told him, I certainly thought so.

All right, Lewis said, let's see what he could do with it. He turned to Morin. How was the cost-center analysis going?

He wasn't quite finished with it yet, Morin replied, but he was getting there. He was still missing a few figures.

Well, said Lewis, let's see what you've got so far, anyway.

They went off upstairs.

When he came back down, Lewis was alone. Feel like some lunch?

At lunch Lewis said he could see the problems now, and understood my frustrations. He said he'd left Morin in an agitated state. When he returned to New Jersey tomorrow, he would get together with Singleton and see where they would go from there. Even Dean was disenchanted, he said. They'd find a new man, and something else for Morin.

Well, I offered, now having severe regrets, Morin may have been the best man in the world for the *Kennebec Journal*. He'd be useful somewhere in Allbritton's organization. I was sorry things had turned out this way for him, but he wasn't right for the *Star*. Find someone else, I urged Lewis, and do it soon. The situation was driving me bananas.

★ 51 ★

Saying Goodbye

After the backfiring, my continued presence was awkward. I was the demoted prima donna whose wagon was still hitched to the old *Star*. I had no right to obstruct the new owner from doing as he pleased. I rationalized that what he pleased was contrary to Allbritton's real interests, and certainly to those of the people at Star Press. But I had deserved to be fired.

I keenly felt the growing alienation between workers and management, meaning, by extension, between my old friends and me. Now there were unseen books and closed-door privacies, and a rich absentee owner. It was assumed that Morin's salary was high, and Singleton's higher. The employees were working to fatten people whose contributions were invisible, if not unfortunate. They were growing listless, unwilling to do more than they were paid to do. I felt the editorial spark going out as the company spirit died.

An unidentified *Star* person was quoted in the *Portland Press-Herald* as saying that *Star* employees had invited a typographical union to make its pitch. The union threat was anathema to Allbritton. When *Star* people asked for my views, I advised them to follow their disposition but hoped they wouldn't organize. I persuaded a reluctant Singleton to give the usual Christmas bonuses and raises to everyone on the first payday of the new year. The employees were watching for them, I told him, and without both, Joe would get his union vote, and he'd lose. Singleton approved both, somewhat reduced. Mollified but nervous, the employees postponed their vote.

Ad manager Steve Hrehovcik left to start his own ad agency; Deanie Hendrick, our page-paster extraordinary, was gone; reporter Frank Gallant left for the editorship of a trade magazine; George Schelling went on to law school; Tom Heslin left for a New Hampshire daily; Jim Martin was preparing to buy an interest in another Maine weekly; Judy Burke had given her notice; George Griffin left for the *Worcester Telegram;* Lynn Langley was leaving Maine with her husband. My dreams of *Star* glory were fading. The hand was writing on the wall, and the middle finger was raised.

I told Bin Lewis that I wouldn't be staying until the Ides of March, after all. We settled on January 12. I wanted to help indoctrinate Morin's replacement — when were they going to tell Morin? All Lewis would say was that Dean was working on it.

November came, and dragged into December. Christmas came and went with a fine, rowdy party, as of old, and me in the thick of it, a warm body covering a cold secret. No one but Morin knew I was leaving, and no one but I knew Morin was. He was spending less time at work than ever — maybe he was out job hunting. New Year's Day came and went, and soon January 12 was a week away. I thought I should tell George Pulkkinen I was leaving. I told him to expect a long, last editorial right on the Tuesday afternoon deadline, and went home for the weekend to write it. I'd have some farewell beers with the Water Street people during my final newspaper-night inserting and bundling session Wednesday, when everyone would know, and then leave.

Monday morning Bin Lewis called to ask me to reserve him a room that night at the Sea Spray. I told him I was ready, and that only George knew I was leaving. He hesitated, and then said something had come up — could I hold back my news and stay on another week? When he didn't amplify, I didn't ask. Sure, I said, what was another week? Maybe, I thought, they wanted Morin to leave before I did, and they would introduce a new man.

Lewis arrived Monday evening and called to ask me to join him for breakfast at the Sea Spray. Breakfast was strange. Two couples greeted Lewis cordially on their way to the other end of the dining area. One of the men walked over to our table and was introduced as "J. D." Schwartz. He inspected me with more interest than seemed warranted — was this the man? He was in his middle forties, accent southern. The other man, Alan Brill, also dropped by to exchange pleasantries with Lewis.

Lewis waited till breakfast was nearly over. Something had come up, he repeated. Instead of going to Kennebunk, would I drive him to Portland for talks with other people connected with Schwartz and Brill? On the way to Portland, Lewis came clean: Allbritton was about to sell Star Press to Worrell Newspapers, of Charlottesville, Virginia. Schwartz and Brill were Worrell executives. In Portland I would meet Dennis Rooker, the company lawyer. If all went well, the deal would close Monday, the conditional tense being due to the union attempt. Rooker would accompany me to Kennebunk to meet employee groups with the request that they give Worrell a year to prove itself before a union vote. None of Worrell's 22 small dailies, 12 weeklies, and two small television stations was organized, and Worrell wouldn't buy the *Star* if a union were in its future. Worrell was a responsible, successful newspaper chain, Lewis said. The *Star* would be its largest weekly, and its only property in the Northeast. While vacationing in Biddeford Pool, J. D. Schwartz had seen the *Star* and liked it. When summer was over Worrell had approached Allbritton about buying it. Worrell would bring in a young publisher, William Kirkland. George Pulkkinen would be associate publisher and editor. Dick Morin would have a place in other Allbritton enterprises. All the others would keep their present jobs.

Hallelujah! I thought to myself; this was good news all around. I could leave with my mind clear.

The employees met with Rooker and me and agreed to give Worrell time to keep its promises before again considering organizing, so the deal was on, with a closing in Portland next day.

On the stroke of our editorial deadline that afternoon I submitted two editorials. In the first I wished the new owners well and wrote that I thought the *Star* would be safe with them. I called my other, more personal editorial "Leavin' Time," from the refrain of the old Arlen and Mercer musical, *St. Louis Woman*. "Everybody has his own leavin' time . . ." it goes. Lyricist Mercer had meant death, though, and the symbolism was strong for me. A lot of what I wrote had to do with my newspaper philosophy; here are some of the other parts:

> I've written about two thousand editorials and personal columns for you in my nearly twenty years of flying the editor's desk at Star Press. Most of them developed easily from the germs of ideas and the word "Editorial" scribbled across the tops of blank sheets of paper. Some came harder. This is the hardest.
>
> Though I've thought and thought about this editorial for years, I've never been able to put together more than a sentence or two at a time in my head, and they were soon forgotten, or mercifully neglected. Writing this one is hard because you can't spend the most productive third of your life pounding away at something you take from your gut with something you take from your bones without strong feelings about what you made. And you don't cut yourself loose from it without gut-wrench and bone-bruise.
>
> This is the last editorial I'll be writing for you — I'm leaving the Star. I still have a third of my life to live, maybe, and I'm looking forward to it. For now I'll tell you some of my thoughts on leaving this business and its people who are so much part of me, some of the things I tried to do, and how I went about them, and what I hope will happen in the future, to Star Press and its publications, and to York County and Maine — a two-Star loaded five-course editorial smorgasbord to go.
>
> A newspaper is part of a business of many parts. The one that publishes this one is complex and delicately balanced. Its production side does commercial printing, a custom operation, meaning that each job differs from the one before it. The custom-manufacturing we do for ourselves includes three separate publications. Every impression, illustration, word, and letter represents a potential mistake, and some of them are actionable. The advertising space we sell is of intangible worth to the buyer, sold on trust in results, filled by us as attractively as time and funds permit. We balance the interest in what you find advertised with what we think will inform and entertain you and make you think as we think you ought to think, all arranged in ways that will make you want to read and look. The mix of talents required to do all these things well is harder to combine successfully than most, and may be as hard as any.
>
> The task of getting it all together, making expenses, keeping it working, and keeping its people not only contented but enthusias-

tic, is what used to be known as a tough job, and is now known inevitably as a "challenge." Thuswise the language she change.

I started here on the lowest rung of the professional ladder, or in a hole behind it, in Recession days. What I did was choose people well, and grow to respect and love them, and they saved me. We walked a business typerope, my good friends and I, or rather scampered along it, because the deadlines came thick and fast, and the wolf was underneath, with his eyes up. What we did, we did unaided, sometimes in the face of ban and boycott.

As Editor, my duties were to shoot trouble and set standards. My commitments to the people of York County were the same. There is a huge power in public print. Like propaganda, it has been used for evil as well as good. If the newspaper is selfless of purpose, courageous, compassionate, analytically sound, and right in its instincts, the community is better for it — far better. But if any one of the alternatives is true, the newspaper is an instrument of the Devil, and the Editor is the Devil's advocate. The editor's chair is not a plaything, like a tricycle to peddle around. It's a locomotive, and you have to feel about it the way Casey Jones did.

I think that without question the *Star* has become an influential force in York County. That is not to say that everyone, or even anyone, permits its words to go unchallenged. It *is* to say that what would otherwise pass unknown is now known. What may help or harm you is brought to your attention, and before the *Star* it was not.

Maine is attractive partly because she's poor. When she gets rich, Maine will be like all the rest of them. I hope Maine will seek out, not what will make her rich, but what will keep her attractive to the people who have made her attractive all along, the people who accept hard scrabble to get the human and natural values that go with it.

I have always assumed that much of the momentum for prosperity that has been generated here in York County was, like the population surge, inevitable. It became one of my goals to help confine its growth to manageable proportions, thereby maintaining the indigenous flavor of man and nature in the part of the world I liked best. But I am haunted by the suspicion that the County has grown faster because the *Star* made it easier. Against this haunt I set a benign spirit that whispers, Yes, but would it have grown as straight?

Now it's time to say good-bye. I'll be better off in terms of peace of mind and security. But I'll miss it. I'll miss seeing my friends every day and working toward something with them. I'll miss the reminders of what we built together. I'll miss not being part of their future, a future I see as limited only by whatever limits apply to the imaginations of the people who carry it on. I'd like to be on hand to see who wins the newspaper popularity contest in York County. I think the *Star* will win it, if anyone does, because we deserve to win it. We're the ones who risked and struggled and did the job down the line for you. We're the ones who cared.

Nobody's writing my obituary yet. What I had a hand in making here will be around for a long time, with some of my blood on it. I'm sure it will continue to give us — you and me — five minutes or three hours worth of diversion every ruddy week, as I tried to help it do for nearly twenty years. I hope I'll be remembered as someone who supplied an extra dimension to your lives, and when they get around to a lapidary inscription, maybe Harry Truman's will do as well as any: "He done his damnedest."

★ 52 ★

Looking Back

I heard later that Allbritton made half a million dollars on the sale to Worrell, partly because there was a *Sanford Star,* and partly because everything else had grown during the 11 months of his ownership. If he had dropped the job printing he sold Worrell, he'd have made nothing, as Dean Singleton appreciated. Dean called me once, several months after I'd gone, to wish me well. Surprised, I reciprocated warmly. He said he'd made some mistakes, and that I'd helped him learn from them. I told him that if he ever got to Maine again I'd be insulted if he didn't help me tear a lobster apart.

During the next three years, still in his twenties, Singleton became publisher of all Allbritton newspapers, including the *Washington Star,* and was chief negotiator during Allbritton's bid to buy the *New York Daily News.* Today Singleton runs a company that publishes 18 newspapers, including the *Houston Post* and *Denver Post.* I read once that

Allbritton had paid $35 million in 1974 for the *Washington Star* and its connected radio and television stations. When he was ordered to divest himself of either the newspaper or the others, he sold the radio station for $16 million, and in 1978, he sold the *Washington Star* to Time, Inc., for $28 million. He kept the television station — which the *Washington Post* said was valued at $138 million by 1982.

For me it was over. For many others, anger and dismay would follow. First thing Worrell did was to stop job printing, in the process getting shed of many of the employees who had led the unionization attempt. All the editorial people but two left within the year, replaced by young journalism graduates. The reporting staff was reduced to five. Within the year only Marilyn Dempsey remained in advertising, manager of a new staff of young women.

The Worrell people lost the food-market fliers and most other newspaper press jobs, and let the superfluous pressmen go. They raised all rates in big leaps. They reduced the news-hole to 40 percent. They stopped covering Biddeford, Saco, and Old Orchard, and deemphasized the southern coverage. Page count dwindled to less than 40. They sold *Clue* to Peter Agrafiotis. When the Hollingworth brothers sold their *York Weekly*, it was former *Star* reporter Patty Hart, not Worrell, who bought it. All the original *Sanford Star* people left, replaced by less experienced people. That *Star* faded in size and profit, and finally, when the new people decided to hold a union vote, Worrell precipitously closed the newspaper down and cleared out of Sanford. There's a new weekly there now.

Once prices had been raised and expenses cut to the bone, Worrell moved publisher Kirkland elsewhere and sent a succession of young publishers, really business managers, to supervise billing and watch expenses. George Pulkkinen was offered a southern job and was let go when he refused it. Peg Hendrick became editor until she too left, in 1982, the year Worrell sold the *Star* and 10 of its southern community dailies to the *New York Times,* which owns the *Star* now. To Worrell and all too many other companies, newspapers are no longer commitments, but commodities.

By any measure other than the standard of living, I call the *Star* successful in my time. It was avidly and thoroughly read. It was quoted, discussed, praised, and reviled. Locked as we were into every topic as a factor of the debate, there was almost no way of discussing local issues without ringing in the newspaper.

Weekly owner-editor-publishers are an obsolescing breed that became one fewer when I left. Before long, I think, none will remain except as strugglers with tiny, one-person or husband-and-wife rural enterprises, printed elsewhere. The individual sparkle of the weeklies will dim as their owners cease to manufacture their products and lose control of makeup and design, which were once parts of their personal statement. The new process is like carving stone with an air hammer — the sculptor loses the intensity of the creative process that comes through his pores in sweat.

There are island people — I am one. I look for islands: succinct, defendable plots of ground. The *Star* was an island of mutually dependent but otherwise free spirits, varied but congenial. Incompatible elements were discarded by the body, and the rest improved by their assimilation into a vigorous organism. Many stayed long, others short. Some influenced island life more than others, or were influenced more by it. The number of lasting friendships engendered, and the nostalgia when old *Star* people meet, is unusual. I like to think it has something to do with both meanings for T.H.W.T.B., To Hell with the Bastards and The Hard Way's the Best. By virtue of my own longevity and intensity of service, the influence on me may have been greatest, but all the others felt it too, in Flecker's words, cutting its pathway slow, and red, and deep.

There is no typical weekly publisher, as there are types for most other callings, because there are no paths in their wilderness. When I was one-and-twenty I wanted a life of fame and high adventure. When I was one-and-thirty I was ashamed to take inventory. Now I am one-and-seventy — how has it gone? Well, it came closer than I thought it would when I was 35, because that was when I left a life I hated in New Jersey for one in Maine I only half expected to be able to find.

In some ways almost everything that happened to me along the way could have been avoided, done wrong for impractical purposes, or done right for the soul of newspapering, to give impracticality its context definition. I haven't written a guidebook for escape from the rat race, or a survival handbook for life in an island environment. I have tried to explain the weekly newspaperman as an extension of his community, and the community as an extension of the newspaper. You may recognize the relationship as the same that inspired Robert Frost to describe himself as a man who'd "had a lover's quarrel with the world."

You may now see the power of the local press more clearly and understand its potential for good and evil in grass-roots America. This power is not the power to entertain, but the power to influence. Influencing *for* is most fun; influencing *against* most dangerous, and so most rare. Of the two, it is also the most important. The first usually has its champions already, with the newspaper in a supporting role. The other is war, with the newspaper as captain. The enemy officers are slipshod elected officials, seekers of special privilege, crooked contractors, religious bigots, patriotic fanatics, false environmentalists, phony educators, and others who prey on human frailties. The troops they lead are spiritual degradation, waste of resources, character perversion, visual abomination, economic injury, and insult to man and nature, and we could almost see the whites of their eyes over the hills in Massachusetts.

The ways and things we tried to promote are in constant danger, or already gone. As soon as they're saved, they're in danger again. Relax an inch, and you've lost an inch — the materialistic enemy, misnamed Progress, is constantly leaning in on you. It needs no champion, as beauty does, as honesty and integrity do. Unless you say To Hell with the Bastards, the bastards'll git you. "T.H.W.T.B." went off the *Star* banner when I left, and the paper went out of the bastard-whupping business.

I'd like to write the other book too, someday, the one about the people, many middle-aged or elderly, the correspondents and guest columnists, and *Star* regulars and news takers, hundreds of them, a long list. And the news *makers* — my God! — many and many of them, tens of thousands, who served on boards and committees, or ran their shops or businesses, or played their high school games — names spattered about my reports, friends and foes and in-betweens, who march before the eye of my mind, always from left to right, the legions of my dreams, like the stream of souls crossing the bridge into Dante's purgatory. They all changed me as I changed them, a drop or a bucketful. They all changed York County too, as much because there was a newspaper to record what they said and did as because of what it was they said and did, or because of what might have been done differently if the words and deeds had fallen unheard in the forest.

After 20 years of marriage, 5 of divorce, and 5 more of marriage, Anneke and I were divorced again, and those memories mingle with the others, bitter and sweet. I am gone now, from York County. I may return to live there again one day, but today there are too many fresh memories. I passed that way once with the people of York County, and that's all I'm allowed. I saw the communities in bad times and good, but better times, I'm convinced, than what's coming. The condominium is proliferating, even invading the big old clapboard homes that are now too costly to heat because the woodlot has been sold and they've been converted to oil, or because they're too much trouble for modern folks to maintain. The person who lives "inium condom" doesn't fix roofs or mow lawns. The lovely line of Pindar's — "For I have come to sing the praise of

Asopichus with Lydian tune and meditated lays, because, thanks to thee, the House of the Minyae is victorious in Olympia" — is spoiled for me. I can no longer think of it without thinking of the creator of the condo who gauges well the spirit of our times, because, thanks to him, the houses of the condominyae are ubiquitous in suburbia.

The unique flavor of dilapidation, somehow reassuring, pleasing to the artist's eye, of rotting pilings and shacks on stony acres, decaying fish houses and wooden mills, is gone, replaced by bland structures no different from the ones in Illinois. There are almost no farms left, and the fishing boats have fiberglass hulls electronically steered. There are fewer sun-leathered faces and wind-squinted eyes. The homes sit freshly painted on small plots of new lawn. In the autumn no one is carting storm windows from the barn or banking cedar boughs against the foundations. No one is building stone walls any more or spending time clearing brush. The service world is crowding in on the old working communities to take care of the new people who are used to service.

There's hardly a road in the Kennebunks that hasn't four houses on it for every one that was there when I came in 1958. And not one — not one — of the new ones seems as gracious to me as the old. Shacks they may have been, but the personal expressions of proud people making what homes they could.

The dead of the weekly newspaper haunt its obituary page. If the paper is small enough, the editor knows almost all the names. They are the ghosts of his other kingdom, where their spirits still roam. The newspaper is a palimpsest over which their names marched, in story or column, until one final time they appeared on the obituary page, next week to be erased from the sheet where other names would march on their sure courses, prologue after prologue into the past. The ghostly impressions appear and reappear, in my dreams, under the new print.

In my dreams the clouds still bundle up over Cape Porpoise Harbor, and the last light comes in under them to strike the green islands and wooden boats, and the white lighthouse on Goat Island. In my dreams I still row out of Paddy Creek in my dory to pull my lobster traps, out past Bass Island where I was married that second time, beyond Vaughn's and Cape Islands I helped save, and Trott's and Green and Stage where we gathered driftwood for our stoves, and storm-beached pot-warp for me, and rose hips for jelly, and found the brown-spotted gray balls of fluff that come from seagull eggs of the same colors. The hush still falls with the first snow, and the cove ice snaps when the tide ebbs under it. One day the snow melts down to patches, and spring comes in starling flocks and crocus spears, and the gulls rise into the warm wind. The pumpkin still turns orange on the vine, and the frost-pale grape turns black-purple when the October morning sun finds the trellis. Everything goes on unchanged in my memory, but changed because I am changed, no longer there. I've done mine, and moved on. It took 20 years to do, and two more to change — maybe better, maybe worse, but changed, because it speaks for different people, in different times.